Chronology of
Religious Life
in America

ALSO BY RUSSELL O. WRIGHT
AND FROM McFARLAND

Chronology of Immigration in the United States (2008)

Chronology of Housing in the United States (2007)

Chronology of Education in the United States (2006)

Chronology of Public Health in the United States (2005)

Chronology of Communication in the United States (2004)

Chronology of Transportation in the United States (2004)

Chronology of Energy in the United States (2003)

Chronology of Labor in the United States (2003)

Chronology of the Stock Market (2002)

Dominating the Diamond: The 19 Baseball Teams with the Most Dominant Single Seasons, 1901–2000 (2002)

A Tale of Two Leagues: How Baseball Changed as the Rules, Ball, Franchises, Stadiums and Players Changed, 1900–1998 (1999)

Crossing the Plate: The Upswing in Runs Scored by Major League Teams, 1993 to 1997 (1998)

Life and Death in the United States: Statistics on Life Expectancies, Diseases and Death Rates for the Twentieth Century (1997)

The Best of Teams, the Worst of Teams: A Major League Baseball Statistical Reference, 1903 through 1994 (1995)

Presidential Elections in the United States: A Statistical History, 1860–1992 (1995)

The Evolution of Baseball: A History of the Major Leagues in Graphs, 1903–1989 (1992)

Chronology of Religious Life in America

RUSSELL O. WRIGHT

McFarland & Company, Inc., Publishers
Jefferson, North Carolina, and London

LIBRARY OF CONGRESS CATALOGUING-IN-PUBLICATION DATA

Wright, Russell O.
    Chronology of religious life in America / Russell O. Wright.
        p.   cm.
    Includes bibliographical references and index.

    ISBN 978-0-7864-4004-7
    softcover : 50# alkaline paper ∞

    1. United States — Church history.   2. United States — Religion.
    3. Christianity and politics — United States.   I. Title.
    BR515.W76   2009
    200.973 — dc22   2009009929

British Library cataloguing data are available

©2009 Russell O. Wright. All rights reserved

No part of this book may be reproduced or transmitted in any form or by any means, electronic or mechanical, including photocopying or recording, or by any information storage and retrieval system, without permission in writing from the publisher.

Cover images ©2009 Shutterstock

Manufactured in the United States of America

McFarland & Company, Inc., Publishers
    Box 611, Jefferson, North Carolina 28640
        www.mcfarlandpub.com

To Terry Ann Wright

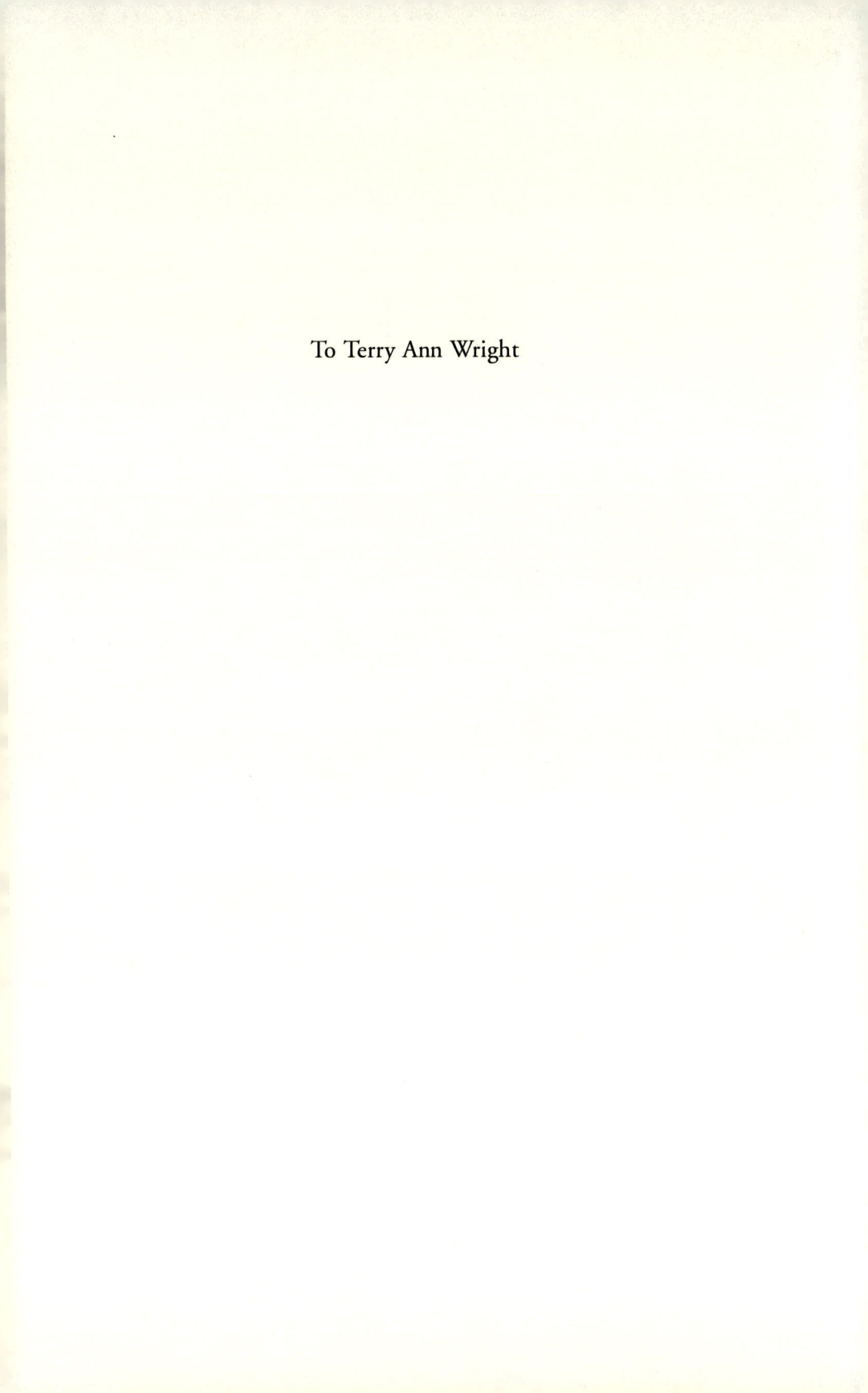

ACKNOWLEDGMENTS

This book, my twentieth, is another product of what I have previously designated as the "Wright writing company."

My wife, Halina K. Wright, served as editor, researcher, and technical troubleshooter on my computer system.

My daughter, Terry A. Wright, used her expertise with Microsoft Word to prepare the manuscript and create the index. She also surfed the Internet to find a large proportion of the information that is contained in the book. There was no reference too obscure for her to find and embellish with additional background information.

The percentage of the creation of these books that is due to Terry's efforts grows with each publication.

Contents

Acknowledgments vi

Introduction 1

Chronology of Religious Life 21

Appendix 1: Religious Groups in the United States 201

Appendix 2: Christian Religious Groups in the United States 203

Bibliography 207

Index 209

Introduction

This book tracks the chronology of religious life in the United States from the initial permanent settlement in Jamestown, Virginia, in 1607, through 2008. As in most things associated with the growth of the United States, the diversity of religious life today is astounding.

The most recent version of the World Almanac lists over 50 major headings for religious groups in the United States, and the list approaches 250 names when all the individual groups within the major headings are listed. Yet this list does not include groups with fewer than 5,000 members or fewer than 50 houses of worship.

Further, although about three-quarters of adult Americans identify themselves as Christians, another source of data for religious groups on which Christians is a single entry, shows 20 additional entries for religious groups in America (the majority being Jewish, Buddhist, Muslim/Islamic, and Hindu).

Perhaps this diversity of religions should not be surprising in a country whose constitution forbids the establishment of any specific religion (or the discrimination against any specific religion), but many countries nominally professing religious freedom often fail to live up to that promise. The United States is certainly a country that does live up to that promise and actively enforces it on a national level.

However, it must be remembered that the Constitution of the United States with its associated Bill of Rights did not go into effect until 1791. This means that for nearly the first two hundred years during which permanent settlers came to the country that would become the United States, they brought with them the religious biases and prejudices that had been developed over the centuries in England and Europe.

There was religious freedom in the colonies in the sense that groups

Introduction

oppressed in England and Europe could practice their religion more freely in the new colonies because they were out of easy reach of their adversaries and not making an undesirable impact in their places of origin, but there was no official religious freedom in all the colonies before 1791.

There are two items that should be noted before starting a history of religion in the United States from 1607 onward. First, there was great diversity in religious practices among the Native Americans who were here before European settlers arrived starting in 1492. Unfortunately, the adherents of these diverse religions declined as the Native Americans declined in response to being pushed further and further west towards near extinction as more and more settlers arrived in the United States. The present diversity of religions simply repeats the large diversity that once existed here.

Second, at the time European settlers arrived just after 1492, the predominant religion to the point of monopoly in Europe was the Catholic religion. Thus, early settlers in the New World from Spain, Portugal, and France were Catholics. But as happens eventually within nearly all monopolies, corruption became rampant among the leaders of the Catholic Church, and a number of reformers arose in Europe. They wanted to correct errors, which in their view had taken the church away from its true mission and into the corrupt practices that were occurring between Catholic leaders and heads of state.

Because these reformers were protesting against the present practices of the church, they and their followers became known as Protestants. Their leaders included such men as John Calvin in Switzerland, John Knox in Scotland, and Martin Luther in Germany. The Protestants made a big convert when King Henry VIII left the Catholic Church and turned to Protestantism in the 1530s. There were a series of wars throughout Europe relating to religion in the 1500s, but as 1600 approached, England, Scotland, Scandinavia and much of northern Germany were firmly in the Protestant camp.

An English preacher named Richard Hakluyt tried to convince Queen Victoria in the 1500s to begin permanent English settlements in the New World, both for the glory (and profit) of England, and to be sure the natives in the New World were led to Protestantism and not the "improper" tenets of Catholicism as Spain and France were trying to implement. Neither Spain nor France had done well with their initial settlements along

Introduction

the eastern seaboard of the New World, and Hakluyt urged that permanent English settlements where settlers could learn the language of and become friends with the natives were required for success. Some early settlements in the late 1500s failed, but King James I, who succeeded Queen Elizabeth I, decided to try again in 1607.

The First Two Centuries: 1607–1791

The English settlers sponsored by King James I had in theory a religious motive to try to spread the gospel among the natives, but it is clear the prime goal of the organizers who sent them was primarily economic. In fact, the widely held belief today that many original settlers came to this country in search of religious freedom is not quite correct. Overall, many immigration studies have shown that 90 percent of the time it was personal economic improvement that drove most immigrants to the United States before 1800. Only about 10 percent came to escape political or religious persecution (which happened to include the initial Puritans about whom we will speak in a moment).

The diverse religious life that evolved in the United States was simply a reflection of the freedom that existed here after 1791 to choose any religion that seemed suitable to any individual. Actually, many early religious groups that were established here in the first two centuries after 1600 practiced severe religious oppression against subsequent settlers. To a large extent, only those religious groups who came initially to the United States realized anything like religious freedom because they were free of direct contact with previous groups they had been part of in England and Europe. Later groups arriving in the New World found relatively little religious freedom (except perhaps in Pennsylvania and Rhode Island) because earlier groups were quite intolerant of newcomers who practiced a different religion.

Analysts have pointed out that the settlers who established Jamestown in 1607 came in order to realize the specific economic rewards that they believed were available in the new colonies, especially land. Many did not plan to settle permanently in Virginia, and it was only after extensive tobacco cultivation began that a sense of permanence took root. Religious activities in Jamestown were essentially the same as they had been in

Introduction

England, including religious oppression towards anyone not strictly following the tenets of the Church of England. The Jamestown (and later much of Maryland) religion was known as Anglican (after "England") and later as Episcopalian. Before the Constitution went into effect in 1789 the local government required all inhabitants to follow the prescribed religion.

In the New England settlements that began near Boston in 1620, the leaders of the settlers were in fact seeking religious freedom. The Pilgrims, as they called themselves, were an especially aggressive part of the Puritans. They had found refuge in Holland almost a decade earlier. The Pilgrims wanted to continue the reformation past the point it had reached in England, and thus they were oppressed there. However, economic pressures, the threat of a war between Holland and Spain, and concern their children were adapting too well to Dutch ways, led the Pilgrims to seek a perhaps better refuge in the new overseas colonies of England. The prime religious mission they recognized beyond being free to practice their religion was they wished was to act as missionaries to the "natives" in this new remote part of the world. An initial group of about 100 people landed at Plymouth Rock on the *Mayflower* in 1620.

A much larger group of about two thousand Puritans began arriving in the Boston area by 1630. By 1640, their number totaled 20,000. The Puritans were not intensely persecuted in the sense that they were driven from England, but they hated the ecclesiastical system they were forced to live under, and they came to the colonies to create forms of both church and state government they felt they could live under. They hoped they would become a model that people in England and Europe would follow.

Unfortunately, as is often the case among various religions, the Puritans felt that theirs was the only true religion, and they were determined to tolerate no other religion. Analysts point out that it is almost a cliché among the history of religion that those freeing themselves from intolerance become more intolerant than their previous oppressors. It was this effect that led to the execution of more than 20 "witches" in Salem, Massachusetts, in 1692. This was the nadir of the story of religious life in the United States between 1607 and 1791.

In other parts of the colonies, the religious aspect was much less intense. Lord Baltimore conceived of his landholdings that became Maryland as a refuge for English Catholics as well as a potential source of eco-

Introduction

nomic gain. However, Catholics were a minority of the initial settlers of Maryland. The generous land policy of Lord Baltimore appeared to ultimately attract more settlers to Maryland than his relatively liberal religious views. The state would later reject his religious views.

The space between the Chesapeake Bay colonies of Virginia and Maryland and the Massachusetts Bay colony of primarily the Puritans was occupied by settlers from Sweden and Holland. They established New Sweden and New Netherlands as trading posts, and the lack of new settlers resulted in the Dutch absorbing the Swedish holdings shortly before the English took over the Dutch holdings in 1664 as a result of yet another war between England and Holland.

These settlements had all been commercial enterprises, and about the only aspect involving religious freedom came in 1654 when the first sizable group of Jews to reach America immigrated to New Amsterdam (soon to become New York) after fleeing Portuguese persecution in Brazil. This movement was one factor in establishing the ethnic diversity for which New York would become famous during revolutionary times and beyond.

To the south, the Carolinas were settled in 1670 by Englishmen seeking commercial gain, and Charleston, South Carolina, became a mix of settlers from the Barbados Islands and French Huguenots. Black slaves were soon brought from Africa to help with the labor-intensive planting activities, and by 1700 the slaves accounted for half of the area's population.

In the middle of this commercial activity, Pennsylvania was established as an area that was built initially on the basic principle of religious freedom. William Penn had been granted land for a "holy experiment" to be a refuge for every persecuted ethnic group and sect. The Quakers, of whom Penn was a member, came first, but Penn's invitation to persecuted groups (and his very favorable land policy) soon attracted other groups.

German pietists, who had beliefs similar to the Quakers, came in great numbers. A group of German Mennonites founded Germantown in 1683 (it eventually became a section of a greatly expanded Philadelphia in the centuries ahead). By the end of the century they would be followed by Dunkers, Schwenckfelders, Moravians and similar German sects. Benjamin Franklin would write a polemic against German immigrants in the mid–1700s, claiming they were trying to take over the state and were fur-

Introduction

ther attempting to make German the official language of the state. But his writing would be an opinion piece, not an official document.

There would be the unfortunately normal conflicts and jealousies between the various religious groups, who tended to live in separate areas and stay isolated from their neighbors, but at least they lived in an area that included both religious and civil liberties. Such freedoms were not available in their places of origin. Pennsylvania was a state that truly was based on religious freedom as we understand it today.

There was a notable decrease of immigrants coming to New England in the second half of the 17th century. This was because the Puritans and their descendants established an atmosphere that discouraged newcomers. They would warn off those who seemed undesirable and urge them to be on their way out of town. Some of this was simply economic in that they did not want to be forced to give aid to those who might become a public charge, but the religious component reached a peak in the infamous Salem witch trials of 1692 as mentioned before.

By 1700 local authorities in New England were urging the governing General Court in the Massachusetts area to permit some white indentured servants to immigrate to relieve a persistent labor shortage. Other parts of the colonies continued to receive a flow of such immigrants for economic, not specifically religious, reasons.

Large numbers of Scotch-Irish came to America between 1700 and the beginning of the Revolutionary War in 1776. These immigrants were primarily Protestant Presbyterians who had been encouraged originally to come to Ulster in Ireland to increase the number of Protestants in otherwise heavily Catholic Ireland. When the favorable terms bringing them to Ireland were not continued by their landlords, the Scotch-Irish emigrated to America.

This again was an economic motive, not a religious one, but many Irishmen from the south of Ireland did not follow their example because in the colonies discrimination against Roman Catholics had already developed. The Scotch-Irish went primarily to the Pennsylvania area after feeling New England's coolness to any kind of strangers. Then many migrated south towards the Carolinas when William Penn's successors abandoned some of his liberal land policies.

The heaviest immigrant flows in the 18th century to America came from the Scotch-Irish and German. As noted, many Germans were

Introduction

attracted by the religious freedoms to be found in Pennsylvania, but most immigrants came for economic reasons. The key religious aspect of the 18th century with respect to American emigration may have been the avoidance of the New England area because of the intolerant nature of the religion being practiced there.

Other religious groups essentially continuing the Reformation in both the colonies and England and Europe by wanting to go further with their reforms included the Baptists and Methodists. They split off from the Puritans (now generally known as the Congregationalists because all local authority was in the congregations) and also arrived as immigrants. They spread into the backcountry of Virginia and the Carolinas where they could find freedom from local religions that oppressed nearly any religion but their own.

The Baptists eventually became the predominant religion in the South and are the most numerous group of Protestants in the nation today. The Methodists became the largest Protestant group in the country for over a century before losing members and influence in the 1960s. Both groups benefited greatly from the constitutional amendment that guaranteed freedom of religion on a national governmental basis in 1791.

In summary, from 1607 to 1791, religious life in the colonies that became the United States reflected the religious life of the places in England and Europe from which the settlers emigrated. The settlers were overwhelmingly Protestant, and they tended to duplicate the religious biases and intolerances of the places from which they came. There was religious freedom in the colonies in the sense that the settlers were far away from England and Europe and thus not as easily oppressed as they could have been at home. But unfortunately the new religions tended to create intolerances of their own, and except for such oases as Pennsylvania and Rhode Island, religious freedom as we understand it today did not exist. The overriding bad influence was that local governments adopted local religious tenets as the law of the local land. For the first time in recorded history the new Constitution and associated Bill of Rights built a wall between church and state in 1791, and this ushered in a time of true religious freedom in the United States. It took time for the official national policy to overcome personal biases and intolerances, but the nation as a whole eventually embraced the brand new concept in the world of religious freedom apart from government intrusion.

Introduction

The Constitution and Religious Freedom

After their success in the Revolutionary War, in which hostilities commenced in 1775 and peace was proclaimed in 1783, the individual states of the new United States began the task of writing a new Constitution to define the government of the new country. The constitution was written in 1787, ratified and adopted in 1788, and declared to be in effect in 1789. However, ten amendments to the Constitution were eventually added to satisfy the demands of the states to help clarify which items were the responsibility of the central government and which were the responsibility of the individual states. These amendments, now known as the Bill of Rights, were submitted to the states later in 1789 and, after ratification, went into effect in 1791.

The now famous First Amendment reads in its entirety: Congress shall make no law respecting an establishment of religion, or prohibiting the free exercise thereof; or abridging the freedom of speech, or of the press; or the right of the people peaceably to assemble, and to petition the Government for a redress of grievances.

The specific clause of interest to this book concerns the issue of freedom of religion, but there is little doubt that the original writers of the amendment never anticipated that such things as the length of hair on a boy or skirts on a girl would become defined as issues of free speech in future generations.

There was some hesitation at first to adopt the idea that religion would become free of government intrusion. At this time this would mean that preferred religions would also become free of government financial support. The state of Virginia, then the nation's most populous state, considered declaring Christianity the official state religion with freedom of choice within the various groups under that religious heading.

But true religious freedom advocates such as James Madison, supported by Thomas Jefferson, got the Virginia legislature to agree to the concept of full separation of church and state, and Madison and Jefferson played key roles in the drafting of the First Amendment. Many persons were still not sure about the then-revolutionary concept even after the Bill of Rights was ratified and declared in force in 1791. It took nearly 30 years for Massachusetts to wean itself from its support of the Congregationalist Church and amend its state constitution to declare true religious freedom in the state.

Introduction

President George Washington got several letters from various minority groups after 1791 asking him if what they read in the Bill of Rights to the effect that they would be free to practice their religions was literally true. Washington's forceful and direct answers that freedom of religion was in fact the law of the land and would be vigorously enforced were widely published and gave strong support to this truly revolutionary new position.

Because the United States was then essentially a homogeneously religious nation with Protestants making up the bulk of the population, initial issues of religious freedom would relate to the protection and creation of other religious groups. They were clearly protected by the First Amendment. But personal biases against such religions as those of Catholics and Jews would exist for a long time in the United States. It wasn't until the election of Catholic John Kennedy as president of the United States in 1960 that Catholics could reasonably feel part of the mainstream in the nation, even though there were no official restraints against their religion and Catholics by then made up a third of all Christians in the country.

Similarly, there were solid although supposedly unofficial quotas in place at many institutions of higher education at least through the 1950s as to how many Jews would be admitted to a given class. Supposedly this system is no longer practiced today, but no one knows exactly what goes through the mind of every admission official. Further, the award-winning movie named *Gentlemen's Agreement* in 1947 demonstrated clearly how Jews were discriminated against in terms of housing and other basic elements of ordinary life. It would seem lawsuits based on religious discrimination would have succeeded, but generally such discrimination was simply accepted as normal at the time.

Thus, for many generations the freedom of religion clause of the Constitution had little apparent practical effect as long as you were a member of the right religion. Public schools routinely included Christian practices in the operation of their schools, and, as discussed later, the famous *McGuffey Readers* of the 1800s, which taught millions of children to read, were filled with examples of Christian faith. This was a prime reason for the establishment of Catholic school systems, and Jewish students either went along or received private instruction of their own.

Then in the 1950s liberals began to test seriously the limits of the amendment. They questioned the long established practices of beginning

Introduction

each day in public schools with prayer and readings from the Bible. This was certainly in their view support of a specific religion (Christianity) in schools supported by public taxes.

Amid headlines screaming "they're kicking God out of school" the U.S. Supreme Court consistently ruled that such activities did violate the First Amendment and were forbidden. These rulings proceeded to bar prayers and invocations at such things as graduation ceremonies. Finally, there was a backlash with persons pointing out that the First Amendment barred the government from prohibiting the free exercise of any religion as well as barring the government from establishing one.

The result has been a careful splitting of hairs by school officials in writing the rules of what is permitted and what is not permitted in school operations and ceremonies. Similar issues have arisen with respect to the use of school properties by various groups after school hours. Even local governments have had to carefully consider such things as city decorations at traditional events like Christmas displays. Official city or state flags have been carefully scrutinized by various groups who find the simple presence of the picture of an ancient monastery a First Amendment violation. If the establishment clause of the First Amendment drew little attention during the first 150 years of its existence, it receives an extremely high degree of attention today.

There may be zealots on either side of the argument who feel their individual rights are not being properly recognized, but objectively analysts agree that the issue of religious freedom is being monitored with great care in the United States today, and that there is a degree of religious freedom in this country today that is not readily matched anywhere else. Individual bigotry is almost impossible to control, but such feelings rarely leak into any form of government without being eventually prohibited.

The Most Recent Two Centuries: 1792–2008

Although it has taken nearly all of the most recent two centuries since the advent of the Constitution and its First Amendment for the amendment to be rigorously enforced in terms of religious freedom, religious life in the United States has evolved in certain notable patterns that steadily advanced positively towards the goal of true religious freedom within a large diversity of individual religions.

Introduction

The issue of religious freedom quickly became entangled with the issue of education after the new country was established. Because the United States was predominately a Protestant nation as the 1800s began, it seemed quite normal that school systems would embody Protestant teachings in their educational systems. The famous *McGuffey Readers* that began to be widely used in 1836 to teach children to read were filled with examples of proper Christian activities. They even were critical of the Pope and clearly inferred that believers of the Catholic faith were inferior.

The *McGuffey Readers* were structured to lead children through stages of increasing difficulty in reading and spelling, and a reader was available for every step through sixth grade. Their popularity was enormous. For the next three-quarters of a century, over 122 million copies were published, and 80 percent of all schoolchildren in the country were taught with the *McGuffey Readers*. Even today over 100,000 copies are published annually, mostly for homeschooling use.

Catholic leaders were understandably upset over the use of the *McGuffey Readers* and the general Protestant flavor of all public (free) schooling, and they set out to establish a school system that would promote Catholic teachings. In 1850, an activist Catholic priest named John Hughes was made archbishop of New York. He used his extensive powers to create a privately funded national chain of Catholic schools. It quickly became, and is today, the largest alternative school system in the United States.

New York City was a natural battleground for such an effort, as the city had been involved since 1809 in trying to establish public (free) schools for the education of the children of immigrants coming in increasing numbers to New York. The city had revised its school system in 1846 to establish an elective system of school board members to counter protests from immigrants (now predominately Catholics from Ireland) that the schools were being run with a Protestant bias and reading materials.

But aside from the battles between those who still assumed the Protestant religion was the official religion of the United States and those of other established religions such as Catholics and Jews who were seeking true religious freedom in all walks of life, there were religious battles among the many denominations contained within the Protestant category to establish the true Protestant faith.

As soon as the basic Protestant denominations realized that their indi-

Introduction

vidual churches could survive very well, and even flourish, with the volunteer actions of their members rather than the funding provided by the state for the official state religion, Protestant churches literally exploded across the nation (and those of other religions exploded right along with them).

The state of Kentucky, considered the beginning of the western territories in the early 1800s, was the site of numerous revival meetings, in which churches established a temporary fixed site for church activities, and widespread settlers traveled to the site for days or even weeks of intense and often flamboyant religious activities.

Even the Catholic Church established a new diocese in the small town of Bardstown, Kentucky, in addition to its dioceses on the East Coast, in recognition of the surge in religious activity that was taking place in the frontier of Kentucky.

The churches traveled west with Kentucky as their new launching pad as settlers moved steadily west into the vast reaches of the Louisiana Purchase. More conservative religious leaders near the East Coast, who saw the activities of the churches in the wilds of Kentucky as not a proper form of their religion, were soon pushed aside by leaders who recognized that west was the new direction of the country and that their religious denomination would enter a period of decline if they did not extend their activities west with the rest of the nation.

The growth of the existing denominations in the country soon became a growth in the number of denominations themselves. In a country with no official religious domination, a new denomination was just as valid as any existing denomination in the eyes of its founder and the followers of the founder.

In the 19th century, new denominations included the Shakers, Mormons, Seventh-day Adventists, Christian Scientists, Disciples of Christ, Nazarenes, African Methodist Episcopal churches, Jehovah's Witnesses, Unitarians, Universalists, the Salvation Army, and several early forms of the Pentecostalists, just to mention some of the most well-known denominations.

The 1800s saw the blooming of new denominations that might have been expected in a country that made it a point to have no official religion, but probably no one could have anticipated the number and diversity of new religions that arose. Further, except for the Shakers that

Introduction

contained the seeds of its own demise in its theology that discouraged having children, all of these listed denominations still exist in some form, and the 20th century added some new ones.

The mainline Protestant denominations like the Presbyterians, Baptists, Methodists, and Lutherans continued to grow steadily in the 1800s and the first half of the 20th century, and would still form the basis of the Protestant religion as the United States continued a steady growth in all religious denominations through that period.

However, many of these mainline denominations would suffer declines in the second half of the 20th century as newer denominations would continue to evolve and the new world of television would create megachurches where specific affiliations would become less important. But the 1800s would be an unprecedented period of religious growth in both total numbers and total denominations.

Another event unique to the 1800s was the Civil War and its effect on religion. First, the mainline denominations such as the Presbyterians, Baptists, and Methodists all split apart a generation before the Civil War over the issue of slavery. Not surprisingly, the northern sections of the denominations found scriptures that supported their antislavery position, and the southern sections of the denominations quoted scripture that supported their proslavery position.

Even priests within the northern and southern portions of the Catholic Church exhibited biases within their conduct of mass that reflected the local position of the location of their churches. The rigid control of the Vatican prevented any thought of a formal rupture within the church, but priests in the north and the south made it clear where their sympathies lay.

The mainline Protestant splits were very deep, and their durations starting about 20 years before the Civil War made them very hard to heal. It was the 20th century before the Presbyterians and Methodists reunited, and the Baptists never came back together.

The number of slaves freed by the Civil War was a little under four million, over 12 percent of the population of the United States at that time. Although some of the slaves had been taking part in religious services under the watchful eyes of their masters before the Civil War, the four million freed slaves represented a significant new gain of members in the religious community.

Introduction

Blacks who had been slaves demonstrated that religion was an important part of their lives. Many joined the religious denominations of their immediate locations, which made black Baptists an early force. However, these newly freed blacks soon preferred to form their own congregations. Even before the Civil War, free blacks in the North had joined churches within the auspices of the Methodist Episcopal Church, but they found a number of biases against blacks in the churches they attended.

These blacks then formed their own African Methodist Episcopal Church (AME), and within a few years the AME in the name of a denomination/church identified it as a black church. The specific church may have had the word "Bethel" or "First" or "Eastern" in front of the "AME," but everyone knew, for example, the First AME Church was a black church.

The blacks took the process further by organizing a completely black church. This meant the preachers, the officers, the laypersons, and even the owners of the church were black. This meant the services and the music and the movements of the congregation were responsive to the needs of blacks and their methods of religious expression.

Blacks had discovered that no matter what denomination their church was a part of, the only way to ensure the church did not exhibit biases against blacks was to make all elements of the church black. Especially after the Civil War, blacks were extremely sensitive to the blatant and even subtle ways biases against them appeared in all phases of their life, and their entirely black churches were an oasis where such prejudices did not appear.

Even when the Pentecostal movement first appeared in the late 1800s and early 1900s, the movement that produced the rapidly growing Assemblies of God denomination, and that also started with whites and blacks on a nearly equal basis, soon evolved into white churches and black churches.

The Pentecostal movement evolved to contain many tens of millions of members, but eventually most of the growth took place outside of the United States in South America and Africa. Only about 10 percent of the members of most branches of Pentecostalism are now located in the United States.

Including the black Pentecostal churches and the other black churches that rose from their Baptist roots and their AME denominations, black churches began to spread across the United States. The black churches

Introduction

tended to differ from white churches not only in the vigorous tone and personal movement involved in the services, but in their involvement in their members' lives.

Blacks could expect help from their congregations in all aspects of their education, job choices, assistance in applying for such social services as welfare, and even in obtaining places to live including their own homes. This aspect of black churches has continued to the present day, with shifting emphasis on different elements of their life as times changed.

As the 1800s closed upon a period of sharp growth in both religious membership and the number of denominations, the War of 1898 with Spain brought a new concept in the view of the United States government towards religion. The United States gained its first foreign empire as a result of the war, gaining control over the Philippines, Puerto Rico, Guam, and, very briefly, Cuba.

Cuba was quickly set on the road to the independence it had been trying to gain from Spain when the war started, and after some hesitation and discussion and insurgent battles, the Philippines were set on a course towards independence over a much longer timescale (they achieved independence in the 1940s). From a religious viewpoint the most important decision was the one not to immediately send teams of missionaries to the Philippines to convert their heathen Catholics to Protestantism.

This decision tended to evolve, but it set an important precedent. Together with freedom of religion at home, the United States was to stand for freedom of religion in other countries it became involved with. Puerto Rico was to become a territory of the United States (as was Hawaii, which was annexed in the same year), and thus would enjoy the same freedom of religion that existed in the United States. And the United States would not try to impose any religion on any land it conquered.

The 20th century saw the establishment of the 18th Amendment in 1919. This amendment, which brought Prohibition to the United States, marked the culmination of decades of effort by many religious groups, most notably the Women's Christian Temperance Union (WCTU). Unfortunately, the advent of Prohibition ushered more than a decade of criminal lawlessness into the United States and only drove the use of liquor out of sight rather than out of existence. Prohibition was a good (or bad) example of the unexpected consequences that can occur when a religious group(s) imposes its view of morality on the rest of the country.

Introduction

The United States also generated laws in the first quarter of the 1900s to greatly reduce the amount and particular sources of immigration into the country. After the number of immigrants had reached record highs in the first decade, bringing an especially large number of Catholics from Italy and Jews from eastern Europe, Congress decided that the total number of immigrants was too high, and that the quality of the immigrants from southern and eastern Europe was much lower than that of previous immigrants from western Europe and England.

Thus, the new immigration laws enacted from 1917 through 1924 not only cut the total number of all immigrants arriving in the United States, the laws essentially ensured that most of the immigrants that did arrive would be Protestant. This would not effectively change until 1965, except for a mix of immigrants/refugees arriving after World War II.

Then in 1965 new immigration laws opened the door to immigrants from Latin America (who were mostly Catholic) and those from Asia. The Asian immigrants from the Philippines were Catholic also, but those from China and India reflected the ancient Asian religions of Hinduism and Buddhism together with Muslim. The United States became a true rainbow of religions, with religious freedom for all.

Beyond the effects of immigration, the growth of existing religions within the United States continued on its upward path that had been established in the 1800s continuing well into the 1900s. However, two very significant events that began in the 1950s had a major impact on religion in the United States through the rest of the 20th century and into the 21st century.

The first of these was a serious attack on the implementation of the First Amendment in the courts. Activists of all types, generally supported by such organizations as the American Civil Liberties Union (ACLU), began to object to the generally assumed idea that the United States was a nominally Protestant country regardless of what the First Amendment said about no official religion in the country.

Lawsuit after lawsuit began to reach the Supreme Court of the United States addressing the commonly accepted practices of reading from the Bible and engaging in regular prayer in the public schools. Once the issues were in the open, the Supreme Court had no choice but to "kick God out of the schools" as some newspapers put it. The First Amendment clearly prohibited actions by representatives of the government, such as public

Introduction

schools, that supported the establishment of any religion (the establishment clause).

These lawsuits became more frequent and more detailed as proponents of supporting the exact meaning of the First Amendment clashed with religious fundamentalists who were trying desperately to get prayer back into public school agendas. The Supreme Court, to its credit, has used a razor blade in carving out decisions that support the elimination of any policy that appears to tend to establish a religion while also supporting the rights of religious institutions to exist without having undue restrictions placed on their activities. The Supreme Court has also permitted things such as Christmas decorations that have passed from religious meanings to simple traditional representations.

The battle appears likely to go on indefinitely, but positive offshoots of the focus on real issues versus lip service have included the elimination of quotas on the admission of Jews to certain educational institutions and similarly bigoted housing issues. The event of taking religious and other rights at their true face value has spread to the elimination of "let's pretend" attitudes in other areas.

The second significant event that started in the 1950s was the advent of television and the emergence of televangelists. A number of preachers started reaching wide audiences via radio networks, and this soon evolved into television networks where their audiences grew even larger and so did their revenue.

The so-called televangelists essentially developed into four broad categories. The first category was those who "did well by doing well." This category included such men as Billy Graham, who started just as the 1950s started, and the Reverend Robert Schuller, of the famous Crystal Cathedral, who retired in the early 2000s and passed his ministry on to his son.

Both men developed huge broadcasting empires with audiences that reached literally around the world. Both were unique in that they were sincerely preaching what they saw as the word of God and were sincerely attempting to convert people to the Protestant version of Christianity and keep them in the fold. On a somewhat smaller scale Bishop Fulton J. Sheen of the Catholic Church tried to do the same thing in the early 1950s.

Unlike many other televangelists, there was never a hint of personal scandal about Graham or Schuller or Sheen and they represented televangelism at its best.

Introduction

The second category, at the other end of the scale, included men like Jim Bakker, who started in the 1960s, and the Reverend Sung Moon of Korea, still plying his trade in 2008. These men spoke of God outwardly, but their real motivation was to enrich themselves personally, and both spent time in jail for their misdeeds. If there is a distinction to be made between them, Bakker turned out to be an outright crook who simply stole from his followers, while Moon enticed his followers to give to his organization, which became wealthy and powerful with Moon enjoying the many side benefits such wealth and power can bring.

In between these two extreme categories was a third group of televangelists who preached the word of God in a sincere fashion at the start of their careers. But as they gathered wealth and fame they became obviously distracted and began to exhibit a degree of arrogance from reading their own press clippings. They evolved into strange on-screen behavior and often wandered into strange off-screen behavior including cavorting with prostitutes. Examples included Oral Roberts earlier in the 1950–2000 period and Jim Swaggart later in the period.

A fourth and final category of televangelists in the 1950–2008 period as what could be called the political televangelists. Notable among these were Jerry Falwell and Pat Robertson. They preached the word of God as they saw it, with a definite conservative southern Baptist slant. Falwell founded and ran the Moral Majority in the 1980s. It was designed to help elect Ronald Reagan and George Bush and other Republican candidates. The Moral Majority may or may not have had the impact Falwell claimed, but its goals were certainly met in the elections of 1980, 1984, and 1988.

Robertson was less flamboyant than Falwell, but Robertson himself ran unsuccessfully for the Republican nomination for president in the 1980s. Robertson apparently was more interested in bending the Republican Party platform to his will than in winning the nomination (which he did not), but both men were more than casually interested in politics.

Both men also wanted to change the First Amendment to the extent needed to get religious aspects back into public schools (of course, only with respect to their particular religions), and their battles to do so were somewhat notorious, especially with respect to Falwell. Many liberal groups were outraged by Falwell's definitely nonpolitically correct religious and personal views, and they attacked him for what they saw as his many misdeeds.

Introduction

But objectively neither Falwell nor Robertson ever appeared to be guilty of enriching themselves at the expense of their followers. Such questionable financial moves may have been made by Falwell on a technically illegal basis, but all moves were made to clearly support their churches and organizations. There was no outright fraud of the Jim Bakker style involved. The main "crime" of the two televangelists was their attempt to get around the separation of church and state.

Most televangelists fell into one of these four categories or into a blend of more than one category. Televangelism became a big business by the end of the 20th century. Its reach was enormous, and its fund-raising potential was also enormous. Here, as in so many other areas of life, the warning of buyer beware was definitely appropriate.

A major religious event of the last two centuries of the 1800–2000 period was the admissions by Catholic priests that they had molested or sexually assaulted over 100,000 members of their congregations. Equally outrageous in the eyes of many in the United States were the attempts by Catholic bishops to try to cover up these crimes and to react to the illegal actions of some priests by simply transferring them to another parish.

The lid blew off, as it always does in these cases, to the tune of about two billion dollars being paid out in damage settlements in the United States in the early 21st century. Even the visit of Pope Benedict XVI to the United States in April 2008 was marred by this issue, but the pope's direct apology for the events, his meeting with some victims, and his acknowledgment that early notices of the events were sometimes handled badly by the churches and the Vatican itself did much to begin a process of healing.

Early in 2008 (the year of the end of this chronology), a new survey was released that showed although the United States remained a Christian nation by a margin of about 75 percent, people were more easily moving from one denomination to another than had been the case in the past. Further, members of one domination were more easily convinced that another denomination could also provide a valid pathway to heaven.

Among this relatively relaxed view of other denominations, members of mainstream Protestant denominations were taking issue with the views of the leadership of the denominations who were trying to be more accommodating to modern issues such as homosexuality. The leaders of the denominations were trying to attract more members outside the denom-

Introduction

ination by appearing to be much more liberal with respect to such things, but the downside was that more conservative churches within the denominations were leaving the national church and its leadership to establish congregations of their own.

The result of these trends was a great deal of flux within organized religion, even though religion in terms of membership was being as much as or more successful than ever. Even the monolithic Catholic Church was undergoing a period of upheaval, but its losses in membership were being masked by the addition of new Hispanic immigrants who were nearly all Catholic (the Catholic Church was approaching a membership where as many as one-third of all members were Hispanic).

Thus, as people easily changed their Protestant denominations, and many mainstream Protestant denominations continued fracturing into smaller and smaller pieces, and megachurches grew via television where the charismatic pastor was more important than the affiliation, the religious life in the United States maintained its importance to most, but the form and dynamics of that life steadily changed as the 21st century continued to evolve.

Chronology of Religious Life

This chronology covers religious life in the United States from 1607 through 2008. The preceding introduction gives an overview of this subject, showing how there were two basic periods in the religious life of the United States. These were the periods in the first two centuries from 1607 to 1791 and the following two centuries from 1792 until the present. The dividing line is the adoption of the Bill of Rights in December 1791 when true religious freedom became the law of the land.

Prior to 1791, religious freedom in the United States suffered from the lack of a national government that could enforce such freedom. Old habits brought with the settlers and the development of intolerance in the new religions established here were major problems. The adoption of a governing constitution that mandated religious freedom was as revolutionary a step in the world as any other result of the Revolutionary War. It has led to a nation filled with multiple religions that have blossomed under such freedom, and it has served as an example to the world of what true religious freedom means.

May 1607—The first permanent settlement from England in the New World was made at a place called Jamestown on the James River in the state of Virginia. The name James came from King James I of England, and the state of Virginia was named after the Virgin Queen, Queen Elizabeth I, who had only recently died after a 45-year reign and had been succeeded by King James I.

The settlers came in three ships, and one of their leaders was Captain Christopher Newport, after whom the eventual nearby settlement of

1609

Newport News would be named. The religious purpose of the group, as spelled out in the Royal Charter of Virginia, under the auspices of the London Company chartered by King James to settle this part of the colonies, was the propagation of the Christian religion to those (natives) who live in darkness and ignorance of God.

The investors behind the voyages were, however, much more interested in tangible returns on their investment. They hoped to reap the rewards the Spanish had gained when they brought back gold from their settlements in the New World in previous centuries. Such rewards were not quickly forthcoming, however, and the initial settlers in Jamestown struggled simply to survive.

There was no issue of religious freedom involved, because the settlers were members of the Anglican (later Episcopalian) Church when they left England and planned to establish the same church in Virginia. The settlers only barely survived, especially after an Indian uprising in 1622, but when they learned how to cultivate tobacco, they found a ready market in Europe and created their version of the Spanish gold of legend.

1609—An event took place in England that would strongly affect the development of the Baptist religion in the New World. John Smyth, a member of the Puritan dissenters in England, who would found Boston in 1630 and colonize the Massachusetts Bay area (see listing), demonstrated his strong belief in adult baptism by rebaptizing himself and several others. This event can be taken as the beginning of the Baptist Church.

The Baptists also stressed a belief in salvation by God's grace for everyone and not just predestined individuals. These differences made Baptists an undesirable minority among the dissenting Puritans, and people with such views were not welcome in the highly intolerant Puritan community that formed in New England after 1630.

The Puritans banned Roger Williams from their region in 1635 (see listing), and Williams is credited by some with founding the first Baptist church in the New World in Rhode Island in 1639. But some historians think that Baptists were emigrating to the New World frequently to escape persecution in England, and the question of the first Baptist congregation is not clearly defined.

At any rate, the Baptists would struggle under discrimination in the New World before emerging as a rapidly growing denomination after the

Revolutionary War. Baptists would ultimately become the largest Protestant denomination in the United States.

1610 — In another part of America that was still under Spanish rule, the town of Santa Fe, New Mexico, was founded by Catholic missionaries. The famous San Miguel Chapel is thought to have been built in the same year, and its remains still stand today as the oldest chapel built in the United States. The Catholics were quite successful in building churches and chapels in the area for some years, but an Indian revolt in 1680 resulted in the deaths of almost 500 Spanish settlers and Franciscan friars. It took some time to restore mission activities.

1614 — A famous historical event took place when one of the English settlers, John Rolfe, married an Indian princess named Pocahontas. The marriage did improve relations between the settlers and the Indians for a short time, but Pocahontas died in 1617 during a trip to London and John Rolfe was killed in the Indian uprising of 1622 (see listing).

There were many romantic stories subsequently written about the marriage, but Rolfe was quoted as saying he primarily married for the political good of the settlement and for the strong religious good of converting an "unbelieving creature" to Christianity. Pocahontas was actually a gentle captive of the colony that hoped to essentially ransom her for some equipment stolen by the local Indians who were ruled by her father. Her father refused, and Pocahontas rebuked him by choosing to remain with the colony because she said he valued some old swords and other items over her.

The couple had a child, and then went to England in 1616 with a group of 11 other native Indians in an attempt by the colony's London sponsors to show that the natives of the New World were not wild animals and thus potential colonists could travel there without fear. Unfortunately, Pocahontas died of an unknown illness in 1617 just as the couple was preparing to return to the colonies. Eventually, many descendents of the couple were left via the one son they had.

1619 — The existing Virginia legislature took its first steps toward making the Church of England the official church of Virginia. This meant it would be publicly supported and would be the sole church in Virginia.

1619

In 1642 and 1662 (see listing) the rulings were made even more restrictive.

This is a good example of the lack of religious freedom as we now understand it in many parts of the early colonies. The settlers brought with them the biases and intolerances of the church they were part of and installed them in the colonies. In some cases, such as in New England, the settlers came looking for religious freedom, but then became more intolerant of other religions than the church they escaped from.

The Virginia legislature became so used to a state-sponsored church that they had great difficulty in 1791 in accepting the concept of complete freedom as espoused in the Bill of Rights. Similarly, it took the Massachusetts legislature almost four decades after 1791 to change the state constitution so that it no longer specified a state-sponsored religion.

The religious life was very important to the original colonists, but only their own religion was readily tolerated in many places.

August 1619—The Dutch brought the first black laborers to Jamestown, Virginia. There is some dispute whether the blacks were brought as slaves or as indentured servants (workers who traded several years of labor for passage and then eventual freedom). Whatever the status of the 1619 group, slavery was legalized in the area and in full swing by 1650. The cheap labor was crucial to the profitable cultivation of tobacco and other crops that were labor intensive. Black slaves made up 20 percent of the population of the United States by 1775.

The efforts made by many people to bring the Christian religion to this sizable group of black slaves will be detailed in this chronology, as well the passionate religious disputes over the Christian position on slavery and the schisms caused in large church groups such as the Presbyterians, Methodists, and especially the Baptists both before and after the Civil War started in 1861. The history of religion in the United States would become very much affected by the history of slavery in the United States.

December 1620—A group of about 100 Pilgrim separatists arrived at Plymouth Rock in Massachusetts after a journey of three months from Plymouth, England on a ship named the *Mayflower*. They had spent nearly a month looking for a suitable harbor and a good place to build a town after reaching land at the tip of Cape Cod after their journey across the ocean.

The Pilgrims were basically part of a Puritan movement in England that was trying to reform the Church of England into an institution more closely resembling the tenets espoused by Reformation leader John Calvin in the previous century. The Puritans were trying to achieve change within the framework of the existing church, but the Pilgrim branch wanted more radical change, essentially wanting to start over from the beginning.

The radical nature of the Pilgrims caused them to be persecuted in England, and in about 1607 they moved to Holland, a country known to be more tolerant of different religions than England. However, the Pilgrims found their children easily swayed by what the Pilgrims saw as too liberal a lifestyle. In addition economic pressures were an issue, and the Pilgrims finally negotiated transportation to the colonies with the grudging approval of King James.

The Pilgrim settlement grew very slowly in Plymouth. They managed to survive, but were eventually absorbed by much larger Puritan settlements to the north around Boston in the Massachusetts Bay area. But the Pilgrims were the first settlement to be established for the specific purposes of religious freedom. They found their freedom in the colonies, even though they and their Puritan compatriots would establish a religion wholly intolerant of religious freedom for anyone else.

1622 — A bloody uprising by the Native American Indians around Jamestown, Virginia, took place (one of the settler killed was John Rolfe of Pocahontas fame — see listing for 1614). This uprising, among others, finally convinced the original English settlers that they were extremely naïve, and probably more than a little arrogant, to think that the Native Americans would welcome them with open arms as the settlers plied them with news of the Gospel while plundering their land.

The issue of the usage and ownership of land would be at the bottom of many disputes and even wars between the Native American Indians and the settlers who flooded into the New World. The Indians believed no one owned the land they all used in common, and the settlers saw land ownership as one of the riches to be gained from settlement. All of the good words the Indians heard from the settlers about obeying masters and

1623

settling land for the glory of God made no sense to them, let alone being expected to be docile laborers for the settlers. With few exceptions such as William Penn, whose sense of religious justice included fair compensation for land taken from the Indians, the settlers and the Indians stayed in permanent conflict on this issue.

May 1623—The Virginia colony enacted the first temperance law. It had very little effect because of the great difficulties in enforcing such a law. Almost exactly three centuries later religious groups (especially the Methodists) would play a big role in bringing Prohibition to the United States, but the "Noble Experiment" would prove a great failure in terms of the costs in money and lives to try to enforce the law.

1629—The Dutch Reformed Church was declared the official church of New Netherlands, the settlement that the West India Company of Holland had established in what is now New York. The Dutch paid little attention to the claims the English made in establishing English colonies to the south in Virginia or to the north in Plymouth, Massachusetts.

The Dutch had previously bought the island of Manhattan from the native Indians and had established Fort Orange for trading purposes near what is now Albany, well upriver from their explorations near the mouth of the Hudson River where they had also established New Amsterdam, later to be New York City.

Holland was then known as a generally liberal country when it came to the question of freedom of religion, and the appointment of the Dutch Reformed Church as the official church of the settlement was mostly an administrative issue. The West India Company did not want religion to be taken seriously enough to interfere with the very profitable trade in furs and other items that was flowing from the New World. Thus, other religions that happened to exist in the area were easily tolerated as long as they caused no trouble.

The appointment of the less liberal Peter Stuyvesant as director general of the colony in 1647 (see listing) led to many problems in this area as Stuyvesant tried to "bring order" to the various religions (Lutherans, Quakers, Presbyterians, and Catholics) that had established a presence in the colony as a result of its general attitude of religious tolerance.

1630 — The city of Boston was established by Puritan settlers who had been slowly arriving around Massachusetts Bay in small groups since the tiny settlement made by the Pilgrims in Plymouth in 1620 (see listing). The Puritans who came after the Pilgrims were somewhat more politically acceptable in England because the Puritans were trying to make religious changes there within the framework of the established church in England.

This made it easier to sponsor immigration to the colonies, and in 1630 over a thousand settlers arrived in the Boston area, with a total of about 20,000 in place by the end of a generation. These Puritans also came in search of religious freedom, but the freedom they wanted was to establish a combination of church and state that they hoped would be followed as a model by those left behind in England (and even Europe).

When the Civil War in England in the 1640s did not work out as they hoped, the Puritans keep emigrating to the colonies and continued to establish the church-state model they desired. This model had many desirable features in terms of thrift, hard work, education, and a democratic form of church administration. But the one thing missing was a complete lack of tolerance for any other kind of religion. This would eventually have tragic and fatal consequences for some people within the tight-knit New England community.

John Winthrop, who would be the leader of the Puritans who settled in the Boston area, came on the ship *Arabella* in 1630. Earlier Puritan (not Pilgrim) settlers had landed at Salem (of later witch trial notoriety in 1692 — see listing) in 1628 and elected Samuel Skelton as pastor of their church in 1629. Skelton created a famous covenant with God that would guide the congregational Puritan Church in New England.

May 1631 — The General Court of Massachusetts issued a decree that "no man shall be admitted to the body politic but such as are members of some of the churches within the limits" of the colony. The decree was one of the first indications of the high level of intolerance that would develop over the coming years within the Puritan colony.

March 25, 1634 — The ships *Ark* and *Dove*, called by some the Catholic *Mayflowers*, arrived on St. Clements Island, Maryland. The state which had been founded by the Catholic Sir George Calvert (Lord Baltimore) in England, and named to honor Queen Henrietta Marie, the Catholic wife

1635

of King Charles I. Calvert's son, Cecil, upon his father's death in 1632, became the second Lord Baltimore and proprietor of the colony. He commissioned his younger brother Leonard as governor of Maryland's first settlers.

Because of its Catholic origins, Maryland was seen as a beacon for Catholics (now out of favor in England) and a place of religious toleration. Catholics were important members of the arrivals in 1634, but they were a distinct minority, and would remain so up to the Revolutionary War in 1776. However, Catholics such as Charles Carroll (the only signer of the Declaration of Independence who was a Catholic) would play an important part in the war.

Cecil Calvert, the second Lord Baltimore, as noted, had carefully instructed the highly educated Catholics on the ships to essentially keep a low profile in the New World because of the potential intolerance they might awaken in the majority of the settlers who were members of the Church of England. The Catholics did so for many generations while quietly building a Catholic presence in Maryland. They helped influence a famous declaration of religious tolerance in Maryland in 1649 (see listing), but political changes in England caused its reversal in 1654. Still, the Catholics went on, quietly building a religious presence.

October 1635—The General Court of the Massachusetts Bay Colony ordered a man named Roger Williams to leave the jurisdiction of the colony. Williams, who had come to Boston in 1631 as a Puritan minister, was charged with disagreeing with the Puritan authority, espousing freedom of religion, and asserting that no attempt had been made to fairly compensate the native Indians for the land the Puritans had simply taken from the Indians.

Williams readily admitted these "crimes," and although the court had agreed to delay his expulsion until the upcoming winter was over if Williams would hold his tongue until then, Williams left the following January when he heard of a plot to send him back to England for continuing to speak out. Williams journeyed south out of the Boston jurisdiction and founded the settlement of Providence in Rhode Island.

Rhode Island would become the first colony to establish complete religious freedom, following the position of Williams that the civil government would have nothing to do with the church in his new settlement.

Williams established a new separate church free of the errors that he found in the New England version, and arranged to buy land for his settlement from the Indians. Williams thus preceded William Penn (see listing for 1681) by almost a half-century in establishing true freedom of religion in the colonies.

The charter that Rhode Island received in 1663 from King Charles II guaranteeing the borders of Rhode Island and affirming permission for its inhabitants to continue its experiment in freedom of religion may have influenced King Charles II in his granting the right for William Penn to conduct his holy experiment 18 years later.

September 1636 — The college that would blossom into Harvard University was established in Boston. The rapid creation of this college, the first in the colonies, was a symptom of the importance placed on education by the Puritans. Because an important tenet of their faith was that guidance came from the Bible (not popes or bishops or such), it was crucial to have learned ministers who could guide their congregations in their personal study of the Bible.

The original intention of such colleges as the one that grew into Harvard University was to train ministers who were capable of providing such leadership to their congregations. With such religious incentives the state of Massachusetts took a leading role in developing educational systems in the colonies and in the United States well into the 20th century.

March 1638 — The Massachusetts Bay Colony continued its reputation of intolerance by expelling a woman named Anne Hutchinson for what they saw as heresy when she dissented from some harsh practices of the colony. Hutchinson eventually made her way to Rhode Island and became a religious activist within the atmosphere of religious freedom established there by Roger Williams (see listing for 1635).

1639 — The Baptists, a new religious group that had emerged out of the Puritan Church in England, settled in Newport, Rhode Island, after having arrived shortly before in Providence to take advantage of the religious freedom promoted by Roger Williams. John Clarke, a physician and clergyman, was the leader of the Baptists in Newport. He was later arrested in 1651 on a trip to Massachusetts to help other Baptists there. The pub-

1643

lic beating of one of his companions by the ever-intolerant Puritans in Massachusetts caused Roger Williams to write a famous letter of protest to Governor Endicott of Massachusetts.

1643—The first notable group of Lutherans arrived in the New World as part of the colony of New Sweden established near what is now Wilmington, Delaware. Most Swedes at the time were followers of Martin Luther, the famous reformer of nearly a century ago. The colony was instructed to follow the "unaltered Augsburg confession" and the basic ceremonies of the Swedish Church.

Too few in number to make a real impact, the Swedes were essentially taken over by the Dutch and Peter Stuyvesant (see listing for 1647) when the Swedes took over a small nearby Dutch fort in 1654. As a result, the colony of New Sweden passed on to the English when the Dutch ceded their colonies in America to England in 1664.

The Lutherans would arrive in much greater numbers from Germany and Scandinavia in future years, but their first entry into America came with New Sweden, and descendants of the original settlement would migrate into other parts of the colonies in small numbers. They would find refuge in the religious freedom of places like Rhode Island and Pennsylvania in the following years.

September 1646—The Cambridge Synod of Congregational Churches convened in Massachusetts to determine what they saw as the correct form of government that they intended all congregational churches in New England to follow. It was part of the design of religion in New England that all churches follow orders from "on high." No dissent was expected or tolerated.

1647—Peter Stuyvesant took over as director general of the Dutch colony including New Amsterdam (see listing for 1629). He was dismayed by the many religions flourishing there as a result of the general religious tolerance practiced by the West Indies Company even though the Dutch Reformed Church was the official church of the colony.

Stuyvesant initially told the West Indies Company he was going to tell some Jews who immigrated in 1654 (see listing) to move on for the good of the settlement, but when the Jewish immigrants protested to the

West Indies Company, the company gave them permission to stay and trade within the settlement as long as their poor did not become a burden to the community. The West Indies Company wanted no religious issue to interfere with what they considered the much more important issue of successful trading.

Stuyvesant also tried especially hard to stamp out the Quakers in his area, but the liberal policies of the West Indies Company stymied him here as well. The citizens complained about Stuyvesant's intolerance, and the company backed them up. Once again, the company wanted nothing to do with any religious edicts that might interfere with their successful trade. Unfortunately, this attitude of religious freedom did not survive the transfer of the Dutch colony to England in 1664 following yet another war between Holland and England.

April 1649—The Maryland legislature passed an Act of Tolerance providing religious freedom for all Christians in the colony. It was a bold step, but pressures brought as a result of political changes in England, and land disputes with the neighboring colony of Virginia, which was governed by adherents of the Church of England, caused the act to be reversed in 1654. Religious freedom was not favored in any way by England, and its followers in the colonies were quick to stamp out the idea wherever they could in the colonies.

October 1649—The colony of Maine passed legislation to give religious freedom to all its citizens. However, there was a caveat that all members of contrary religions must behave acceptably to realize the benefits of the legislation. The term "acceptably" was, of course, as viewed in the eyes of the legislature.

1651—Shortly after their founding by George Fox in England, some members of the Society of Friends, known as the Quakers, moved to Rhode Island to take advantage of the religious freedom offered by the colony of Roger Williams. The Quaker settlement soon grew in size enough that the Quakers became a force in the civil government of the colony. They would join with their counterparts in Pennsylvania (see listing for 1681) to become an influential force in the colonies through the 18th century.

1653

December 16, 1653 — Oliver Cromwell was made lord protector of England, Scotland, and Ireland. This event essentially capped a period starting in 1642 and running through Cromwell's death in 1658. The English Civil Wars in that period had variable effects on religious life in the colonies as the predominant church powers swung from Puritanism (of which Cromwell was an advocate) to Catholicism to Anglicanism to forms of Presbyterianism.

Chaos was present throughout England and subsequently through the various religions that had been brought to the colonies by various settlers. Chaos was again the result of the return to power of the Royalists in 1660. But no one religious group could wield full power for about the next three decades. The Anglicans were the major group, with the Catholics and Puritans (with other similar radical groups) nibbling at the edge.

It wasn't until the Glorious Revolution of 1688 and the ascension of William and Mary to the throne in 1689 (see listing) that a reasonably peaceful period ensued with the establishment of some degree of religious toleration. The effects of this period were also felt in the colonies. During this long period of instability, Baptists, Quakers, Presbyterians, and ultimately Methodists started to develop in England and then emigrate to the colonies as they were oppressed by the various changes in England.

1654 — The first sizable group of Jews in America arrived at New Amsterdam (which became New York ten years later). The Jews were fleeing religious prosecution by Catholics in Brazil. They were told to move on by the director general of the area, but they made a successful protest to the West Indies Company which prized trade over religious differences (see listing for 1647).

The Jewish immigrants were permitted to stay, and they flourished and ultimately organized the first synagogue in America in 1729 under the Congregation Shearith Israel. This cemented the long relationship members of the Jewish faith would have with New York City during the history of the United States.

July 1656 — The first Quakers to arrive in Boston, women named Mary Fisher and Ann Austin, were arrested and deported back to England five weeks later. Eight more Quakers arrived in August, and they were immediately imprisoned by the Puritan authorities. The Puritans regarded Quakers as religious and political subversives.

Only four years later a female Quaker teacher would be executed for refusing repeated orders to leave the Bay Colony (see listing for June 1660).

June 1, 1660 — A Quaker teacher named Mary Dyer was hanged on Boston Common after defying edicts of banishment. This was a sobering symbol that even though the New England Puritans led the colonies in many ways in education, emphasizing hard work and thrift, the democratization of church proceedings with town hall meetings and power vested within their congregations (causing them eventually to be known as Congregationalists), the Puritans had absolutely no tolerance for opposing religious views. There was no freedom of religion in areas controlled by Puritans.

Some Puritan descendants later regretted the hanging of Mary Dyer enough to build a statue in her memory as a martyr. The statue stands today in downtown Boston. But this Puritan strain of intolerance would lead to the execution of 20 women as witches in Salem, Massachusetts in 1692 (see listing).

1662 — The Virginia legislature provided for the governance of each church parish through the creation of a board of 12 of the most able men to manage the parish. Each man was to swear allegiance to the King of England and to the king's church. The men were to pledge to observe the doctrine and discipline of the Church of England. Thus, the church and state were bound ever tighter together, a bond that would be difficult to break when the Bill of Rights came along 129 years later.

May 1664 — Increase Mather, then a colonial theologian who was only 24 years old, became the minister of Boston's Second (Congregational) Church. He would hold this influential position until he died in 1723 at the age of 83. Along the way Increase Mather would serve as president of Harvard University.

Increase Mather would also play an important role in ending the Salem witch trials (see listing for 1692) after breaking with his equally famous son, Cotton Mather, over the issue of permitting spectral evidence at the trials. However, both Mathers would act very irresponsibly in writ-

1670

ten and spoken words at the beginning of the trials and fan the flames that led to the deaths of 24 people.

April 1670—The city of Charles Town (Charleston), South Carolina, was established while the Carolina Territory was settled by a mix of about 100 English men and women who sailed from London to establish Charleston. Their mission was essentially economic, and they were aided by a number of small planters wishing to escape the overcrowded island of Barbados in the West Indies.

However, by 1680, a group of French Huguenots (Protestants) trying ultimately to escape religious persecution by the Catholic Church, joined the settlement. To that extent, Charleston was a place of religious freedom. The persons from Barbados were familiar with using black slaves from Africa to help with the crops, and by 1700 about half the population of the 7,000 then in the settlement were black slaves. By 1750, the colony had reached about 64,000 people, of which nearly 40,000 were black slaves.

The colony would attract many different religious groups, and the representatives of the Church of England would be hard pressed to obtain the order and obedience they wanted to impose on the people of the colony.

1674—In St. Augustine, Florida, a community generally thought to be the oldest continually occupied European settlement in the continental United States (founded by the Spanish in 1565), seven men were ordained into the Catholic priesthood. This was a significant church spectacle at the time.

Although Florida was not part of the British colonies at the time, the missions around St. Augustine remained in some form until all of Florida was finally ceded to the new United States in 1821. The British had taken over much of Florida in 1763, but their religious activities there were at a much lower level than the Spanish who preceded them.

May 1675—The very long sermons preached in typical Puritan/Congregationalist churches in New England caused some church members to make an early exit from the church services. Accordingly, Massachusetts passed a law requiring church doors to be locked during services.

September 1678—The famous book *Pilgrim's Progress* by John Bunyan was published in England. Three years later it was reprinted in colonial America and widely read in the Puritan areas of the colonies. The book is considered a Christian allegory, has been printed over time in more than 200 languages, and supposedly never has been out of print.

The full title of the book is *The Pilgrim's Progress from This World to That Which Is to Come*. The book was praised for its effective simplicity, which allows it to be read by both adults and children. Bunyan wrote it during stints in English jails for holding religious services outside the auspices of the Church of England, a common punishment in many places when church and state were closely entwined.

Bunyan wrote many other books and even a hymn, but none gained the popularity of *Pilgrim's Progress*. Its simplicity and careful cadences were not possible to reproduce successfully in his other works.

May 1681—William Penn was given land by King Charles II for what would become Pennsylvania. Penn founded Pennsylvania as a holy experiment, seeing Pennsylvania as a refuge for people of different nationalities and religions to live together in freedom and peace. The king owed a large debt to Penn's father and discharged it by granting Penn a large tract of land west of the Delaware River. Penn tried to carefully plan his colony to avoid the mistakes made by prior colonies.

Penn cautioned his potential colonists to expect to struggle for a few years before reaping the benefits of the new land. He also advised them that he intended his colony to be one of religious freedom and that all religions were welcome but none would be given a preference. Penn spent so much time in preparing his colony that even today some sources disagree on whether Pennsylvania was founded in 1681 or 1682, but in 1681 Penn was already writing his cautionary words for prospective settlers. Penn himself did not sail for Pennsylvania until August 1682.

Penn was a member of the Society of Friends (Quakers) in England, and it was his efforts to stop the persecutions against the Quakers in that country that led him to envision a colony in the New World that was based on true religious freedom. Accordingly, when Penn laid out the city of Philadelphia (city of Brotherly Love) in Pennsylvania ("Penn's Woods"), Quakers flocked to the new city. Penn's holy experiment attracted other religious groups to follow the Quakers. Penn had also established very lib-

1682

eral policies for the eventual ownership of land in his new colony, and this was another factor that attracted new settlers. Pennsylvania thrived from the beginning.

May 1682 — The General Court of Massachusetts repealed two laws having to do with religion as practiced in the state. The first law repealed was one which prohibited people from observing Christmas. The second was one that established capital punishment for Quakers who returned to the colony after being banished.

Unfortunately, the repeal of the capital punishment law was too late to save the life of the Quaker teacher Mary Dyer who had been hanged in Boston in 1660 (see listing) for returning to the colony after being banned.

June 1683 — Another one of the mistakes William Penn wanted to avoid in his new colony (see listing for 1681) was mistreatment of the native Indians that had caused so many problems in other colonies. Penn had sent agents to America before his own arrival there to assure the Indians that he wished to compensate them for the land used by his colony and otherwise demonstrate proper respect as a neighbor.

It would take until 1701 to complete a comprehensive treaty, but Penn showed that he was true to his word in 1683 by signing an initial treaty with the Delaware Indians and making an initial payment for lands he was incorporating into his Pennsylvania colony. As a result, Pennsylvania generally had much less trouble in its initial years with Indian uprisings than other colonies.

Also, during this year the first sizeable continent of German immigrants came to America and settled Germantown near Philadelphia. They were soon followed by the Mennonites and the Amish who settled a little further west in Lancaster County. Penn had visited parts of Germany when he was living in England, and he had talked with some of the groups now seeking religious freedom in his new colony.

The German groups were fleeing religious intolerance in Germany where they were seen as different, and Pennsylvania was an ideal destination. It was out of reach of their German oppressors, and the promise of religious freedom from other groups already in Pennsylvania was a promise carefully kept, not to mention the liberal policies for eventually owning land in Pennsylvania. Germans quickly became a large proportion of the population in Pennsylvania.

1685 — The growth of religious intolerance in France, capped by the revocation of the Edict of Nantes, resulted in a surge of emigration by French Protestant Huguenots fleeing Catholic persecution. They headed for the Protestant American colonies, and although in some places they faced continuing discrimination because they were not quite the right kind of Protestants, the degree of discrimination was much less than they faced in France.

The number of Huguenots was not especially large, but they had a strong influence on the colonies they settled in because they had a high proportion of merchants, professional men, and craftsmen among their ranks. They tended to settle in established cities like Charleston, Philadelphia, New York, and Boston, where their descendents achieved considerable commercial and political influence by the time of the Revolutionary War in 1776.

February 13, 1689 — A document called (in short form) the English Bill of Rights was presented to the proposed new rulers of England, King William III of Orange (Dutch) and Queen Mary II (a daughter of the deposed James II). Upon signing this document, the couple was offered the throne and crowned a few months later in April 1689.

This was a momentous event in English history, but it also had a substantial effect on the religious life of the colonies in America. The crowning of the new rulers was a result of what is called the Glorious Revolution of 1688. This revolution deposed the Catholic King James II, and gave or confirmed many individual rights to the English (and Scottish and Irish) people. It reestablished the Protestant religion as the official religion in England and gave various branches of that religion new freedoms.

But the Catholic religion was absolutely devastated in England. Catholics were denied the right to vote or to become members of Parliament. Catholics were denied commissions in the British Army, and any British monarch was forbidden to be Catholic or to marry a Catholic. This ensured the succession of Protestants to the throne and reinforced the idea that only a Protestant religion (Anglicanism) would be the official religion of England.

1692

The full title of the English Bill of Rights was An Act Declaring the Rights and Liberties of the Subjects and Settling the Succession of the Crown. It also had statements of tolerance for other forms of Protestantism, but it was a long time before such groups gained full legal rights. In some of the colonies, arrogant members of the Anglican Church fully embraced the establishment of their church as the official church, but preferred not to show any signs of tolerance towards other religions (see listing for 1707 — New York).

Other than the impact the events of 1689 had on religious life in the colonies as they attempted to follow new edicts from England, the English Bill of Rights ultimately had a strong influence on the writing of the Declaration of Independence, the Constitution, and The Bill of Rights of the United States. Many statements in these documents were taken directly from the English Bill of Rights. However, only the United States took the bold step of the separation of church and state. It can be argued that establishing both freedom of religion and **from** religion was the key step in realizing true individual liberties that so many other countries failed to realize in spite of their truly good intentions.

1692, Maryland— Political changes in England caused Maryland to become a royal colony under the control of a Protestant king and Parliament. As a result, Maryland's assembly passed an act making the Protestant religion the official religion of the colony. Thus, Maryland, which had begun on a theme of religious tolerance in 1634 (see listing) became just another Anglican colony transplanted from England as was nearby Virginia. However, simply issuing a declaration of an official religion did not automatically make all members of the colony follow that religion, as was also the case in nearby Virginia.

1692, Salem— In the town of Salem, Massachusetts, the infamous Salem witch trials and resulting executions took place. During the year, over 200 people were arrested on suspicion on being witches. In the spring and summer, 14 women and 5 men were hanged, another man was pressed to death under heavy stones, and 4 more people died in jail awaiting trial.

These 24 deaths were later identified as total miscarriages of justice, and they gave rise to the name of "witch trial" when similar hysterical conditions resulted in hasty investigations, indictments or trials based on

1692

very flimsy, if any, real evidence. Unfortunately, even three centuries later, such events still occur (see listings for day care trials in the 1980s and 1990s).

The notorious Salem trials were religious events in the sense that actions were perceived as being taken against representatives of the devil himself. The tightly controlled Puritan religion of the time created an atmosphere in which such events could take place. Further, famous Puritan minister Cotton Mather proclaimed the position that witches were a real manifestation of the devil and should be sought out in the community. Thus, leaders of the Puritan Church like Mather were certainty culpable in the tragedy that eventually took place in Salem.

A small industry has grown up in modern times in writing books purporting to tell the story of what really happened in Salem in 1692. Many of these books simply try to essentially excuse the people for their behavior by finding reasons for their actions in terms of other events occurring in and around Salem at the time. The bottom line is that the people still reflected the ignorance and superstitions of their cultural roots in Europe, and their prime religious leaders like Cotton Mather encouraged their actions rather than trying to stop them. In that sense, the Salem events were clearly Puritan religious events and Cotton Mather can be charged with acting in a completely irresponsible way.

There were many conflicting motives behind the trials that were circulating around Salem at the time. In 1689, a new minister named Samuel Parris was installed in Salem. His household included his daughter Betty, then about nine, his niece Abigail, about 11, and a slave couple from Barbados. The elite Putnam family, which had initially contacted Parris, was feuding with the elite Porters, and there was bad blood overall between the merchant families of the port of Salem and the farmers of Salem Village surrounding the port. Parris eventually became embroiled in disputes over his salary, and he refused finally to move out of the parsonage until he was paid.

In the middle of this acrimony, the young girls in the Parris household began having fits and exhibiting strange behavior. They were soon joined by other neighborhood girls their age and older, including some 17 years old. The girls claimed to being attacked by witches in spectral (ghostly) form which only they could see. The older the girls were, the more fanciful their stories. As unbelievable as it may seem now, these claims

1692

led to the deaths of 24 people. Various members of the Salem population pursued their personal agendas and Cotton Mather poured verbal gasoline on the sparks and ignited a blaze.

Most experts today believe the girls were basking in the attention they received, and their claims eventually became wilder and wilder until they passed the point of credulity for even their most ardent supporters. Their spectral evidence was admitted at trial until Increase Mather, father of Cotton Mather, broke with his son and condemned the practice in October 1692. After that, the hundreds of suspected witches were slowly given reprieves and/or found not guilty at trials where spectral evidence was not admitted.

Sir William Phipps, governor of the state, took a leading role in dismissing the cases, and Cotton Mather and some judges asked forgiveness for their actions. But William Stoughton, the deputy governor and one of the most aggressive witch-hunters did not ask forgiveness and was furious he could not continue riding the colony of witches no matter how many needed to be executed. It is perhaps an indication of the mind-set of many of the Puritans in the state that Stoughton became the next governor of Massachusetts.

Many of the accused witches were older women, as has been the normal case in the history of witch hunts, but several were widows with property while most accused witches were poor. Some analysts have claimed simple land grabs were behind the actions of some of the inhabitants of Salem who condemned the so-called witches.

There was certainly a mixed bag of motives in the trials, but there is little doubt that the lack of leadership, or the wrong kind of aggressive leadership played the biggest part in the executions. There are many things of which the New England Puritan Church can be proud, including an emphasis on hard work and thrift, the importance it placed on education, and the democratization of the leadership of the church. But the degree of intolerance it practiced that played a big part in the tragedy of Salem is a black mark that greatly dims the light of its positive accomplishments.

Perhaps the strongest lesson to be taken from the Salem episode is that even with the fresh start made in the New World, the old mistake of entwining religion with the affairs of state and creating a state-preferred religion led to tragedy as it had so many times in the past. If the Founding Fathers of the United States needed a good example of what could be avoided by creating the First Amendment (see listing for September 1787) by separating church and state, Salem was that example.

1693— Virginia, alone among all southern colonies, created a college called the College of William and Mary (Harvard had been created in 1636 in Boston — see entry). A man named James Blair, a bishop's representative, had been the prime mover in getting the Virginia legislature to create the college, named after the then-present king and queen of England.

The stated purpose of the college was to educate men to become clergy, provide a pious education for other young men, and help convert the Indians. Initially not many men undertook to be educated as clergy because they would have to travel to England to be ordained. The Indians were also little affected by the college. But the college did become an educational force in Virginia and eventually trained many of its leaders.

April 1693— A tragic footnote to the Salem witchcraft trials of 1692 (see listing) came when the four-day-old son of minister Cotton Mather died of unspecified causes. In spite of essentially being rebuked by his minister father Increase Mather for his inflammatory part in the Salem witchcraft trials, Cotton Mather still suspected that witchcraft might have been the cause of his son's death.

Cotton Mather was a noted minister in the Puritan/Congregationalist Church of his era, but his obsession with witchcraft demonstrated how deeply ancient superstition was embedded in even the ministers of the time.

January 1697— Citizens of Massachusetts observed an official day of repentance and fasting for their roles in the Salem witch trials of 1692 (see listing) and the incredible miscarriages of justice that took place during the trails.

1699— Thomas Bray of England put together philanthropic forces in the country to create literature to be sent to all the colonies in North America to help support the many struggling churches there. Problems of widely scattered parishes over large distances in the colonies were making it difficult to establish the normal tight-knit church communities known in England.

1700

In 1699 the groups created a Society for Promoting Christian Knowledge to aid members of congregations. The groups also helped send clergy to the colonies, and in 1701 created a Society for the Propagation of the Gospel to aid the clergy in their work.

May 1700—William Penn, founder of Pennsylvania (see listing for 1681) as a beacon of religious freedom, used his position as a Quaker leader to begin a series of monthly meetings for blacks that advocated emancipation from slavery.

1701—The university that became Yale University was founded in Connecticut. It was also intended as a way to achieve the education esteemed by the Puritans (now generally known as Congregationalists because of their emphasis on the congregation as the leader of the church) as had been achieved with the founding of Harvard in 1636 (see listing).

1704—Joining the movement of other religions to Rhode Island to take advantage of the religious freedom to be found there, the Anglican Church of England established a presence in Rhode Island. Then, true to form, the Anglicans in Rhode Island ultimately wrote to England to complain about the many different religious groups they found flourishing in Rhode Island, thus making it difficult to make more converts to the Anglican cause.

1706—The Reverend Francis Makemie, who had arrived in the colonies from Ireland in 1683, led the organization of the first American Presbytery in Philadelphia. Makemie was a Presbyterian, a religion that had been founded by John Calvin in Geneva, Switzerland around 1537 as part of the Reformation of the 1500s. John Knox, a Scotsman, had studied theology with Calvin, and he took the religion back to Scotland. Scotland and England became the bastions of Calvinism/Presbyterianism.

Makemie was arrested in New York in 1707 (see listing) for preaching his religion against the wishes of the dominant Anglican Church, but gained his freedom in a jury trial and continued his preaching efforts. The Presbyterians became an active evangelistic denomination, as many Scotch-Irish immigrants brought their Presbyterian faith with them as they immigrated in large numbers to the colonies when times turned bad at home.

1707, New York—The present English governor of New York City, Lord Cornbury, decided to further impose the will of the Anglican Church upon the settlement won from the Dutch in 1644. He had already ignored the terms of the 1644 surrender granting freedom of religion to the Dutch Reformed Church, and now he proposed to rid the area of other religious groups.

Cornbury arrested a Presbyterian preacher named Francis Makemie for preaching without a license. When Makemie protested at trial that Cornbury was violating the terms of England's 1689 Declaration of Religious Tolerance (English Bill of Rights—see listing), Cornbury replied in essence that he was above following the declaration without specific royal instructions to do so, and Cornbury instructed the judge in the case to tell the jury to find Makemie guilty.

The jury then found Makemie innocent. Cornbury found, as had other arrogant Anglicans before him, that Americans were not as willing to automatically follow English orders as were English in the old country. Cornbury was soon recalled to England, and the Anglican cause in New York, New Jersey, and Delaware was helped primarily by the efforts of Thomas Bray and the Society for the Propagation of the Gospel (see listing for 1699).

1707, Philadelphia Baptists—Enjoying the religious freedom they found in Pennsylvania, a number of Baptist churches banded together to form the Philadelphia Association, the first such interchurch fellowship among Baptists in America. Baptist churches grew rapidly in Pennsylvania for the rest of the century.

1709—A mass exodus from the German Palatine (later known as the Rhineland) began for a number of reasons, only partly religious. But many Germans headed for existing settlements in Pennsylvania, which were initially settled for reasons of religious freedom (see entry for April 23, 1683). German religious groups, including the Lutherans and the Amish (the Pennsylvania Dutch), would establish firm religious roots in Pennsylvania before later extending into Ohio and even further west.

December 1712—The colony of South Carolina, under pressure from the representatives of the Anglican Church of England, passed what was

1718

known as the Sunday Law. The law required everyone to attend church each Sunday. It also required everyone to refrain from any type of skilled labor and to avoid traveling by horse or wagon beyond what was absolutely necessary.

Violators were either fined or spent two hours in the village stocks — or both. It was another example of the tie between church and state that would not be broken until the adoption of the Bill of Rights in 1791 (see listing).

1718, William Penn— William Penn died at the age of 74. Penn had been very successful in establishing his colony of Pennsylvania as a place of true religious freedom, and he had also set an example of dealing honestly with the Indians whose land he had utilized for his colony.

Pennsylvania was thriving when Penn died, and it continued to thrive after his death. But Penn had encountered many deep disappointments by the time of his death. He found the constant enmity between different factions of his beloved Quakers to be disillusioning, and he disliked the petty jealousies between them and among and within other religious groups that he found disheartening. Various trustees within the colonial management proved greedy and dishonest, as did members of his family.

Penn was not the first to find evils within the paradise he tried to create, and he certainly was not the last. But the ongoing success of his colony stood as a monument to his earnest efforts to create something different in a positive way.

1718 — Scotch-Irish— The British Parliament prohibited the emigration of skilled artisans. This was triggered by the increasing number of Scotch-Irish emigrating to America. Regardless of prohibitions, it is estimated that in the next half-century as many as 250,000 Scotch-Irish came to what would become the United States.

The Scotch-Irish were dedicated Presbyterians, but what triggered their emigration to America was the termination of land leases on favorable terms that had been granted 30 years before to encourage the Protestant Scotch to settle in otherwise Catholic Ireland. The Irish were hit with the same unfavorable leases, but they stayed in Ireland for another century before famine forced them to leave en mass for the United States.

The Scotch-Irish generally fared well in America, but their strong

Presbyterian faith was not equally welcomed in all parts of the colonies. One favorite destination became the ever-tolerant Pennsylvania, where they acted as a buffer in the western part of the colony between the settlers and the Indians being stirred up by the French. Many of the Scotch-Irish later drifted down into the backlands of the South.

1726—Presbyterian minister, William Tennant, founded a ministerial log college in Pennsylvania. This urge to develop educational facilities led to the founding twenty years later of what became Princeton University in nearby New Jersey (see listing for 1746).

August 1727—A group of French Ursaline nuns arrived in New Orleans and established the first Catholic charitable institution in America. There was an orphanage, a hospital, and a school for girls. New Orleans belonged to France at the time, but its Catholic churches and institutions generally remained in the United States when President Thomas Jefferson made his famous Louisiana Purchase in 1803.

April 1730—The first synagogue in America was dedicated in New York City. It was built by Shearith Israel as noted in the listing for 1654.

1730—A report from London deplored the lack of progress in converting the black slave population in the colonies to Christianity. By the time of the Revolutionary War in 1776 slaves would represent over 20 percent of the population in the colonies, and the fact that this sizeable group was not being converted raised concern in England. Missionaries had been sent out from England for that very purpose, and results were meager.

What the English did not fully realize was how important slaves had become to the economy of the colonies, especially in the South. Authorities in the South did not want to upset this economic balance and they were hesitant to make (or permit) any overt effort to convert the slaves to Christianity.

February 1732—A Catholic mass was celebrated for the first time at St. Joseph's Church in Philadelphia. Although early Catholicism in the colonies was often associated with Maryland because Maryland was nominally founded as a Catholic refuge (see listing for 1634), Catholics tended

1740

to keep a low profile there because of potential and actual harassment from the later government of the state.

However, Catholics did find true religious freedom after 1681 in William Penn's Pennsylvania, and Philadelphia quietly became a Catholic center in the colonies. St. Joseph's Church became the only Roman Catholic Church built and fully maintained in the American colonies before the Revolutionary War.

1740, George Whitfield—George Whitfield, an Anglican minister from the Church of England who had been located in England, arrived in the Charleston area in South Carolina (see listing for April 1670). His preaching produced great consternation for the Anglican commissary already in the area, Alexander Garden. Whitfield wanted to embrace members of all the religions in the area, and he soon was preaching a message of inclusion and goodwill. Whitfield felt the missionaries being sent to the Carolinas (and Georgia) were poor representatives of the Church of England, and were, to put it simply, bigots.

This was a good example of the problems the Anglican Church of England was having in the colonies. Most representatives of the church, like Alexander Garden wanted strict obedience to the church, and they saw the multiple religions springing up in America as obstacles to the rule of the Church of England. Men like Whitfield saw the Presbyterians, Baptists, and Congregationalists (from New England) as fellow Christians working for a common goal.

Whitfield became famous throughout the South for his preaching, and he even raised funds to start an orphanage in Savannah, Georgia. Whitfield was a symbol of what could have been accomplished in America before the Revolutionary War if the Church of England had taken a less arrogant position in its dealings with the colonies.

1740, *The Garden of the Soul* — During the period in the colonies (and England) when Catholics were generally prevented from public worship, prayer manuals were published quietly to assist Catholics in private worship. One such book was written by Richard Challoner and published in 1740 with the name *The Garden of the Soul*. It was an especially popular version of the genre and was widely used among Catholics.

The book stressed personal piety rather than public worship, and urged Catholic laity to stay involved in the tasks and professions around them even if they had to keep their practice of Catholicism private.

July 1741— Noted Congregationalist minister Jonathan Edwards delivered his famous sermon "Sinners in the Hands of an Angry God." This sermon is considered by historians as a key step in the Great Awakening that took place in the American colonies (and England) from about 1730 to 1760. But there is considerable historical debate about the timing and nature of the Great Awakening if, in fact, there was such an event.

Many who claim the existence of a Great Awakening from 1730 to 1760 tie its beginning to the sermon by Jonathan Edwards, although this sermon did not take place until 1741, as noted. George Whitfield (see listing for 1740) is also noted as a leader of the Great Awakening, but he also began his most active work in 1740. But if the Great Awakening as a period of more intense, more personalized preaching, the period from 1730 to 1760 certainly demonstrated many examples.

Not all who preached during this time were necessarily happy with this evolution in the style of preaching. There were New Lights who took readily to the new style, and Old Lights who were not happy with change of any sort in religious protocols. The New Lights were by far the most popular. Further, the New Lights encouraged people to read the Bible on their own at home and a more personal interest in their religion. Old Lights disapproved of this idea. They wanted to interpret the Bible for their church members.

Some historians think that the Great Awakening may have had a political as well as a religious affect. The sense of democratization within the hierarchy of the church and the then-radical movement to individual responsibility for salvation can be viewed as leading to independence politically from the corrupting policies of old mother England. The Great Awakening could easily have led to thoughts of political independence in the same way it led to new thoughts about the practice of religion.

1742, Chauncy— Charles Chauncy wrote "Enthusiasm Described and Cautioned Against," which took a different position on the Great Awakening presently going on (see listing for July 1741). As can be guessed from its title, Chauncy's polemic did not favor the stricter view each individual was being encouraged to take regarding religious views. Unitarians later would consider this the true beginning of Unitarianism in America (see listing for 1825).

1742, Muhlenberg— Henry Muhlenberg, an accomplished linguist and preacher, arrived in Philadelphia at the age of 31. Muhlenberg could preach in Dutch and English as well as his native German. Muhlenberg was a Lutheran, but he traveled widely throughout the colonies, preaching wherever he went in whatever language seemed appropriate for the place in which he found himself.

Muhlenberg was a great missionary, but he found fault with the pacifism of the Quakers and several German sects. He found them inappropriately standing by when the French-Indian Wars demanded action, and he fought against such pacifism as the Revolutionary War took shape in 1775 and after. In his view, true religion was one thing but a refusal to defend yourself and your neighbors against a common enemy was quite another.

1744— A Presbyterian preacher named Samuel Davies migrated into Virginia from Pennsylvania and began to attract converts to his religion. Davies was violating the strict tie between the Anglican Church and state in Virginia, and was soon prosecuted by the Virginians. When Davies protested that the authorities in Virginia were going beyond the Declaration of Religious Tolerance issued by the king and queen of England (William and Mary), he was supported by English authorities who decreed some degree of religious toleration was needed to support the free trade efforts of a trading nation like England.

Virginia essentially backed down, but only to a degree. It was another example of how some of the colonies became more intolerant of other religions than the home church in England. The powers that be in Virginia wanted no evangelical efforts in their colony, especially when some of those efforts sought to bring Christianity to black slaves.

1746— Presbyterian churchmen in all the colonies and even the British Isles combined their forces to found The College of New Jersey, later to be known as Princeton. In 1776 its president, John Witherspoon, who was also a clergyman, was the only minister to sign the Declaration of Independence.

1753

The Presbyterians were becoming very strong around this time because of the arrival of hundreds of thousands of Scottish immigrants, both from Scotland proper and especially the Scotch-Irish from the Ulster area.

1748—Jonathan Mayhew delivers his famous "Seven Sermons" (which would be published in 1750). Mayhew stated that not only does everyone have the right to make private judgments in religious matters, they have the duty to do so. It was another attack on the almost dictatorial nature of the Puritan/Congregational Church. It was also another step in the development of Unitarianism in America.

June 1750—Famous (or perhaps notorious by now) Congregationalist/Puritan minister Jonathan Edwards (see listing for June 1741) was dismissed from his ministerial post at the Congregationalist Church of Northampton, Massachusetts. Edwards had been at the church for 23 years, but over time his super-conservative theology and his complete inflexibility on even administrative issues had worn thin with the church members.

Thus, the democratic arrangement within the church hierarchy, in spite of the basic rigid intolerance of the church towards any other religion, supported the decision of the congregation to dismiss their minister, no matter how famous he might otherwise be.

1750—Taking advantage of the freedom of religion in Pennsylvania, Catholics, regarded with much suspicion and dislike in America, migrated over the years into Philadelphia from Maryland (see listing for 1634) and even arrived directly from Great Britain and Europe. By 1750, there were only 30 Catholic churches in the colonies, and 26 of these were in Pennsylvania or Maryland.

During the early years of the French-Indian Wars in 1757, British authorities ordered a census of the Catholics in Pennsylvania, fearing the Catholics might be tempted to intercede on the side of Catholic France. The census showed a total of only 1,400 Catholics in the whole colony, most of whom were German.

1753—Jonathan Mayhew now occupied the pulpit of the West Church in Boston from which he preached the unity of God as part of the effort

1754

to develop Unitarianism in America (see listing for 1748). In 1755 Mayhew published a book called *Sermons*, which contained 14 more sermons in addition to the seven previously published in 1750.

Mayhew continued to attack the Calvinist views on predestination, justification by faith alone, and original sin.

1754, Baptists— Shubal Sterns, a Baptist preacher, emigrated to Virginia from Massachusetts and began to make converts to his religion. The relatively simple message of the Baptist theology attracted many followers, and even though Sterns himself soon moved on to North Carolina, he left many converts who continued spreading the Baptist form of Christianity.

1754, King's College— The Anglican leaders in New York City decided to create a college to advance learning in the area, and they further determined that the Anglican religion and liturgy would be the only one used at the college. The college was named King's College after King George II who chartered the college.

Presbyterian lawyer and Yale graduate William Livingston led a protest against the Anglican monopoly at the college, pointing out that the many members of the other religions in the area outnumbered the membership of the Anglicans. The Anglican Church agreed that attendance at the college would be open to all, even though the college president would be an Anglican "forever after."

The word "forever" turned out to encompass a very brief time in this case. After the Revolutionary War, the name of the college was changed to the more patriotically sounding "Columbia" and the Anglican leadership was soon gone.

1759, Ebenezer Gay— Ebenezer Gay delivered the Dudleian Lecture at Harvard University. Gay, who in 1750 had assumed leadership of the Hingham Association (a group of ministers in southern Massachusetts committed to the fight for freedom from "unreasonable doctrines"), titled his lecture "Natural Religion as Distinguished From Revealed."

Gay's thesis was that revelation can teach nothing contrary to natural religion or the dictates of reason. It was a basic Unitarian position.

1759, Anglicans—An Anglican Church leader complained about the rapid spread of Baptist converts in Virginia by stating that this "shocking delusion" threatens to subvert "true religion" in the area unless its proponents are "apprehended or otherwise restrained." It was another example that religions brought from England in the colonial period believed in religious freedom only for their specific form of religion.

1763—Members of the Jewish religion, who had earlier migrated to Rhode Island to enjoy its climate of religious freedom, completed their building of what was claimed by others to be the finest synagogue in the colonies. The synagogue, named the Touro Synagogue after the rabbi presiding there at the time of construction, was built by the congregation of Jeshuat Israel, and is still in use 250 years later.

1764, Brown University—The college that would become Brown University in Providence, Rhode Island, was started with the help of Baptists from Pennsylvania and other parts of New England. The original charter of the school, true to its origins in Rhode Island, stated that no religious test would ever be required for admittance, and all members "shall forever enjoy full, free, absolute, and uninterrupted liberty of conscience."

1764, St. Louis—The community of St. Louis was founded with French Jesuit missionary Sebastian Meurin as the first pastor of the church established there. French Catholic missionaries had been active in Canada and the northern part of America since the early 1600s. Many had met horrific deaths at the hands of Indian tribes in the area, even though the Catholic priests had set out to "civilize" and convert the "savages" of the New World. But many had considered the natives of Canada and the northern tier of what became the United States as subhuman and their attitude probably was easily discernible.

The French missionaries began working their way down the Mississippi River towards the Gulf of Mexico, establishing parishes in Mississippi and Alabama around 1700. But probably the most lasting reminders of the French missionary presence were created in New Orleans (founded in 1718) based on the religious work they did there (see listing for August 1727).

1765

1765— The Dutch Reformed Church followed the lead of other religions in opening a college to train its ministers and to provide a proper education for its young men in general. The college was initially named Queen's College, but it was later named Rutgers.

1768— Presbyterian minister William Livingston, commenting on the efforts of various leaders of the Anglican Church to send more bishops to the colonies from England to impose stricter efforts on the colonies to obey the edicts of the Anglican Church, was quoted as saying this effort "posed a threat to liberty, property, and conscience even greater than the obnoxious Stamp Act." The Stamp Act had recently been another issue of contention between the colonies and the English government.

It was becoming clear that the colonies were ready to revolt against what they saw as the tyranny of the English Church as well as the tyranny of the English government.

July 16, 1769— A Catholic mission was established at San Diego by Franciscan Junipero Serra. Following Serra's initiative and continuing mission building, a total of 21 missions were finally built between 1769 and 1821 (Serra died in 1784) in a chain spreading up the California coast. Junipero Serra ultimately took up residence at the San Carlos Mission in Carmel where he lies buried today.

The road built to link the missions was named El Camino Real (the "Royal Road") and is a major highway in California today. The missions were intended originally to civilize and convert the Native Americans, but in many ways they became glorified prisons of free Indian labor for the settlers and priests who prospered in the community-like missions. Many of the Native Americans died from exposure to new diseases common to the settlers and missionaries but fatal to the Native Americans. By the 1830s, the Indian population was only a quarter of what it had been when the mission building started. It was a microcosm of what was taking place in the entire United States at that time.

When Mexico gained its independence from Spain in 1821, Mexico adopted its own version of separation of church and state. It began a program of dissolving the missions and appropriating their land.

1770— Dartmouth University opened its doors for classes (it had been chartered in 1769). Named after its patron, the earl of Dartmouth, the college was founded by the activities of Eleazer Wheelock, a graduate of Yale University, class of 1733. Wheelock was especially interested in converting the Indian population to Christianity. He intended Dartmouth to be a school for Indians, opening it to both Indians and the white population.

The Indians failed to show much interest in the college, and it quickly became another college operating under Congregationalist traditions. The emphasis placed by the Puritans on education in the highly religiously intolerant state they were building in the New World would become a marker as unique as their high degree on intolerance.

Dartmouth would become the centerpiece in a landmark U.S. Supreme Court decision in 1819 (see listing) giving religious and private groups the right to operate their colleges without interference from the state in which they were located.

March 29, 1772—Emmanuel Swedenborg of Sweden died on this date at the age of 84. Swedenborg was a Swedish scientist who became a Christian theologian at the age of 56. He claimed to have dreams and visions in which he saw God who instructed him to write a heavenly doctrine to reform Christianity.

The writings of Swedenborg (often called the Third Testament) gained him a following in England and the American colonies and subsequently the United States. His followers sometimes used the name Swedenborganism to define their religion, although they also have used such names as the New Christians, Neo-Christians, The New Church, and Church of the New Jerusalem. Noted Americans influenced by Swedenborg included Ralph Waldo Emerson, Helen Keller, Henry James, Sr., and John Chapman (Johnny Appleseed).

The followers of Swedenborg in the United States are estimated to have peaked in the 1850s, with about 10,000 remaining in the early 1900s. There are less than that today, although worldwide membership is estimated to be about 25,000.

1772—Quaker Anthony Benezet in Philadelphia called for an end to the slave trade both in Africa and the countries that imported the slaves. Baptist John Allen in Boston made the same plea in even stronger terms, saying that all Christians who follow the Gospel of Christ were duty-bound to oppose slavery. Such sentiments would continue to grow in the north-

1773

ern part of the country for almost a century until the Civil War would bring the issue to a head in 1861.

The issue of slavery would split the three largest Protestant dominations in the early 1800s, the Baptists, Methodists, and Presbyterians, into northern and southern factions divided by protests against and support for slavery based on geographical location. The Catholic Church would not split per se because it was a monolithic organization directed from afar by Rome, but priests in northern parishes would oppose slavery while priests in southern parishes would defend slavery.

The Civil War would not only split the nation, it would split the churches in the nation. The nation would finally recover officially from its split, but some churches would not. And a legacy of bitterness would remain for a long time.

1773—The first annual conference of Methodists in the New World was held. A few years earlier Philip Emery from Ireland had begun to preach in New York and Robert Strawbridge founded a Methodist congregation in Maryland. In 1769, founder of Methodism John Wesley sent several preachers from England, and John Asbury (see listing for 1784) arrived in the colonies in 1771.

These various groups put together the first annual conference in 1773, and laid the groundwork for the official creation of the Methodist Episcopal Church in the United States in 1784 (see listing).

August 1774—An English religious leader named Ann Lee arrived in America with a small group of her followers. This group would be the basis of the American development of the Shakers. The name preceded the group as they had been named Shakers in England because of the rather wild dancing that was part of their religious observances. The group consisted of Quakers, and the name progressed from Shaking Quakers to simply Shakers.

Ann Lee was an illiterate worker in a textile mill in England. She married when she was 26, but all four of her children died. This might have been a factor in her subsequent belief that celibacy was necessary to be a devoted follower of Jesus. Lee was imprisoned in 1770 by English authorities during a period of persecution of religious minorities such as the Quakers. While in jail she had a series of religious visions.

Upon her release from jail in 1771, Lee founded a religious sect called the United Society of Believers in Christ's Second Appearing, but because of her prior association the sect was called the Shakers. Still unwelcome in England, Lee, now called "Mother Ann" by her followers, migrated to the American colonies with her husband and a few followers to spread her gospel in the New World.

Lee was imprisoned again in 1780 during the Revolutionary War because of her pacifist views and refusal to sign an oath of allegiance. She died in 1784, and the Shaker religion was led thereafter by Elder Joseph Mecham and Eldress Lucy Wright. They guided the movement to great success in terms of growth in membership and a reputation for great craftsmanship in their established communities.

However, the Shaker belief in celibacy and not having children carried the seeds of the eventual disappearance of the sect. The Shakers believed they essentially represented the second appearance of Jesus (as did Mother Ann) and they must create a heaven on earth as his followers. The sect peaked in 1840 with 6,000 members (see listing for 1840) and then slowly declined. They left a reputation for harmonious communal living, great craftsmanship and building techniques, and equal rights for women.

1774 — An arrest in Virginia of some Baptist evangelists for disturbing the peace near the home of future president, James Madison, then only 22 years old, set Madison on the road to espousing the religious freedom he would manage to insert into the Bill of Rights 17 years later when it was written in the years following the Revolutionary War.

At the time of the arrests, Madison wrote a condemnation of such persecution, stating that the "diabolical, hell-conceived principle of persecution" must cease. Madison was not a Baptist, but he felt that all such dissenters should be free to practice their religions.

July 1775 — The American Army began employing chaplains to look after their religious needs. There was no formal Declaration of Independence yet, but hostilities between the British and the American Army were already under way in Massachusetts. George Washington of Virginia was placed in charge of the Army there.

1776 — In the year the writing and publication of the Declaration of Independence marked the formal beginning of the Revolutionary War, a man

1777

named John Leland arrived in Virginia from Massachusetts. He immediately began to support Madison's concept of religious freedom (see entry for 1774). Leland later observed that state establishment of religion had done more harm to the cause of Christ "than all the persecutions" ever did.

Leland's influence was evident when the Baptists and Presbyterians joined together to petition the Virginia legislature for relief from the oppressive laws that favored the Anglican Church and suppressed dissent. The Baptists also joined with the followers of Thomas Jefferson to promote religious freedom.

1777—Thomas Jefferson, in his capacity as the governor of Virginia, wrote a Bill for Establishing Religious Freedom and sent it to the Virginia legislature. Some members of the legislature, while agreeing that the bill was in the spirit of the Declaration of Independence, worried that complete freedom of religion might be too big a step and sought for a compromise that would prevent prosecution of different religious groups but still designate the "Christian Religion" as the official religion of the state. James Madison undertook the role of leading the fight for full religious freedom (see entry for 1785).

1782—The Jewish community in Philadelphia built the Cherry Street Synagogue. Members of the Jewish faith had also taken advantage of the true freedom of religion to be found in Pennsylvania, and they had located there steadily over the years. By the end of the colonial period, the Jewish community in Philadelphia was the largest in the nation.

1784, Catholics—John Carroll of Maryland was named superior of missions in the United States, removing the Catholic Church in the United States from the authority of the vicar apostolic of London (Carroll was subsequently named America's first Roman Catholic bishop in 1789—see listing). Carroll was a member of the wealthy and powerful Carroll family in Maryland that had played an important role in keeping the Catholics established in Maryland as the fortunes of the church waxed and waned with changes in the political climate. He was the cousin of Charles Carroll, the only Catholic signer of the Declaration on Independence in 1776.

With the ending of the Revolutionary War also ending the dominance of the English Anglican Church in the United States, Rome felt free to name its first bishop in the new nation as noted above. In 1791, Carroll chose Baltimore as the site for his cathedral, and the famous architect Benjamin Lathrobe (architect of the United States capitol) designed a cathedral modeled after the Parthenon in Rome. Carroll recommended proceeding with great caution in promoting the Catholic church in the new country so as to avoid any negative reaction to a church only recently feared and disliked in many of the colonies. Maryland and Pennsylvania became the prime centers for the Catholic religion in the early days of the United States.

1784, Methodists—The Methodists formally organized themselves as a strong Protestant church group at a meeting in Baltimore, Maryland. The Methodists felt much more secure in their efforts to spread the teachings of their religion now that the Church of England had no official voice in the United States following the end of the Revolutionary War. The leader of the Methodists at this key point in their history was Francis Asbury, often recognized as the first American Methodist bishop (Thomas Coke also shared this title). The Methodists in Maryland especially reached out to the black community, and eventually the Methodists would become the largest individual Protestant church group in the country for over a century.

Thomas Coke had been consecrated as the first English bishop of the Methodist Episcopal Church in England by the founder of the religious denomination, John Wesley. There was some dispute over whether Wesley, still a member of the English Anglican Church, consecrated Coke as a superintendent in 1784 and then a bishop or whether the title bishop just evolved and Coke adopted it permanently. Either way, Coke sailed for the United States in 1784 and went on to play a key role in the growth of the Methodist Church in both the United States and as a missionary to foreign lands. Both Coke and Asbury were later recognized as the first American Methodist bishops rather than simply Superintendents.

1784, Chauncy—Charles Chauncy (see listing for 1742) published a treatise called "The Mystery Hid From Ages and Generations." The treatise dealt with the subject of universal salvation and continued the break from conventional theology that was going on in New England.

1785

1785, Madison—James Madison presented his famous "Memorial and Remonstrance" arguing for freedom of religion in Virginia. The Virginia legislature was considering a bill proposed by Patrick Henry (of "give me liberty or give me death" fame) to make "the Christian Religion ... the established Religion" of the state.

The old Anglican Church previously brought from England had been renamed the Protestant Episcopal Church, but Virginians (as were many others) were uneasy about not having an official state religion. It was what they had known all their lives, and more practically they were concerned that any church would not survive if the state could not coerce citizens to contribute to its support.

Madison, however, was determined that freedom of religion really meant freedom of religion. He stated that a state-favored religion created "pride and indolence in the Clergy; ignorance and servility in the laity; in each, superstition, bigotry, and persecution." Madison added that Christianity was not created by human power and did not depend on human power for its survival.

Madison's position won in the Virginia legislature (see listing for January 1, 1786), and he carried it over into the writing of the Constitution during 1787 (see listing) and the Bill of Rights that finally went into effect in 1791 (see listing).

1785, King's Chapel—The well-known King's Chapel in Boston, which formerly claimed allegiance with the Episcopal Church, ordained Unitarian James Freeman as its minister. Accordingly, all references to the Trinity were removed from its prayer book. King's Chapel became a center of Unitarianism.

January 1, 1786—The Virginia Statute for Religious Freedom, a modified version of the bill Thomas Jefferson had written in 1777 (see listing) and that James Madison had supported with his famous "Memorial and Remonstrance" in 1785 (see listing) was adopted. Although Jefferson was now in Paris in continued service as a diplomat for the new United States, his words would form the basis for the all-important Bill of Rights that became effective in 1791 (see listing).

Jefferson wrote that "Almighty God hath made the mind free," and thus mere men should not assume the power to exercise "dominion over the faith of others." For those who fear that without state authority errors and heresies would spread, Jefferson pointed out that errors can only be conquered by truth, and "truth is great and will prevail if left to herself."

Although none of the words of the Virginia statute found their way into the Constitution and Bill of Rights that followed (see listings for 1787 and 1791, respectively), they formed the basis for the important words in these documents that were concerned with religion.

The Virginia statute read "Be it enacted ... that no man shall be compelled to frequent or support any religious worship place, or ministry whatsoever." Further, no one shall suffer for his or her religious opinions, and whatever opinions they express shall in no way affect their citizenship or their rights. In essence the statute made it clear that there shall be both freedom of religion as well as freedom from religion.

Jefferson and Madison then turned themselves from religious freedom in the state of Virginia to religious freedom in the entire nation of the new United States.

April 1787 — In Philadelphia a black minister named Richard Allen, who had been appointed assistant pastor of St. George's Methodist Church in 1786, joined with fellow black activist Absalom Jones and other ex-slaves to form the Free African Society. This was a combined benevolent/religious group, supported in part by wealthy Quakers, that offered fellowship and mutual aid to free Africans and their descendents.

Allen was an ex-slave who had bought his freedom from his owner, located in Delaware, when the owner was converted to the Methodist faith and was convinced by the process that slavery was wrong in the eyes of God. Allen sawed cordwood and drove a wagon during the Revolutionary War period to earn money to buy his freedom. Allen became a "licensed exhorter" for the Methodist Church, preaching along the East Coast. His actions were noted by Methodist leaders, including Francis Asbury, the first American bishop of the church (see listing for 1784), and this led to his appointment as assistant pastor of St. George's Methodist Church in Philadelphia as noted above. Allen would later become famous for his roles in other Methodist activities in Philadelphia (see listing for 1794).

September 1787 — One of the most important events affecting religion in the United States took place when the Constitution was signed by the members of the commission appointed to create it and then shortly sent out to the states for ratification. The only basic mention of religion in the original Constitution was in Article VI that forbade any religious test to be applied to any person seeking to hold any "Office or public Trust" in the United States. However, the Constitution specifically allowed those taking the oath of office to "affirm" their allegiance rather than "swearing" their allegiance. This was in deference to religious groups like the Quakers and others who believed that the Bible forbade such swearing of allegiance.

The primary purpose of the Constitution was to define the form of the new government of the United States, not define its religious makeup, but the sixth article clearly signaled that the United States was going to be a country of religious freedom. That point was made much more explicit in the Bill of Rights that would grow out of the ratification process for the Constitution. The Constitution was declared ratified and in effect in March 1789. The Bill of Rights (see listing for 1789) was declared in effect December 15, 1791. A number of states had made their approval of the Constitution contingent on the adoption of the amendments that became the Bill of Rights, and these amendments were submitted to the states for ratification in September 1789.

March 1789 — The Constitution, written in 1787 (see listing) was declared ratified and in effect after going through the ratification process from September 1787 through July 1788. Other states continued to ratify it after it had been declared in effect.

During the ratification process, some states had said their approval of the Constitution was contingent on the addition of some amendments that would better clarify certain issues and make the division of power between the states and the central government more explicit. The amendments that would become the Bill of Rights were sent to the states for ratification in September 1789. James Madison, who had guided the development of the Constitution, then guided the writing of the amendments, taking care to note the work he and Jefferson had done on the issue of freedom both of and from religion.

There were originally 12 amendments, but two were not ratified promptly by the required number of states. Thus, the original amendments numbered 3 through 12 became numbers 1 through 10, and these amendments became the famous Bill of Rights. From the standpoint of religion the First Amendment was the key amendment (see listing for December 15, 1791). The two amendments not initially ratified had to do with the apportionment of representatives and the compensation of members of Congress. The compensation amendment was ratified two centuries later in 1992 and became the 27th amendment.

November 1789— Father John Carroll of Maryland was confirmed as the first Roman Catholic bishop in the United States. As noted in the listing for 1784, the Carroll family had long been prominent in Maryland and John Carroll and his cousin Charles (the only Catholic signer of the Declaration of Independence) had traveled with Benjamin Franklin and Samuel Chase to (Catholic) Canada in 1776 to try to get Canada to support the colonial cause. When Franklin was later in Paris, he responded to a papal inquiry that he recommended John Carroll as the head of the Catholic Church in America.

Carroll served as superior of the missions from 1784 until 1789. Then, with the United States firmly established as a new nation, Rome gave the Catholic Church in the country the status of a full diocese. The Catholic clergy in the nation were invited to choose their new bishop. They chose John Carroll, to no one's surprise.

However, the consecration of a new bishop required another bishop to lay hands on the head of the new bishop's head per ancient ceremonies. Because John Carroll was the only bishop at the time in the United States, Carroll ultimately traveled to England to arrange to meet other bishops and go through the official ceremony. There were an estimated 25,000 Catholics in the eastern part of the United States when John Carroll became a bishop. This was about 1 percent of the total population. There were about an equal number of Catholics in the western part of the United States that was still under the rule of Spain. None of them at the time could believe that in another 50 years or so the Catholic Church would represent the largest single Christian denomination in the United States.

In this momentous year for John Carroll, he also made time to found what became Georgetown University, the oldest Catholic University in the United States.

December 25, 1789— This was the first Christmas under the aegis of the new Constitution, but Congress was holding a regular session. This

1790

was because Christmas did not become a national holiday until 1870. In fact, at the time the celebration of Christmas was held in low regard by many Christians. They saw it as a time of many anti-Christian excesses and partying.

In the strict religious atmosphere of Boston, celebrating Christmas was actually illegal between 1659 and 1681. The law was finally repealed in 1682 (see listing), but the general anti-Christmas celebration sentiment in the North was what kept Christmas from becoming a national holiday until 1870.

1790, George Washington — Even before the Bill of Rights was ratified in December 1791 (see listing), people who were aware of the wording of the First Amendment and its specification of religious freedom, wrote to new President George Washington to ask essentially if it really meant what it said. The idea of freedom both of and from religion was so new and revolutionary in the world of 1790 that many could simply not believe it.

On March 12, 1790, Washington replied to a group of Roman Catholics, one of the most harassed religions in the nation, that he hoped to see "America among the foremost nations in examples of justice and liberality." With reference to the Catholics in particular, he added, "I presume that your fellow citizens will not forget the patriotic part which you took in the accomplishment of their Revolution and the establishment of their government." He noted the critical role France, "a nation in which the Roman Catholic religion is professed," played in the success of the revolution.

The Jewish Congregation in Newport, Rhode Island, asked if the United States would continue to offer asylum to the persecuted of the world. Washington replied on August 17, 1790, that liberty of conscience applied to all Americans without discrimination. He confirmed that "happily the Government of the United States ... gives to bigotry no sanction, to persecution no assistance." He concluded with the hope that the "children of the Stock of Abraham" would continue to enjoy and merit the goodwill of all other inhabitants of the nation. Washington concluded that he envisioned a future where "everyone shall sit in safety under his own vine and fig tree, and there shall be none to make him afraid."

Washington wrote in a similar vein to many other religious groups, including the Quakers and the Baptists. He tried to assure them that even if the words of the First Amendment seemed too good to be true, this was one instance where such good words really were true.

1790, Leland—John Leland (see listing for 1776) proposed to Virginia Baptists that they condemn the practice of slavery as inconsistent with the teachings of their religion. Slavery should also be condemned as inconsistent with the new government being built in the United States now that the Revolutionary War was over and the United States was developing a new constitution. The Baptists adopted his resolution, but it would be many years before a concerted effort would be made to change the institution of slavery.

November 10, 1791—The only Catholic bishop in the United States, John Carroll (see listing for November 1789), wrote a prayer meant for the president's inauguration that asked God's blessing not only on the president but on all the key government officials charged with leading the nation. Carroll was a close friend of George Washington, and the prayer was much praised. It is still in regular use today.

December 15, 1791—The Bill of Rights was declared ratified and in effect. The ten amendments making up the Bill of Rights had been written in 1789 (see listing). By far the key amendment relative to religion was the first of the ten amendments. It stated at the beginning that "Congress shall make no law respecting an establishment of religion, or prohibiting the free exercise thereof...." These relatively few words created a revolution in the relationship between the government and religion in the United States and eventually around the world.

Even though there had been passionate calls for the freedom of religion, some states did not applaud the idea when they recognized fully what the law entailed. Massachusetts, for example, took nearly four decades to revise its state constitution to reflect the freedom of religion as espoused in the Bill of Rights. The objection was not so much a refusal to permit other religions to operate freely within its borders (although many were even opposed to that idea), but rather an objection to the fact that without specific state sanction as a preferred religion, their beloved Congregationalist Church could not depend on the resources the state could supply through taxation and thus would have to survive on the resources it could

1793

raise on its own. The members of the legislation had never experienced in their lives the situation of the lack of an official state church and the idea took time to get used to.

Other states had similar hesitations, but as the churches continued to survive on their own the idea of no state-sponsored church began to be accepted. Other religions that had been oppressed as not being the official church, such as the Presbyterians, Baptists, and Methodists, underwent even more rapid growth and continued to expand throughout the United States.

There was no magic switch thrown when the First Amendment went into effect, and many members of the establishment continued to act as though their church was the preferred one and they still expected the privileges that came with their position of being members of the right church. Their attitudes were handed down to their children for generations to come, but the key aspect that started in 1791 was that there was no official backing to their assumptions.

Even though there was no official backing, for example, to the Protestant position that their form of Christianity at the least was the preferred religion, all public schools reflected the Protestant form of religion in terms of readings from the Bible and classroom prayers, not to mention the use of materials such as the popular *McGuffey Readers* to teach children to read. These books were filled with religious versions of events and took the time to poke fun at the pope and present Catholicism as an undesirable religion.

It was not until the second half of the 20th century that activists would successfully attack such practices, and among headlines screaming "they're kicking God out of schools" get the United States Supreme Court to affirm that the First Amendment really means exactly what it says.

The rest of this chronology covers the many instances where this kind of attitude affected the daily lives of many Americans, but the efficacy of the First Amendment in 1791 did permit the explosion of new religions in the United States and that explosion goes on today. There were many individuals who decried this explosion, but there was no official barrier to the creation of new religions after 1791.

1793— Now that the United States had its first Catholic bishop (see listing for 1789), the first Catholic priest to be ordained in the United States

1794

was the next step. Stephen Badin was ordained and sent to the frontier in Kentucky by Bishop John Carroll. Subsequent Catholic activities in Kentucky would result in the rather obscure place of Bardstown, Kentucky, being established as a new diocese in 1808 together with the more notable places of Boston, New York, and Philadelphia.

1794— English Unitarian Joseph Priestly arrived in the United States and helped to establish Unitarian churches in Philadelphia. This moved Unitarianism to some other place beyond its base in Boston.

July 1794— In a ceremony led by American Methodist Bishop Francis Asbury (see listing for 1784), black Methodist minister Richard Allen (see listing for 1787) and a small group of other free black Methodists formally opened Allen's Bethel African Methodist Episcopal Church.

A few months earlier, Allen had declined to become pastor of St. Thomas's African Episcopal Church, the church that been built by the Free African Society Allen had founded in 1787 (see listing). Allen explained that he felt bound to stay with the Methodist Church because it had played such an important role in obtaining his freedom, and for which he had been an active preacher for the last decade. Allen's friend, black activist and preacher Absalom Jones finally accepted the position. The Episcopal Church had essentially replaced the Anglican Church with which many free blacks had long been associated.

But Allen had felt the need for several years for a church operated entirely by and for blacks. He had led a withdrawal in 1789 from the Free African Society when the Quakers associated with the society wanted to adopt certain Quaker practices such as 15 minutes of silence at its meetings. Allen and others wanted more enthusiastic Methodist practices. In 1792, Allen led a walkout from St. George's Methodist Church, where he had been appointed an assistant minister in 1786, because the church practiced racial segregation in not permitting blacks to be buried in the church cemetery and, in 1792, building a separate gallery in which blacks were to worship.

Allen later explained that he wanted blacks to have the power "to call any brother that appears to us adequate to the task to preach or exhort as a local preacher, without the interference." So Allen led the creation of the Bethel Church in an old blacksmith's shop in southern Philadelphia,

1800

with "Methodist" carefully inserted into the title and with the blessing of Methodist Bishop Francis Asbury. The Bethel Church prospered with its emphasis of a black church operated by and for blacks, growing from 121 members in 1795 to 457 in 1805 and on to 1,217 in 1813.

Allen would later become the first black bishop of the Methodist Church and would continue to play an influential role in creating denominations within the church to expand his idea of churches operated by blacks for blacks. The African Methodist Episcopal (AME) Church would eventually become a separate denomination.

The concept of black churches owned and operated by and for blacks was greatly expanded after the Civil War when black ex-slaves flocked to mainly Protestant churches. Blacks would become very sensitive to any undercurrent of antiblack racism in the country, and they would soon realize black churches were one place where there was no such racism. The black churches went on to expand into supporting elementary schools and colleges and other such elements of everyday life. The black churches today are like a government within the national government where blacks can worship in their own way and otherwise prosper without encountering any sense of racism.

May 1800—The earliest known Methodist camp meeting was held in Logan County, Kentucky. Camp meetings became a popular way to spread the Gospel in the generally sparsely populated areas of the western frontier. People would travel significant distances to gather for a few days or more in the almost carnival atmosphere of the camps, where many preachers from many denominations would also gather.

The state of Kentucky was a popular place for this kind of meeting because at the time Kentucky was considered the beginning of the western frontier to residents of the original colonies (now states) on the eastern seaboard. The Methodists, Baptists, and Presbyterians appeared to benefit most from these camp meetings/revivals in terms of gaining new members, but even Catholics, now at least officially free of religious discrimination, were also active in Kentucky. In fact, in 1808 the obscure community of Bardstown, Kentucky, would join the large population centers of Boston, New York, and Philadelphia as being designated as the center of new Catholic dioceses.

This surge in religious activity in Kentucky and elsewhere caused the period from 1800 to about 1830 to be described by historians as the Second Great Awakening in the United States (the First Great Awakening was from about 1730 to 1760—see listing for July 1741). The Second Awakening featured evangelistic travel by preachers of the major denominations to reach the rather sparsely populated areas of the frontier through the method of camp meetings and revivals. The message of the Gospel was delivered in a joyous fashion showing how believers could be given salvation by a loving God and how those believers should apply the lessons of their faith to problems in everyday life.

One of the earliest and most famous of these camp meetings took place at Cane Ridge, Kentucky (see listing for August 6, 1801). It was one of the largest known and triggered many other such events, even if on a smaller scale.

February 16, 1801—The African Methodist Episcopal (AME) Zion Church made official its separation from its parent church, the Methodist Episcopal Church. The new denomination later became part of the African Methodist Episcopal Church created by Richard Allen (see listing for 1794). This made it part of the process of establishing black churches operated by and for blacks to eliminate any trace of antiblack racial discrimination within the churches attended by blacks. The AME Zion name is often confused in historical references because there are several black churches carrying that name (see listing for 1821).

August 6, 1801—One of the most famous camp meetings that were a fixture of the period took place at Cane Ridge, Kentucky. The organization of the event was credited to a Presbyterian minister Barton Stone, but Baptist and Methodist preachers took part as well. A crowd estimated at from ten to twenty-five thousand people attended the event held over six or seven days and nights. The size of the crowd can be best appreciated when it is realized that nearby Lexington, the largest city in the state, then had a population of just over 2,000.

The Cane Ridge camp meeting was, as were all camp meetings, a very emotional event. The attendees were mostly farmers who lived generally in a high degree of isolation. Observers noted that the huge number of wagons flanking the hastily assembled tents created an unusual environment for the people assembled there. The singing of songs amid

1805

flickering fires at nighttime certainly created a new emotion for people who commonly arose with the sun and slept when it went down.

There was much dancing and writhing and shouting as people claimed to be accepting Jesus as their savior. Some critics said they noted a greater increase of "fleshly lust" among the emotional crowd than of spirituality, and they were further quoted as saying "more souls were begot than saved." There was obviously a strong social element involved in the camp meetings, and how many of the highly visible conversions were lasting is open to question.

However, it was consistently noted that church attendance in the relatively few churches that existed in the region always increased after a camp meeting. The new nation was now peopled with individuals who were growing used to the freedom to express their religion in any way they pleased. The camp meetings were obviously fulfilling a need.

1805— Elizabeth Baley Seton, who would become the first American-born canonized saint, converted to the Catholic faith. Seton was the daughter of a distinguished colonial family named Baley, and the widow (at age 30 in 1804) of a wealthy merchant named William Seton. She and her husband had five children, but when she was widowed so young she decided to convert to Catholicism and do God's work. She only lived to age 47, but she left a substantial mark on the Catholic Church in her relatively few years (16) as a Catholic.

Seton moved to Baltimore in 1808 because it was the center of the Catholic Church in the United States at the time. She established both a school for girls and the core of a group that eventually became the Sisters of Charity. In 1809 Seton moved to Emmetsburg in western Maryland and established the nucleus of a parochial school system.

St. Joseph's Academy was founded by Seton in Emmetsburg, and she led her growing group of sisters as a writer, teacher, nurse, and administrator, teaching them to staff schools and orphanages. She was an active woman in all phases of her religion at a time when women were still expected to stay in the background.

1811— Priest Bendick Joseph Flaget arrived in Kentucky as the first bishop of the Bardstown, Kentucky, diocese that had been created in 1808. The diocese covered a huge area, from the Great Lakes to the Deep South and from the Appalachian Mountains to the Mississippi River (an area that would ultimately be split into more than 30 dioceses).

Flaget had spent nearly two years trying to avoid being made bishop of this large area, but Archbishop Carroll of Baltimore finally appointed him in 1810, and Flaget took up his post the following year. In spite of his initial reservations, Flaget remained as bishop for the next 40 years, and made a great success of his tenure.

April 1812— The Sisters of Loretto were founded in the Bardstown, Kentucky, diocese under the direction of a Belgian missionary named Charles Nerinckx. This sisterhood was the first established in America that was not linked to a "motherhouse" in Europe. Just eight months later, the Sisters of Charity of Nazareth were assembled by Father John Baptist David, the rector of the St. Thomas Seminary.

1813— Unitarian Andrews Norton took over Harvard's Dexter Lectureship in Biblical Criticism. This action, following the 1805 election of Unitarian Henry Ware to be Hollis Professor of Divinity at Harvard, increases the Unitarian influence at the oldest university in the nation.

1815— Father William DuBourg was appointed Bishop of Louisiana and the Floridas by Archbishop John Carroll of Baltimore. The appointment was made essentially as a result of the Louisiana Purchase from France by President Jefferson in 1803. This transferred many French Catholic priests to the control of the United States, which they initially resisted. The Spanish priest in the Floridas took their direction from the bishop of Havana. Thus, DuBourg had a difficult time exercising his authority.

The problem with the Spanish priests was resolved in 1819 when Spain ceded its Florida territory to the United States. However, the difficulties with the French priest who had been entrenched in New Orleans for a long time not was so easily solved. DuBourg moved the location of his headquarters northward to Saint Louis and waited for the French priests to undergo normal attrition and/or absorption into other parts of the Catholic Church within the United States before he moved back to New Orleans.

In spite of his initial problems with the resistive priest, DuBourg did good work among the Indians in his area, and was responsible for getting

1816

Jesuit Pierre Jean DeSmet from Belgium to come to the United States where he did excellent work with the Indians (see listing for 1840).

1816, John Adams—John Adams, the ex-president, wrote to his son (who also would later become a president himself), that in respect to religion, one must "Let the mind loose. It must be loose" uncramped by dogmatism, and unfettered by superstition. Adams felt that religion had done a lot of good things, and was a necessary part of life, but it was best when taken in a simple way without a lot of complicated theologies.

1816, Bible Society—The American Bible Society was formed by a group of individuals who were concerned that the new separation of religion and state might lead to a decline in religious beliefs. The society saw a need to distribute the scripture widely across the nation (and beyond). The Bible would have to be inexpensively printed and methods would have to be created to distribute it inexpensively as well. Such an accomplishment would require much free voluntary labor.

1817—Noted Baptist missionary John Mason Peck arrived in Saint Louis and began working along both sides of the Mississippi River. He kept at it for most of the next 40 years, founding schools, distributing tracts, organizing denomination activities, and preaching an almost endless number of sermons. Peck was a symbol of the ceaseless missionary actions of the major denominations in settling the early West.

1818, Connecticut—The state of Connecticut finally modified its state constitution to remove Congregationalism as the preferred religion in the state. It had taken 27 years since the adoption of the First Amendment to the nation's Constitution (see listing for December 15, 1791) for the state to wean itself from having a preferred state religion. Massachusetts would take several years longer.

Thomas Jefferson wrote to his friend John Adams, that he, Jefferson, rejoiced to see that "this den of priesthood is at length broken up, and that a protestant popedom is no longer to disgrace American history and character." Jefferson was quite sure of the need to firmly separate church and state, but at his death in 1826 (Jefferson and John Adams both died on July 4, 1826, exactly 50 years after the issuing of the Declaration of

Independence), much of the United States was still trying to adapt to the revolutionary idea.

1818, Presbyterians—At the General Assembly of Presbyterians, there was a unanimous declaration on the evils of slavery. The declaration read "We consider the involuntary enslavement of one part of the human race by another as a gross violation of the most precious and sacred rights of human nature; as utterly inconsistent with the law of God ... and as totally irresponsible with the spirit and principles of the Gospel of Christ."

There was a general feeling among religious groups that slavery in the United States would simply wither away because it was so evil on its face. But the harder the push for its elimination, the harder the resistance became for those on the other side. Positions would continue to harden until the outbreak of the Civil War in 1861.

1819, Channing—Noted minister William Ellery Channing delivered his famous sermon titled "Unitarian Christianity." This was one of the final steps that would lead to the founding of the American Unitarian Association in 1825 (see listing).

1819, Dartmouth—The United States Supreme Court ruled that religious groups and private trustees could continue to control colleges without interference from the state in which they were located.

The specific case concerned a battle over control of Dartmouth University (see listing for 1670), but the ruling gave encouragement to many religious denominations to continue to found colleges for both the education of their ministers and to provide what they saw as a proper Christian education to all young people.

Spring 1820—Joseph Smith, Jr., who would found the Mormon Church in 1830 with the publication of the *Book of Mormon* (see listing), saw a vision at the age of 14 in Palmyra, New York. He saw God and Jesus, and in his vision was told that all denominations of all religions had strayed from the truth and he should not join any of them. These instructions fit Smith's concern that local denominations tell different stories, in his view, and make him unsure of which to join.

1821

Smith continued his life as a farm boy unchanged in any way by the vision. When he told a local minister about his vision, Smith was scorned. He revealed this vision to no one else for nearly the next two decades.

1821—The African Methodist Episcopal (AME) Zion Church was officially formed in New York City. This particular church grew out of the John Street Methodist Church of New York City. There was considerable activity in the area of forming African Methodist Episcopal churches in Philadelphia and New York near the turn of the century (see listing for Richard Allen in 1794), and considerable confusion can result when trying to track the evolution of these churches.

However, there was one consistent theme. Free blacks who were drawn to Methodist Episcopal churches found themselves the objects of racial discrimination within the churches. There was no official policy of such discrimination in the Methodist Church structure, and the Methodists were especially active in recruiting blacks as well as whites, but in mixed congregations, such issues as not permitting burial of blacks in church graveyards and urging blacks to worship in separate areas of the church constantly arose.

The result was the creation of separate black congregations with black ministers under the heading of African Methodist Episcopal (AME) churches to which the nearly generic name of Zion or something similar may or may not have been added. Today, the designation AME immediately defines the church as a black church operated by blacks for blacks. It's one of the few places blacks can go and be sure of not encountering any trace of racial discrimination, no matter how subtle.

As usual, these churches act as a state within a state to assist blacks in any way possible. In 2008, the First African Methodist Episcopal (FAME) Church in Los Angeles was trying to attract financing to arrange to buy foreclosed homes resulting from the housing crisis to assist the sale of such homes to members. Blacks who get involved in such sales if they occur will be able to be sure there will be no trace of racial discrimination in any transaction that may take place. It is an example of the multifaceted ways black churches attempt to serve black members beyond the issues of religious faith. It is a process that has been going on for more than two centuries, and helps to explain the especially strong attraction blacks feel for their local churches.

1822 — Bishop John England, who was assigned to lead the newly created (1820) diocese of Charleston, South Carolina, founded the first Catholic newspaper in the United States. It was called the *United States Catholic Miscellany* and was symbolic of how far the Catholic Church had come since it was essentially a persecuted church in most colonies before the Revolutionary War.

September 21, 1823 — Joseph Smith (see listing for Spring 1820) had a vision of an angel named Moroni who tells Smith of a book written on gold plates that are buried on a nearby hillside. Smith found a box containing the gold plates on a small hill named Cumorah about three miles from the farm on which Smith lived. Smith claimed he was told to return annually for the next four years to find the mission God had for Smith. The angel Moroni said the book on the plates contains the story of people who used to live in America, and the book contains the "fullness of the everlasting Gospel." In March 1830 (see listing) Smith would publish what be believed to be that story in the *Book of Mormon*.

1825, Tract Society — An organization called the American Tract Society set as its goal the printing and distribution of "short, plain, striking, entertaining, and instructive Tracts" that would lead to good morals and the exercise of basic religious principles.

The society noted that a ten-page tract could be produced for a penny and thus the tracts were ideal for the poor, even to the extent of being given away. In the view of the society, "travellers may scatter them along the roads and throughout the inns and cottages.... Merchants may distribute them to ship-masters, and ship-masters to seamen; men of business may transmit them, with every bale of goods, to remote corners of the land and globe." In this way, for very little expense, the Gospel could be widely spread.

1825, Ann Randolph — Demonstrating how even women were now taking part in the evangelical outreach of the church after 1800, Ann Page Randolph of Virginia wrote about the slaves whom she felt were being seriously neglected by the churches.

Randolph wrote that those "who inhabit the smoky huts and till our fields" had souls that were as dear to God as those of their masters. It was

1825

our solemn duty, she declared, to care for both the bodies and souls of our slaves, "knowing that we must give an account of our stewardship."

July 19, 1825—Some of the more liberal members of various Congregationalist churches in New England came together to form the American Unitarian Association. Unitarianism was a new denomination that had been given a strong boost by a sermon delivered by William Ellery Channing in 1819 (see listing). Channing stressed the importance of the New Testament of the Bible over the Old Testament and the sense of a loving God over the strict Calvinist view of man as a hopeless sinner.

Unitarianism remained mostly centered around Boston, but its influence grew out of proportion to its relatively few members because of the fame of some members. Ralph Waldo Emerson was one such member whose stress on self-reliance evolved into what became called transcendentalism. Other preachers like Howard Bushnell deplored what he saw as theological hairsplitting and called for unity between denominations without requiring every group to realize every possible aspect of its viewpoint.

The total freedom of religion and from religion contained in the 1791 Bill of Rights gave rise to an almost endless view of religion as seen by an almost endless expansion of preachers and theologians with a new view to offer. However, Unitarianism traced its roots to 1742 and the writings of Charles Chauncy (see listing).

February 13, 1826—The first American Temperance Society was formed in Boston. The society would later be renamed the American Temperance Union and grow within a decade to more than 1.5 million members in 8,000 similarly-minded groups.

The Temperance Union was not a religious group per se, but it was strongly supported and influenced by most members of all religious faiths. It would become an example of how religious groups would come together to achieve religiously oriented goals without the taint of imposing a specific religion on the nation as was forbidden by the Constitution.

The Temperance Society/Union would give rise to groups known as the Abstinence Society, the Independent Order of Good Templars, the Sons of Temperance, the Templars of Honor and Temperance, the Anti-Saloon League (see listing for 1895), the National Prohibition Party, the

1830

Women's Christian Temperance Union (WCTU — see listing for 1874) and many others that shared similar goals.

These many organizations would ultimately cause the creation of the 18th Amendment, which ushered in the sadly lawless era known as Prohibition, after the amendment was adopted in 1919. The failure of this amendment (repealed in 1933) to achieve its intended goals would demonstrate as clearly as possible that no amount of good intentions could be used by one group to legislate morality (in the view of that group) on the nation as a whole.

1829 — The first provincial meeting of the bishops of the Catholic Church in the United States was held in Baltimore. There were ethnic tensions involved with this meeting because the French-born archbishop of Baltimore, Ambrose Marechal, had resisted such a meeting that had been repeatedly called for by the Irish-born bishop of Charleston, John England (see listing for 1822). This was because Marechal did not like the growing power of the Irish within the Catholic Church in the United States. Politics can rear its ugly head in nearly every setting.

Only when Marechal was succeeded by the English-born James Whitfield was England able to convince his superior that such a meeting was needed and it finally took place in 1829. But ethnic issues in the rapidly growing United States would continue to arise in the Catholic Church because eventually German and Polish Catholic immigrants, for example, would resist parishes controlled by Irish priests who did not speak their language. The monolithic Catholic Church would struggle for years in this way in the pluralistic United States.

March 26, 1830 — The *Book of Mormon*, as translated by Joseph Smith (see listing for September 21, 1823), was published. After a series of adventures (and misadventures), Smith translated the book inscribed on the golden plates he finally unearthed in 1827. The book was written in "reformed Egyptian," which Smith translated with the aid of special eyeglasses and dictated to his wife and various other helpers.

Smith's translation claimed that the Garden of Eden actually was located near what is now Independence, Missouri. Israelites from the Middle East later traveled to America around 600 years before the birth of Christ and split into two warring tribes. Jesus appeared in America after

1832

his crucifixion and produced about 200 years of peace, but the tribes finally started fighting again. Finally, near the year 400, a prophet named Mormon completed a book inscribed on gold plates about the history of his people and then was mortally wounded at a place called Cumorah (the hill on which Smith found the plates in 1823 and which became a shrine for future Mormons). Mormon's son Moroni completed the book and appeared to Smith in a vision in 1823 to direct Smith to the golden plates.

There was much skepticism about the *Book of Mormon* when it was published, but the angel Moroni had reclaimed the golden plates and thus they are no longer available. Smith's family and others (who become members of the new church) claim to have seen the plates, but there is no objective verification of their claims. However, historians point out that most religions are based on the claims of people to have seen visions/revelations and/or to have spoken to God in dreams, and the basis for Mormonism is little different from these other religions.

The official name of the new church is the Church of Jesus Christ of the Latter-day Saints (LDS). The church immediately began to send out missionaries to convert others to the new religion.

January 1, 1832—A handshake between Barton W. Stone (the pastoral host to the great revival at Cane Ridge, Kentucky) (see entry for August 6, 1801), and "Raccoon" John Smith (the selected representative for the famous Campbell father-son preaching duo and their followers) sealed the formation of the Christian Church (Disciples of Christ).

The irony of the name was that it showed how the new denomination, which was primarily formed to bring simplicity and basic agreement on styles of worship to denominational doctrines, could not initially agree on the name of their new denomination and simply used both that had been proposed. Even the date of the handshake, which most documentation shows to have actually occurred the day before (Saturday, December 31), was in dispute. But the January 1st date has been used historically to satisfy some issue or another.

Both Barton Stone and the Campbells were raised as Presbyterians but broke with the church over use of creeds and worship procedures that were not specifically noted in the Bible. They and their followers wanted a denomination that would more directly follow the Bible and end the proliferation of denominations. Their movement became known as the

"Restoration Movement." One key motto was that "where the scriptures speak, we speak; where the scriptures are silent, we are silent."

Some followers wanted to be known simply as Christians, others to be known simply as disciples. Hence the combined title as noted above. The denomination has grown to about 750,000 members today, but rather than reduce the number of denominations in the Christian world, it has increased the total, and it has undergone the fractures and splits common to all such religions in the United States.

1832— Noted congregational preacher Lyman Beecher (of the famous Beecher family of preachers) moved his residence from New England to Cincinnati to be in the middle of the American West. Beecher originally had been distraught at the thought of a clear separation of church and state leaving churches unsupported by the state, but he came finally to believe that such a separation was a great success because it brought volunteerism into the church. Beecher found as others did that people responded much more favorably to being asked to do things rather than being told to do things.

Beecher moved west because he came to believe that the West had the potential to essentially fulfill the American dream. He foresaw how the population of the relatively new part of the United States would grow dramatically, and he said that Bibles and Sunday schools and colleges and clergy would help God bring the West to the "mighty" status He had prepared for it to occupy in the world.

1833— This year marked the end of the number one position in membership held by the Congregationalist Church in Massachusetts. The dominant religion in the state was now Unitarianism. Andrews Norton (see listing for 1813) published "A Statement of Reasons for Not Believing the Doctrines of Trinitarians."

Massachusetts, the state that was perhaps the most rigid and conservative in terms of religious theology before the Revolutionary War, was now one of the most liberal. New views of theology were arising continually.

1834— Anti-Catholic events began to occur as the membership of the Catholic Church increased steadily, fueled by the growth of Irish and Ger-

1835

man immigrants. A convent and orphanage were burned down by a mob in the Charlestown area of Boston. The mob may have been exhibiting a mix of both anti–Irish and anti–Catholic sentiments.

Irish immigrants were flooding into Boston because it was the cheapest port to reach from Ireland, and "NINA" (No Irish Need Apply) signs would be familiar in advertisements in the Boston area for a good part of the 1800s. Nearly all Irish immigrants were Catholic, and thus anti–Irish and anti–Catholic actions would be very closely linked for many years.

The next year, 1835, Samuel F. B. Morse (the inventor of the telegraph) published a book with the title *The Foreign Conspiracy Against the Liberties of the United States*, also listed by some sources as *Imminent Dangers to the Free Institutions of the United States Through Foreign Immigration*. Either way, it was a diatribe against the pope and his rumored attempt to take over the United States.

The following year, 1836, a woman named Maria Monk wrote a book titled *Awful Disclosures of the Hotel Dieu Nunnery of Montreal*. The book purported to tell of her unwilling stay in a Canadian convent, and was filled with lurid tales of sexual liaisons between priests and nuns.

Anti-Catholic actions that had taken place in the colonies before the Revolutionary War were now being repeated in the United States, but because the Catholic Church had increased its size dramatically, the number of people being affected was much larger. Many speakers on both sides of the issue tried to find a peaceful middle ground to avoid efforts to try to divide the country along religious lines. Such a division was exactly what the First Amendment was intended to avoid.

For about the next two decades, incidents similar to those that took place in Boston would occur sporadically, but by 1860 the anti–Catholic sentiments were primarily a war of words. A century later in 1960, the election of John F. Kennedy, a Catholic, as president of the United States would demonstrate that the Catholic Church had effectively joined the mainstream of American life.

1835, Finney—Charles G. Finney, a professor of theology at and even president for a time of Oberlin College (founded in 1833 as the first college in the United States to accept women as well as men), was famous for his active role in the revivalism that was part of the Great Awakening in religion during the first part of the 19th century.

1836

Commenting on the effort to promote revivals, Finney wrote: "In the bible, the word of God is compared to grain, and preaching is compared to sowing seed, and the results to the springing up and growth of the crop." He went on to say that it was the job of religious leaders to thus prepare the way and not just sit back and wait for something to happen.

1835, Channing—Noted Unitarian clergyman William Ellery Channing produced in Boston a famous treatise against slavery. Channing argued that it was the duty of every Christian to oppose slavery. It was a test set by God, and if Christians failed this test they were failing "him who came to raise the fallen and save the lost."

1836—The first of the famous *McGuffey Readers* was published. The books were intended to permit children to learn to read and advance through progressively more difficult levels. Over the next three-quarters of a century over 122 million copies were sold, and with five to seven children sharing each book, their influence was enormous.

But the *McGuffey Readers* were written with a definite Protestant view of life. They contained excerpts from the Bible, and the morality tales they told as reading lessons made it clear to the children reading them that attending church and Sunday school was expected of them. Any mentions made about the pope and Catholics were made in a disparaging way, and Catholics were identified as the "enemy."

The *McGuffey Readers* would certainly not pass First Amendment muster today, and the readers did in fact help motivate Catholic leaders create a public school system of their own so that they had control over the content of the textbooks used by their students. The popular *McGuffey Readers* were just another example of the fact that most citizens considered the United States to be a Protestant country regardless of the meaning of the First Amendment.

March 27, 1836—The first Mormon temple was dedicated in Kirkland, Ohio. The Mormons moved from New York to Ohio in 1831 following a vision by Joseph Smith in late 1830 to do so. The Mormons had found an inhospitable environment in Ohio, as had their missionaries elsewhere, due to their claim of being people selected by God and their perceived attitude of banding closely together and not welcoming others who are not

1836

members of their church (Smith was tarred and feathered in front of his house in 1832 by townspeople resentful of growing Mormon influence). But the church continued to attract new members and continued to grow.

A book was published in 1835 containing 138 of Joseph Smith's revelations and some "Lectures on Faith." The book was called *Doctrines and Covenants* and is today a key part of Mormon literature. With the *Book of Mormon*, the *Doctrines and Covenants* is used to expand the Mormon faith in both the United States and Europe.

July 17, 1836— William White, who had been the first American Anglican bishop, died at the age of 88. White was credited with adopting the term "Protestant Episcopal" for the new Anglican denomination. The term was used to describe what had been the Anglican Church when the aftermath of the Revolutionary War made the English Anglican Church no longer acceptable in the new United States.

November 7, 1837— Presbyterian clergyman and determined abolitionist Elijah P. Lovejoy was shot and killed in Alton, Illinois. Lovejoy had a small printing press to publish what were, in his area, unpopular antislavery views. He had had three previous printing presses destroyed and thrown into the Mississippi River, and he had fled to Alton where he was using a fourth.

Lovejoy appealed to the citizens of Alton in his publication that even if they did not agree with his very passionate antislavery views, he be permitted the right to publish them as all citizens were in the United States. He said every persecuted person must make a stand somewhere, and he had determined to make his stand in Alton. He insisted that local authorities grant him the protection his rights required.

But the debate over slavery had "ceased to be a matter for polite or rational debate." Some saw Lovejoy's death as an issue about the freedom of the press rather than just a religious issue concerning differing views about slavery. Either way, his death showed conflicts over slavery had reached the boiling point.

1838— Ralph Waldo Emerson delivered his famous Harvard Divinity School address criticizing mainstream Unitarianism. Only two years before, in 1836, Emerson had published his essay titled "Nature." This was considered the start of what became called transcendentalism, but many Unitarians considered this only a branch of their basic denomination. Emerson disagreed.

This specific dispute spawned a series of discourses on both sides of the argument that went on for a decade and then into the 20th century. Different organizations arose, and a dispute broke out concerning whether Unitarianism should even have a focus on God. Among all these issues, Unitarianism never became a sizeable denomination.

1840, Shakers— During this year, the religious group called the Shakers (see listing for August 1774) reached their peak of about 6,000 members. They lived in 19 communal villages ranging from New England to Ohio. The Shakers believed that the nature of God was both male and female. Jesus of Nazareth was the male form, and their founder Mother Ann was the second appearance, this time in female form. Subsequently, Jesus appeared "in all in whom the Christ consciousness awakens." The Shakers thus believed it was the duty of all to live purely (including celibacy) in "the kingdom come" and to strive for perfection in everything they did.

The practice of celibacy essentially limited the growth of the Shakers to the number of new members they could attract, and that limit was reached in 1840. But with all their energy turned to the practice of perfection in their daily lives, the Shakers while they existed were a model for all utopian communities.

The Shakers built beautiful communities, the products they built for sale were highly regarded (especially furniture), and in their carefully attended gardens they were self-sufficient with enough left over to give to the poor. In their southern areas they freed the slaves belonging to their members and bought other blacks out of slavery. With equal rights for women and communal ownership of property they created the kind of heaven on earth they wanted to establish.

The Shakers created many clever implements from the clothespin to the circular saw, and they shared them without any question of patents or royalties (some entrepreneurs launched successful industrial careers using Shaker inventions). Shakers owned one of the first cars in New Hampshire and had electricity in their village while the state capital was still burning gas.

1840

When the Civil War broke out, the Shakers sent elders to see Abraham Lincoln to be granted an exemption from the draft because of their religious pacifism. Lincoln granted it and the Shakers were among the first in the United States to be given the status of conscientious objectors.

Many stories have been told about the Shakers and many words written about them, nearly all of which are favorable. They truly were a unique religious group, and no one duplicated their success in utopian living. Few, if any, Shakers are known to survive today, but their legacy is proud and historic.

1840, Pierre DeSmet—Jesuit Pierre Jean DeSmet, who had come to Saint Louis from Belgium to work as a missionary with the Indians in the West at the request of Bishop William DuBourg (see listing for 1815), left Saint Louis for the first of the many trips he would make among the Indians.

DeSmet developed a great deal of respect for the culture of the Indian tribes he worked among, and he complained that they were generally called savages whereas he found their cultures to be of a high level until they "learned the vices of the whites."

DeSmet's regard for the Indians was returned in kind, and ultimately in 1868 the secretary of the Interior of the United States asked DeSmet to be his representative in the negotiation of a peace treaty with the Sioux Indians, who, as all Indians, were being pushed further and further west as the United States expanded ever further westward. DeSmet was a shining example of the benefits of treating the Indians he worked among with respect rather than a condescending attitude.

December 1840—The Mormons received a city charter establishing both extensive home rule and a local militia in Nauvoo, Illinois. Nauvoo was a city named by Joseph Smith after the Mormons bought land near Quincy, Illinois, where the Mormons had previously taken refuge from their problems in Missouri. Joseph Smith became both mayor and military leader, and the community became a state within a state, ruled by Smith and the Mormon Church. Nauvoo grew rapidly, bolstered by an influx of Mormon converts from Europe. Within four years, Nauvoo was nearly as large as Chicago.

The Mormons came to Illinois in 1839, after encountering violence that was essentially continuous in Missouri from the time Joseph Smith moved his headquarters there in 1838. Mormon missionaries had encountered a hostile reception there since beginning their activities in 1831. Smith had been driven out of Ohio, and things became much worse in Missouri, including a clash between Mormons and the Missouri militia. The governor of the state finally ordered the Mormons to be driven out or wiped out. A massacre of 17 Mormons at a place called Haun's Mill followed.

Smith was arrested for treason in 1838, spared execution by a militia officer who refused to shoot Smith without a legal trial, and after five months in jail Smith "escapes" to join his fellow Mormons in Illinois. The Mormons had been led to safety there by Brigham Young.

March 21, 1843— This date marked the beginning of the period of the "Great Disappointment." The specific disappointment on this date was that the prediction of preacher William Miller that the world would end on this date and Jesus would come again to usher in the Kingdom of God. The devil would be overcome and the earth cleansed of all unrighteousness. These were things some viewed as being promised in the Book of Revelation. A period of 1,000 years of peace and virtue was expected, giving rise to the name of Millennialism to the movement for making such predictions.

Miller's prediction did not take place, and the fact that he had originally said it would be this date or a year later (see listing for October 22, 1844) did little to assuage those who sold their earthly goods in 1843 and anxiously awaited the Second Coming. Revisions in the predicted date were made by others, and the Seventh-Day Adventists grew out of this effort. The Shakers (see listing for 1840), whose official title was the United Society of Believers in Christ's Second Appearing, were especially interested in the prediction. Their essential religious belief, after all, was to forsake all normal earthly activities, including having children, because they and their founder believed the second appearance of Jesus had already happened in their sect and they were already striving to create heaven on earth.

July 12, 1843— Joseph Smith, leader of the Mormons, revealed his most controversial vision by saying that plural marriage (polygamy) is not only permissible, but in certain cases required. The announcement would not be officially made outside the church until 1852, but rumors quickly spread

1844

in the outside world, and the declaration of the latest revelation produces substantial divisions within the church.

Smith would be dead in almost exactly 12 months (see listing for June 27, 1844), but he is recorded as having more than 25 wives. That means he must have, on average, took two new official wives each month during the last year of his life.

January 18, 1844— Senator (later President) James Buchanan introduced a resolution in the Senate that the United States be declared a "Christian Nation" and acknowledge Jesus as America's savior. The resolution was rejected, but several similar resolutions would be introduced in the following years, including one that would call for amending the Constitution as required.

This was the latest demonstration that more than 50 years after the adoption of the Bill of Rights (see listing for 1791), many people were still uncomfortable with the still revolutionary idea that the United States had chosen to be a nation without an official state religion. It also demonstrated why it would take another century until the 1950s before the Supreme Court would take a truly active role in turning the nation away from nominally supporting a national religion with beginning the school day with prayer and readings from the Bible.

June 27, 1844— Joseph Smith and his brother Hyrum were shot to death by a mob in Carthage, Illinois. The Smiths were being held in jail after Joseph Smith had surrendered to authorities in connection with charges being brought once more against him for trying to take the law into his own hands by ordering the smashing of the presses of an opposition newspaper and using his militia to suppress church dissidents and to protect his city against outside authority. The jailers holding Smith arranged with the leaders of the mob to fire blanks in Smith's defense and then to permit the mob to enter the jail. No one was ever convicted of the crime.

Smith wanted badly to be free of any authority other than his own. He had announced plans to run for president of the United States in 1844, and he had gone to Washington in 1839 to see President Martin Van Buren to complain about what he saw as the illegal treatment his Mormons had received in Missouri.

Smith wanted to run for president because he was convinced being

1845

president was the only way he could run his church as he wished without interference from the various governments and personal entities he had struggled with in every state he had been located in so far. It was this general attitude of being above his neighbors and the recent revelation of polygamy that turned his latest Illinois neighbors against Smith and the Mormons and resulted in his death at the hands of the most recent angry mob.

Smith's death caused a major crisis within the leadership of the Mormon Church. Brigham Young was selected as the new leader of the church two months later. Others formed groups that split off from the church to form new branches, including Smith's first wife Emma and their son Joseph (the branch they started still exists today). But most Mormons remained with the church now established under the leadership of Brigham Young.

October 22, 1844— The peak of the "Great Disappointment" (see listing for March 21, 1843) occurred when another calculation for the end of the world and the Second Coming of Jesus proved once more to be wrong. It was estimated that more than 100,000 disillusioned followers of minister William Miller (see listing for March 21, 1843) returned to their original church denominations or left Christianity altogether. But many went on to continue in one group or another whose basic religious belief was centered on the fact that the Second Coming of Jesus was due soon, even if the date was not precisely known. These groups were generally called Adventist churches.

1845— A Catholic lay organization named the Society of St. Vincent de Paul, which had begun in France, moved to the United States. By 1865, the society had 75 chapters (or conferences) in the nation. It provided industrial schools and boarding schools to give young people the training and religious discipline needed for future success.

The society collected contributions wherever it could, whether or not the sources of the funds were Catholic. The society felt required to offer its services wherever they were needed.

May 1, 1845— Disaffected members of the Methodist Episcopal Church organized the Methodist Episcopal Church, South, in Louisville, Kentucky, as a new denomination. The split was over the different attitude of

1845

the church in the north and in the south towards slavery. All of the major denominations (Methodist, Baptist, and Presbyterian) would split over the slavery issue, and the splits would remain for a long time after the Civil War ended in 1865. The split of the Baptists (which occurred also in this month — see listed for May 12, 1845) would be permanent.

Even in the Catholic Church, which did not split officially over the slavery issue because of its monolith nature in that it was ruled from Rome, there were splits in the sense that priests in the North support the northern position and priests in the South support the southern position.

The Methodist Church per se is still a major denomination in the world and in the United States, but perhaps its most notable characteristic is to undergo splits in its prime branches and then splits within the splits to accommodate different points of view. The number of churches with some form of Methodist in the title of the church is extremely large.

May 12, 1845 — The Southern Baptist Convention (SBC) was formed following a series of meetings that began on May 8, 1845. The meetings were held at the First Baptist Church in Augusta, Georgia. The creation of the SBC officially split the Baptist churches in the south from those in the rest of the nation. The prime reason for the split was the different position the churches took on the issue of slavery (the SBC supported slavery), but the SBC also wanted a more centralized structure in the church.

The SBC became a very successful denomination on its own. Today, with over 16 million members, it is the largest Baptist group in the world, and the largest Protestant denomination in the United States. The SBC is second to the Catholic Church among Christian churches in total membership in the United States, but the SBC has more congregations.

Although there have been attempts to make changes within the SBC in the last few decades (as listed later in this chronology), the SBC has been primarily an organization for whites throughout its history, and it has been a significant political force within both the South and the nation as a whole.

February 4, 1846 — Brigham Young led the majority of the Mormons out of Nauvoo on what Mormons would come to call the Great March West. Since Joseph Smith's murder in June 1844 (see listing), there were continual acts of vengeance and tit-for-tat reprisals between the Mormons

1846

and their neighbors, including burning of homes and even some killings. Young realized there was no possibility of achieving peace in Illinois, and he offered the governor a truce in which the Mormons promised to leave not only the state of Illinois but the entire United States if there was a cease-fire in which the Mormons could build wagons for their journey out of the United States.

The Mormons wanted to find a place that would be far from present settlements, and would likely stay isolated for years to come. That way the Mormons could establish a community that would have the church/state mix the Mormons wanted. Such an arrangement would not be subject to outside authority, which the Mormons saw as interference with the free practice of their religion. They considered the West Coast and even Canada, but chose the Great Basin in what is now Utah. It was essentially a desert and was owned by Mexico. The Mormons decided it would be only sparsely settled for a long time, and the Mormons could build a settlement where they would dominate indefinitely.

The Mormons planned to wait until the spring of 1846 to begin their exodus, both to make their travel easier and to have grass on the trail to supply forage for their animals, but a rumor began to circulate that the authorities planned to arrest Brigham Young on a charge of harboring counterfeiters. The Mormons decided to leave early, even though it was the middle of winter, to avoid any further battles with outside authority.

The 1,300 mile journey to the Great Basin would take nearly 18 months, including a stop to near what is now Omaha, Nebraska, to wait out the winter of 1846-1847. About 6,000 Mormons went west in the first group, and others followed later. It was a grueling trip on which many would die of various hardships and disease, but it was a very determined group that reached the Great Salt Lake in the summer of 1847.

It should be noted that the Mormons who reached their destination after the arduous journey had undergone a special sort of bonding process. The Mormons who were doubtful and in disarray after the death of Joseph Smith had left the basic church before the journey west. Only those who were the true believers had followed Brigham Young. They had undergone many difficulties together before heading west, and those who arrived in Salt Lake City were ready to follow the dictates of their leaders and establish themselves in their new home where they expected to be free of the persecutions they had encountered previously.

1846

It would be another 75 years before the Mormons would join the mainstream of the American family in the 1920s. One could say they made many mistakes of bad judgment in their conflicts with the United States government during that time, especially concerning their insistence on continuing polygamy when it became illegal in the country and not just the individual states, but the Mormons who settled in and controlled the state of Utah had a sense of "us against them" to a degree rarely, if ever, seen in the history of religious life in the United States.

1846—Famous ex-slave and abolitionist Frederick Douglass spoke before a packed house in London. Douglass was such a powerful speaker that in addition to speaking throughout the United States, he was invited to speak overseas as well.

Douglass told his audience that one of his largest complaints about slavery was that its prisons in the South stood side by side with the churches. "The church bell and the auctioneer's bell chime in with each other." He was dismayed that the churches accept the profits from buying and selling slaves to build more churches.

Douglass had a point. Christian churches supported slavery in the South. But churches in both the North and South, had a common scenario. There was no absolute truth quoted from scripture. Church leaders essentially supported whatever attitude was held by their congregations. Ministers from both the North and South quoted phrases from the Bible supporting the attitude toward slavery in their geographical area. Even Catholic priests did the same depending on their location. There was no overriding right or wrong guidance from the Bible. Only a war would settle the issue.

April 26, 1847—The Lutheran Church-Missouri Synod was officially organized. The new denomination of Lutheranism was a reflection of the fact that although Pennsylvania was the initial destination of Lutheran immigrants, many came to the Midwest near and after the Revolutionary War.

1847, Theological Society—The Society for the Promotion of Collegiate and Theological Education declared, after a spate of college building following the Dartmouth decision in 1819 (see listing), that religion must be prepared to do for the frontier "what Yale, and Dartmouth, and Williams, and Amherst have done for New England: to call forth ... a learned and pious ministry; to send life, and health, vigor through the whole system of popular education; and, to ... found society on the lasting basis of religious freedom and evangelical truth." The society concluded that the greatest opportunities to do so were in "the valley of the Mississippi."

1847, Oneida— The religious group that became known as the Oneida Community moved from Putney, Vermont, where it was founded by John Noyes, to Oneida, New York. The Oneida Community, like so many other "utopian" groups had an unusual view of marriage (called "complex marriage") that developed the ire of neighbors (the move to Oneida was due to exactly such problems in Vermont), and it had a different view of the Second Coming of Jesus.

Noyes believed marriage should be only among persons selected by the group to obtain the best results (not unlike the breeding of horses his enemies claimed), and his vision of the future was based on his unique interpretations of the Bible. The group practiced communal living and was very industrious, but never grew to more than about 300 persons in the three decades of its existence before it began to break up.

Probably the most memorable part of the Oneida Community for most people is the excellent silverware produced there when the community needed to have an economic base for continued survival.

March 31, 1848— This is the date set by adherents of Spiritualism as the beginning of their movement. Their religion's basic belief is that the spirits of the dead can be contacted by mediums. Thus, the dead can provide people who are alive with information about the afterlife.

Although often controversial, and not considered a true religion by many, Spiritualism had an estimated eight million followers in the United States and Europe at its peak in 1897. There is today a Spiritualist Church, which embraces many New Age ideas, which basically represents the surviving element of the Spiritualist movement.

On March 31, 1848, Kate and Margaret Fox of Hydesville, New York, reported that they had made contact with the spirit of a murdered peddler. The spirit communicated via rapping noises that were audible to

1848

onlookers. This type of evidence appealed to many in the so-called "Burnt-over District" (see listing for 1876) in which the sisters lived. Spiritualism especially appealed to women because it gave them a vehicle as mediums for a position of leadership in addressing mixed crowds in public.

The Fox sisters became a sensation and soon were earning a good living providing both a form of entertainment for many and a spiritual catharsis for some. Mediums found it easy to attract paying audiences, and with many opportunities to earn money via simple fraud, the emergence of fraud soon became associated with Spiritualism.

But as in any such enterprise, true believers developed and helped spread the word about Spiritualism and its claims. To these believers, Spiritualism was as real as any religious faith, especially for those who sincerely believed they had communicated with the spirit of a departed loved one or friend.

Demands for mediums peaked after the many deaths in the Civil War (as would happen later after World War I). Even Mary Todd Lincoln, wife of President Lincoln, while grieving over the loss of her young son to typhoid fever, arranged séances in the White House to which she was accompanied by President Lincoln.

In 1887 the Sebert Commission (a group of faculty members at the University of Pennsylvania) reported that they uncovered fraud or suspected fraud in every case they had studied of respected Spiritualist mediums from 1884 to 1887.

Famous magician Harry Houdini also reported similar results. Houdini had a special bond with his mother, and was greatly affected by her death. When mediums tried to make contact with her, Houdini found that the contact via "automatic writing" was fraudulent because the message was in English and his Hungarian immigrant mother spoke almost no English.

Houdini became convinced all mediums were frauds, and he undertook to debunk them using his great knowledge of magic and illusions. He was part of a committee from the magazine *Scientific American* which offered a cash prize in the 1920s to anyone who could successfully conduct a séance of any type without Houdini finding the fraudulent technique. There were several famous test cases, but no medium ever collected the prize.

All of this made no difference, as usual, to true believers. They continued to believe what they wanted to believe, but the business of being a medium trying to contact a departed spirit faded over time (but has never entirely ceased). Fortune tellers and such have been with us since the beginning of time, and they, like the mediums, probably will exist forever.

June 9, 1848—According to Mormon legend, a flock of seagulls arrived on this date in what is now Salt Lake City to begin eating the locusts that were destroying the crops the Mormons had carefully planted and cultivated to support them in their first full year in their new land. As a result, a monument (which still stands) was erected to the seagulls, and the California seagull (the species involved in the miracle) is the state bird of Utah. This miracle is seen as God's way of ensuring the survival of the about 4,000 Mormons who had traveled to Utah to escape persecution in Illinois and Missouri (see listings).

As is often the case in such events, more objective views tell a somewhat different story. The crops of the Mormons were certainly attacked by a swarm of flightless insects that travel along the ground in seemingly endless numbers. Swarms of these insects are reasonably common in the mountain areas around May. They belong to the katydid family, although they are now often called Mormon crickets because of this event.

The seagulls involved were actually native to the Salt Lake area, and there are differences in the estimates of how many insects, a natural part of their diet, the gulls actually ate. Some accounts state the Mormons saved many of the crops by traveling in lines through their fields and driving the insects to adjacent areas where the gulls fed on them as usual. Many accounts infer that the miracle occurred in thoughts after the fact.

But the crops were saved, the Mormons were safely installed in their new home, and miracles generally being in short supply in modern times, the miracle of the seagulls remains well established in the history of the Mormons.

1850—As a result of the dramatic rise in immigration that took place in the first half of the 1800s (and after), especially from Ireland and Germany, the Catholic population in the United States as of 1850 was 1.5 million. That was a startling increase from the estimated Catholic population of just under 0.2 million in 1820. By most estimates this made the Catholic church the largest single denomination in the United States.

1850

From this new baseline, the number of Catholics more than doubled to over three million in the next 10 years (1860). By 1920 the total would stand at 18 million. The growth would make the Catholic Church a more powerful institution in the United States, but it would also produce an anti–Catholic backlash that would grow well beyond the events that took place before 1850 (see entry for 1834) as the immigrant-fueled growth began.

September 9, 1850— Brigham Young was appointed governor of the new territory of Utah. The land making up the Utah Territory was ceded to the United States by Mexico following the treaty that ended the war between Mexico and the United States in 1848. Following the annexation, Young had petitioned to make Utah a state, but Congress was still leery of the Mormons after the Nauvoo events, and chose to make it a territory instead. Congress felt it would have more control over a territory than a state, but the Mormons would continue to resist control of any sort by anyone.

Young had asked for the name Deseret to be applied to his new proposed state. It was drawn from the *Book of Mormon* and meant honeybee. Young thought the honeybee was an apt symbol of the industry with which the Mormons addressed their work, and also a symbol of the church in which there was a belief that personal freedom should be submerged to meet the goals of the whole.

Congress instead used the name Utah after the Ute Indians who had originally populated the region. The Mormons continued to call the region the Kingdom of Deseret and showed it as such on all their maps. The state seal of Utah today contains the image of a beehive, as do all state highways. The second largest newspaper in the state today is owned by the Mormons and is called *The Deseret News*. In all of their actions in the nineteenth century, the Mormons practically had a reflex action to oppose any position taken by the outside world.

December 29, 1851— The first Young Men's Christian Association (YMCA) was established in the United States in Boston. The YMCA had been created in England in 1844 to address the needs of young men flocking to London to find work. The Y, as it became known, offered Bible study and assistance in finding housing and other needs to these mostly

1852

rural young men in place of life on the mostly corrupt and dangerous streets. The YMCA idea spread throughout England and crossed the ocean to the United States in 1851.

The YMCA benefited from the fact that although it was founded as a Christian organization, it did not espouse the tenets of any single denomination and it accepted people from all churches and social classes. The Y offered exercise classes of all types, cheap summer camps, and various training classes in addition to cheap housing. Its symbol became a triangle showing its emphasis on spirit, mind, and body.

The YMCA evolved into a social services organization with a light Christian background, and every reasonably sized community in the eastern United States had its Y with its accompanying gymnasium and swimming pool.

One unintended consequence of the YMCA program was the literal invention of the games of basketball (1891) and volleyball (1895) at the International YMCA Training School in Springfield, Massachusetts, and the game of racquetball (1950) at the YMCA in Greenwich, Connecticut.

To some extent, the popularity of its sports facilities has caused many people to overlook the social services the YMCA provides in its function as a Christian organization. The YMCA served as a model for the Young Women's Christian Association (YWCA — see listing for 1858) and the Young Men's Hebrew Association (YMHA — see listing for 1854).

1852 — Black minister Daniel Payne became a bishop in the African Methodist Episcopal Church after stints as a Lutheran clergyman and then a Presbyterian minister. Payne became an abolitionist along the lines of Frederick Douglass (see listing for 1846).

Payne had been quoted as saying that he condemned slavery "not because it enslaves the black man, but because it enslaves man." Payne's position was that slavery corrupts masters as well as slaves.

August 29, 1852 — Brigham Young made it official to a church-wide assembly in Salt Lake City that the Mormons practiced polygamy. The announcement was meant to stress the benefits of polygamy as seen by Young, but it was a public relations disaster. The steady flow of Mormon converts from Europe was interrupted, and the aggressive way in which the Mormons pursued polygamy within their church set them on a colli-

1853

sion course with the rest of the United States. This latter effect was irrelevant to the Mormons. To them it was their way or no way.

There were about 20,000 Mormons now living in the Salt Lake area, and their influence throughout the West would grow as their numbers continued to grow. In just a few years Mormon missionaries would establish settlements in what would become Las Vegas and in California and Wyoming.

1853—Antoinette Brown Blackwell, a graduate of Oberlin College (the first coeducational college in the United States), became the first woman to be granted ordination as a minister in a major denomination (Congregationalist). There had been Quaker ministers (Lucretia Mott was a good example), but Quakerism was not considered a mainstream religion at the present time in the United States.

There were many male preachers who objected strenuously to the idea of female ministers, claiming women's activities in this area were not supported by the Bible, and controversy over this issue would go on through the next century.

1854—Following the model of the Young Men's Christian Association (YMCA—see listing for December 29, 1851), the Young Men's Hebrew Association (YMHA) was established in Baltimore. The initial focus of the YMHA was to provide help to Jewish immigrants, and an annex organization was created in New York City in 1888 to help Jewish women. It was called the Young Women's Hebrew Association (YWHA). An independent YWHA was organized in 1902.

These two organizations were taken over by the Jewish Welfare Board in 1917 and later renamed Jewish Community Centers (JCC). However, many such groups prefer to maintain the old name, or to be called simply the Y, especially in the New York City area.

The Jewish Y's are similar to Christian Y's in that they offer a range of recreational and social activities with generally a light religious background. They are active around the world and an asset to the communities they serve.

1857—The Presbyterians split into north and south divisions because of differences between their views on slavery. The Presbyterians were the last of the three major Protestant denominations to do so, as the Methodists and Baptists had split more than a decade earlier.

In all three denominations, the splits would go on into the next century as after the slavery issue ended in 1865, hard feelings would continue between the North and South for a multitude of reasons.

July 13, 1857—President of the United States James Buchanan selected Alfred Cumming to replace Brigham Young as governor of the territory of Utah. Buchanan was responding to reports that Young was ruling the territory as a personal theocracy in which the predominance of Mormons on all juries and in all judgeships enabled the Mormons to be sure the church triumphed whenever there was a conflict between federal law and church law. Young was running a nation within a nation.

Buchanan declared the territory to be in a state of rebellion and sent 2,500 troops west from Kansas to restore order and install Cumming as the new governor. The Mormons were outraged and threatened resistance at every turn. But when push came to shove, the Mormons relented.

In September 1857 a wagon train of settlers heading west from Arkansas was attacked by Mormons led by fanatic John Lee. The Mormons killed 120 people in what was known as the Mountain Meadows Massacre. It would take two decades to get a Mormon jury to finally convict Lee and have him executed for the crime (see listing for March 1877).

June 26, 1858—Troops of the United States Army entered Salt Lake City and marched through the streets. This amounted to a symbolic, formal installation of Alfred Cumming as the new governor of Utah replacing Brigham Young. Young and the Mormons had issued defiant statements when Cumming was announced as the new governor in July 1857 (see listing), and had threatened military action against troops sent to Utah.

But no shots were ever fired in anger, and the Mormons, at least officially, accepted Cumming as their governor and bowed to the will of Washington, D.C. President Buchanan declared the Mormon War over and issued a blanket amnesty.

1858, Revivalism—The year 1858 was a period of intense revivalism, and it is credited with beginning a Great Awakening in the United States from the late 1850s to 1900. Some historians record this as the third Great

1858

Awakening, the first taking place from 1730 to 1760 and the second from 1800 to 1830. Other historians have commented that such designations leave relatively little time in the 1800s when the nation was not in the grip of a Great Awakening of one sort or another.

Whether it fitted some special definition of a period of time or not, 1858 had an unusually high number of revivals and religious conversions, at least in the North. The fact that such activity took place to a much lesser extent in the South eventually dampened the hopes of those who felt such revivalism was a sign that the intensive religious period would lead to an agreement between the North and the South on the subject of slavery before a war broke out.

Harriet Beecher Stowe, a sister of the famous preaching Beecher brothers, and the author of the abolitionist novel *Uncle Tom's Cabin*, had ended that 1852 novel with a plea to both North and South to repent of their respective injustices and cruelties relative to slavery while there was yet time to "avoid the wrath of Almighty God" for failing to settle the issue.

In 1858, Stowe renewed that plea, hoping the great revival of 1858 would become the great reformation of 1858. But animosities had grown too large on both sides to prevent the Civil War that started in the spring of 1861.

1858, YWCA — The Young Women's Christian Association (YWCA) was established in the United States. Although the organization was started in England and concentrated on social services for rural young women seeking jobs in the cities as had the Young Men's Christian Association (YMCA — see listing for December 29, 1851) before it, the YWCA was a completely separate organization.

The YWCA provided recreational and social services for young women for many decades, while moving steadily into the fields of women's rights and social justice. In some areas the link to Christianity was submerged to concentrate on political issues.

November 24, 1859 — In England Charles Darwin's famous book, *The Origin of Species by Means of Natural Selection* was published. All 1,250 copies of the first printing were sold out on the first day. The book was a landmark in the field of science.

1863

However, the book would begin a controversy among religious groups that persists to this day. Those who believe every word of the Bible is to be taken literally find the story of evolution foreign to their beliefs, and they certainly wanted no part of a theory postulating that mankind as we know it descended from the apes. It is a controversy that shows no signs of ever ending, no matter how may court battles concerning the teaching of evolution are fought.

1862— President Abraham Lincoln signed the Morrill Anti-Bigamy Act that made polygamy illegal in territories of the United States. The act was specifically intended to "punish and prevent the practice of polygamy in the Territories of the United States and to disapprove and annul certain acts of the territorial legislature of Utah."

The Morrill Act was a legal blow to the practices of the Mormon Church in Utah. Before coming to Utah the Mormons had struggled with the laws of individual states in many ways, with polygamy, which was a felony in most states, being the final straw. By coming to the Utah area, then owned by Mexico, the Mormons hoped to avoid such problems with state laws.

Even when the United States took over the area following the United States-Mexico War, the Mormons were relatively free to do what they wanted with Brigham Young as the territorial governor. Territories were governed under federal law, which had no specific law against polygamy. The Mormon War (see listing for July 26, 1858) was over Brigham Young's usurpation of federal prerogatives, not polygamy per se. The practice of polygamy was certainly offensive to Washington, D.C., but not technically illegal.

The Morrill Act changed that. Because Lincoln was involved with the Civil War at the time, the Morrill Act went essentially unenforced. But it was a throwing down of the gauntlet, which the Mormons ultimately would be unable to ignore.

September 10, 1862— Rabbi Jacob Frankel was appointed as the first Jewish chaplain to serve in the army of the United States.

January 1, 1863— President Abraham Lincoln issued the Emancipation Act, freeing all slaves, or at least those areas where federal authorities could

1863

make such an act a reality. Lincoln later observed in 1863 that Americans as a people have grown too accustomed to success, too self-sufficient, "too proud to pray to the God that made us." He added that it is time, therefore, for humility and confession and earnest pleas for divine forgiveness.

May 23, 1863 — The Seventh-Day Adventist Church was formally organized. The church grew out of the Adventist Movement that followed the Great Disappointment resulting from the failure of the prediction of William Miller of the Second Coming of Christ in 1843–1844 (see listing for October 22, 1844). Most followers of Miller left when the prediction failed, but some decided that a Second Coming was due although parts of Miller's prediction were in error. These persons became known as part of the Adventist (the "coming") movement.

One group believed that Miller misinterpreted the meaning of what he found in the Bible, and that Christ moved to the "Most Holy Place" in heaven on the predicted date rather than returning to earth. Thus, a process began in 1844 in which Christians would be judged to verify their eligibility for salvation. The Second Coming was still imminent, but the date unsure.

A seventeen-year-old girl named Ellen Harmon (later White) had visions in 1844 that led her and other followers to believe she was chosen by God to establish what became the Seventh-Day Adventists. Ellen White wrote her first book in 1851, and her writings are held in high regard by Seventh-Day Adventists today.

The Seventh-Day Adventists are so named because they believe the seventh day meant for worship is Saturday, not Sunday, which is actually the first day of the week. Others joined Ellen White (including her husband James White) in officially founding the Seventh-Day Adventists, but Ellen White is usually identified as the founder because of her visions and her writings.

The Seventh-Day Adventists now have over 15 million members around the world, and are especially known for promoting health and nutritional issues. The popular cereal empire of the Kellogg Company was developed by W. K. Kellogg (a member of the Seventh-Day Adventists) in Battle Creek, Michigan, in an attempt to create a nutritious cereal that was both healthy and tasty.

1868

April 22, 1864—For the first time, the motto "In God We Trust" appeared on a coin issued by the United States. The specific coin was a bronze two-cent piece issued while the Civil War was still ongoing. No one at the time could imagine an era when such things would evoke protests about violation of the First Amendment.

1865—Following the assassination of President Abraham Lincoln earlier in the year, famous clergyman Howard Bushnell gave a commencement address at Yale University that placed Lincoln's assassination in stark terms.

Bushnell said that, as Christians, we have been taught that without the shedding of blood there is no remission of sins. So it is that "without shedding of blood, there is almost nothing great in the world ... for the life is in the blood, all life." Great has been the sacrifice, and great the suffering. But what has been given to us thereby is a nation reborn: "In this blood our unity is cemented and forever sanctified."

July 28, 1868—The Fourteenth Amendment to the Constitution was ratified. It had been proposed June 13, 1866, and by this date 28 of the then 37 states had approved the amendment, thus causing it to be ratified.

The amendment was written primarily to protect the slaves recently freed by the Civil War, and the southern states were required to approve it as part of being readmitted to the Union. Most refused, but official ratification by the remaining states made the issue moot.

The amendment made any person born or naturalized in the United States a citizen of the United States and of the state in which they live. It provided that no state shall abridge the privileges and immunities of citizens, or deprive any person of life, liberty, and property without due process of the law, or deny to any person the equal protection of the law.

Southern states initially passed many state laws to dilute the protections of the Fourteenth Amendment, but ultimately it would serve as the basis for the end of segregation in public schools in 1954 (see listing), and the equal protection and due process clauses would become some of the most known legal justifications for lawsuits brought in the 20th century and afterwards.

The Fourteenth Amendment did not start out as a religious issue per se, but many black churches used its protections to get established and

1870

prosper, both in the South and elsewhere. It added to the protections of the First Amendment in many circumstances.

June 26, 1870—With the concurrence of President Ulysses S. Grant, Congress officially declared Christmas to be a national holiday. Once again, at the time, no one could anticipate an era in which the observance of Christmas and the degree to which local governments would take part would become a controversial issue dealing with the First Amendment. The unspoken (or often firmly spoken by politicians and preachers) assumption was that the United States was a Christian nation.

1870—About 100,000 blacks withdrew from the Methodist Episcopal Church, South (see listing for May 1, 1845) to form what was initially called the Colored Episcopal Methodist Church. The church would grow for almost a century, and then the word "Christian" was substituted for "Colored." The original splitting off would follow the persistent trend among blacks to found churches operated by blacks for blacks.

October 2, 1871—As pressure increased on the government of the United States to bring what many saw as the renegade Mormons to heel, Brigham Young was arrested on charges of polygamy (Young had married his 27th and last wife in 1868). Young was not ultimately convicted of the crime, but pressures continued to make Mormons conform to the laws of the nation.

In the meantime, the Mormon Church headquartered in Salt Lake City, increased its membership to 60,000 in 1866 on its way to 110,000 members in 1878. The legal problems of the church did not stop its growth (today the church has about 13 million members around the world).

1872—A man named Charles Taze Russell, then only 20 years old, started what was essentially a Bible study group to deal with the differences between what Russell felt was true based on his study of the Bible and the general doctrine of most Christian churches. Russell was seen as a heretic by most church groups, but the organization he founded grew into the Jehovah's Witnesses association with seven million members around the world.

Russell denied not only the concept of eternal damnation and hellfire for sinners; he denied the Trinity, the deity of Christ, and the Holy Spirit.

1874

To spread his ideas, in 1879 he copublished a magazine called *The Herald of the Morning* with its founder, N. H. Barbour. By 1884 he took control of the publication and renamed it *The Watchtower Announcing Jehovah's Kingdom*.

Russell also founded the Zion's Watch Tower Tract Society. When he started, his magazine published about 6,000 copies per month. Today, his successor organizations publish a total of almost a million books and magazines a day. They are distributed worldwide, and the *Watchtower* magazine claims the largest monthly circulation in the world at just over 37 million copies.

There were many changes in the name of the organization and its leaders after Russell died in 1916, and many of these are noted further on in this chronology. The Witnesses originally believed there would be a great cosmic battle between Jehovah and Satan, and Christ would return to earth to mark this event. Further, this battle was thought to be near at hand, and they stated "millions now living shall never die." But this belief was later modified as other aspects of the denomination also changed.

August 1874—The first organizational meeting of the Women's Christian Temperance Union (WCTU) was held on the Chautauqua meeting grounds at Chautauqua, New York. The first national convention of the WCTU was held three months later in November 1874, in Cleveland, Ohio.

The WCTU was an outgrowth of the temperance movement that had been under way in the United States among Protestant religions for most of the past century (see listing for February 13, 1826). By 1879, the WCTU had grown to about 1,000 local unions in 23 states containing over 26,000 members.

Under the leadership of its first national president, Annie Wittenmeyer, the WCTU in 1877 adopted a pledge of total abstinence from alcohol as a requirement for membership in the WCTU (the requirement is still in place today).

Frances E. Willard, the second national president starting in 1879, pushed the WCTU in the direction of women's rights issues in addition to its general temperance work. Willard became nationally known for her work, and after she died in 1898 a statue was erected in her memory in Statuary Hall in the Capitol in Washington, D.C., in 1905.

1875

But in retrospect, analysts have pointed out that the dilution of the efforts of the WCTU among so many issues reduced its influence in achieving its initial goal of prohibition. The Anti-Saloon League (see listing for 1895), which focused specifically on political issues, was given the primary credit by most observers for achieving the success of the 18th Amendment that ushered in the age of prohibition in 1919.

1875, Blavatsky—During this year Madame H. P. Blavatsky and others organized the Theosophical Society. It was intended to blend the ancient wisdom of India with the many religions of the West for the benefit of all humanity.

In the next decade, metaphysical clubs, mind-cure institutes, and new thought proponents added to the already explosive mix of new religious denominations that was taking place in the nation following the Civil War. The concept of religious freedom was rarely to be exercised more thoroughly in the United States than it was in the second half of the 19th century.

The woman who called herself Madame Blavatsky had what can most charitably be called a checkered past. She was born in Russia in 1831, married for the first time before she was 17, and traveled the world in one way or another before emigrating to the United States from Russia in 1873. Having been previously involved in occult phenomena, Blavatsky easily moved into the medium business of Spiritualism (see listing for March 31, 1848).

Blavatsky wrote a great deal about the theory of theosophicality, and her writings have served as the basis for the nearly inevitable splitting of the Theosophical Society into several branches, some of which still operate today.

Unfortunately, some of her writings about "Root Races" were used (or misused) by Adolf Hitler and his followers to support their theory of Aryan superiority and the anti–Semitic themes that followed.

1875, Moody—Evangelist Dwight L. Moody had one of his most notable successes at Madison Avenue Hall in New York City. About 5,000 persons crowded into the Hall with several hundred left standing outside straining to hear the sounds within. Moody was accompanied by his new partner, song leader and hymn writer Ira D. Sankey. A reporter sent to cover the event wrote about the great air of expectancy, the joy of the hymn singing (from the *Moody and Sankey* hymn book), and the quiet and rapt attention paid to Moody's preaching by what one would expect to be a boisterous crowd. The scene was often repeated in large cities around the nation. As an evangelist, Moody was a star.

However, Moody knew that such fame and good revival feelings can easily decline, and he concentrated on creating longer-lasting institutions, especially in the field of education. Moody had not passed the seventh grade himself, and as an unconfirmed preacher, never had a formal education of any sort. But he recognized the power of education, and throughout his career he had been active in educational projects.

In 1879 Moody opened a school for girls in Northfield, Massachusetts (his old hometown), and then founded the Mount Hermon school for boys in 1881. He returned to his old stomping grounds in Chicago to transform by 1879 the Evangelical Society into a coeducational religious school. It became the Bible Institute for Home and Foreign Missions, and then changed its name to the Moody Bible Institute after Moody died a decade later.

The beginning of Moody's career occurred in 1856 when he was 18 years old. He was a Boston shoe clerk and had just joined the Congregationalist Church because he was deeply impressed by the earnestness of his Sunday school teacher. He continued thinking about a career in church work when he moved to Chicago the same year to start a career in a suitable business. By 1860, after working after business hours on church work, he decided to devote himself to religious work fulltime.

While working among Chicago's poor and among soldiers in the Civil War, he began to develop a reputation as an evangelist. His plain spoken words about the Gospel were well received everywhere. Moody traveled to Great Britain where he became famous for his preaching, and it was as a result of this fame that he returned to the United States to make his mark in 1875 as noted above. Moody was indeed a self-made man, and he made a great success in spite of his lack of education and formal ordination, which could have well barred him from his chosen field in an earlier time.

October 3, 1875— Rabbi Isaac Meyer Wise led the founding of the Hebrew Union College in Cincinnati. It was the first Jewish college in the

1876

United States that trained Jewish men to become rabbis. Wise had previously founded the Union of American Hebrew Congregations in July 1873. It was his second attempt to do so, and the first purpose of the Union was accomplished when the rabbinical seminary was opened.

1876 — The autobiography of noted evangelist Charles G. Finney (see listing for 1835) was published and made the first known reference to the "burned-over district" of central and mostly western upstate New York.

The expression came from the fact that western upstate New York had a frontier aspect about it in the early 1800s as the Erie Canal was being built from New York City to Lake Erie. Professional clergymen were scarce in the area, and many self-taught and self-proclaimed preachers led many of the relatively few inhabitants to adopt folk religions as well as the more well-known mainstream religions.

The rate of such conversions was quite high in the revival atmosphere, and the saying became common that the area was so heavily evangelized that there was no fuel (potential converts) left over to burn (convert). The area was a ripe one for the establishment of new religious sects. These included:

1. The Mormons. Their founder, Joseph Smith, Jr., lived in the area and claimed to have translated the *Book of Mormon* from the golden plates he was led to by the angel Moroni near Palmyra, New York (see listing for March 26, 1830).

2. The Millerites. They were the followers of William Miller, a farmer who lived in Low Hampton, New York, and as a preacher predicted the end of the world and the Second Coming of Christ based on his calculations from the Bible. Neither of the dates he predicted over the period of a year (the second being October 22, 1844 — see listing) came true leading to the Great Disappointment.

Millerism was extremely popular in western New York State. After the failures of Miller's predictions, some followers still felt his predictions were accurate but his calculations were flawed, and other religious sects were founded flowing from Millerism. One of these was the Seventh-Day Adventists (see listing for May 23, 1863).

3. Spiritualism. The Fox sisters of Hydesville, New York, conducted the first séances in the area, maintaining that it was possible to communicate with the dead. The movement known as Spiritualism grew out of

these activities and spread widely over the nation (see listing for March 31, 1848).

4. Shakers. The Shakers were very active in the area and located several of their communal farms there (see listing for 1840).

5. The Oneida Society (also known as the Oneida Community) had located in the area to be near the border to Canada in case an escape was needed due to its controversial views on group marriage and related protocols (see listing for 1847).

In addition to these religious sects, the area was noted as the home of feminist Elizabeth Cady Stanton, who was a resident of Seneca Falls, New York. She and others initiated the Seneca Falls Convention dedicated to woman's suffrage.

Stanton was also an activist for women's rights in church leadership, and helped to produce *The Women's Bible* to support her position (see listing for 1895).

March 23, 1877— Mormon John Doyle Lee was executed by a firing squad in Mountain Meadows, the scene of the massacre he led twenty years before in 1857 (see listing). Lee was the only person prosecuted for the massacre, and he was initially the benefactor of a hung jury in 1875 until Brigham Young took action to obtain a conviction in 1876, essentially offering Lee as a sacrifice to remove pressure on the church from the authorities determined to prevent the Mormons once again from ignoring the laws of the United States.

Lee realized he was being sacrificed, and while he was in prison awaiting execution, he wrote a book titled *Mormonism Unveiled*. The book was published posthumously and became a national bestseller. In the book Lee took the position taken so often in such circumstances that he was only following orders of the Mormon Church, and that he was finally deserted by Brigham Young.

As a footnote, Lee's family claimed that Lee had predicted that if he was an innocent man and was executed, then Brigham Young would die within six months of Lee's death. Brigham Young did in fact die five months later in August 1877, of apparently a burst appendix. Young was 76 years old.

Young was replaced as president of the Mormons by John Taylor, who had been severely wounded by the attack that killed Mormon founder

1879

Joseph Smith in 1844 (see listing). Taylor was even more truculent towards the federal government than Brigham Young had been, but legislation that would cause the Mormon Church to officially (if not actually) renounce polygamy in 1890 (see listing) was already in process.

1879— The first Church of Christ, Scientist was chartered this year. The denomination grew out of the experiences of Mary Baker Eddy, who had suffered much from ill health in her youth, and found conventional remedies of little help. She uncovered a "science of health" in the 1860s during her association with Phineas P. Quimby, and this led to her book, *Science and Health* in 1875.

Her book explained her theory that science alone could not produce healing; a special religious understanding was also required. In her view, disease was caused by mental error, which required proper understanding of the scriptures to be overcome. By 1883 Eddy provided a *Key to the Scriptures* that was intended to be read as a part of her original *Science and Health*.

Christian Science expanded slowly across the nation, reaching a total of more than a thousand churches by the time Mary Baker Eddy died in 1910 at the age of 89. Christian Science reading rooms and public lectures were part of the usually well-controlled centralized organization that got the message of Christian Science out to the nation. The world headquarters of the church is in Boston. The estimated number of its followers today ranges from 100,000 to 400,000.

In many ways the church has always been controversial, because each story about persons gaining their health through practicing the teachings of the church is often matched by stories of people who died due to refusing timely medical care that might well have saved their lives. A number of critics have claimed that Christian Science is not a true Christian denomination because of its unusual teachings. But as in any religion, true believers pay little attention to the critics of their beliefs.

Mary Morse Baker (who became Mary Baker Eddy after her third marriage) was born in 1821. She was what was called a fragile child, and suffered a long list of illnesses throughout the first 40 years of her life. The exact nature of her illnesses is not clear, and some observers felt they were mainly psychosomatic. At any rate, she never obtained what she felt was proper relief from her ailments.

1881

At the age of 41 in 1862, Mary Baker Eddy became a patient of Phineas Quimby. He was known as a magnetic healer who used hypnosis among other unconventional methods on his patients. Mary Baker Eddy initially gave him much credit for helping to relieve her nervous conditions, but Eddy later broke with Quimby. However, Eddy began to think more deeply about the effect of mental thinking on illness as a result of her association with Quimby.

In 1866, when she was 45, Eddy suffered a fall in the city of Lynn, Massachusetts, which she claimed caused her a severe spinal injury. She then claimed to cure herself by reading the Bible and later withdrew the lawsuit she had filed against the city of Lynn. She isolated herself from society for about three years to further study the Bible, and then conducted experiments on herself and others to confirm the results of what she had learned.

By 1875, at the age of 54, Eddy had completed her book *Science and Health*, which led to the foundation of the Church of Christ, Scientist in 1879. Widowed in 1882 at the age of 61, Eddy devoted the rest of her long life until her death at age 89 to writing the highly detailed by-laws of the church and lecturing on its mission. She founded the *Christian Science Monitor*, a highly regarded newspaper covering current events in 1908 at the age of 87. The newspaper continues to be published today.

October 2, 1881— Father Michael J. McGivney held an organizational meeting for the group that would become the Knights of Columbus (they were incorporated March 29, 1882). McGivney had seen firsthand the financial disasters that could befall a family when the breadwinner died without any kind of life insurance. McGivney himself had to leave temporarily his seminary studies to help his family when his father died.

Catholics had a special problem in this area because at the time they were often excluded from labor unions and other organizations that provided such services. Further, Catholics were barred from fraternal organizations or, in the case of groups like the Freemasons, forbidden by their church from joining.

McGivney felt Catholicism and fraternal organizations were not incompatible per se, and he believed a suitable organization could provide the benefits he sought and also offer Catholics a way to be proud of their heritage and demonstrate their patriotism. McGivney found defects with

1882

existing groups such as the Catholic Order of Foresters in Massachusetts and the Catholic Benevolent League in New York, so he and his followers decided to start a new group from scratch.

They decided to name their organization after Columbus because Columbus was a hero to many Catholics. The 400th anniversary of the discovery of America was fast approaching and there was generally renewed interest in him. The group felt the use of Columbus as a patron saint would help bridge the gap between Irish-Americans such as themselves and new Catholic immigrants of other nationalities.

The Knights of Columbus was quite successful and began to expand to include education, charity, and other social services. By World War I, among many other ventures, the Knights was operating over 300 recreational centers for servicemen in the United States and a similar number overseas. By that time the Knights had some 300,000 members. Today there are some 14,000 councils around the world. The Knights is a multi-billion dollar organization with more than $60 billion worth of life insurance policies in force.

But there is much more to the Knights than life insurance. It gives more than $135 million annually to charitable causes and uses an endowment fund of over $50 million to support church-related causes. It especially supports those with physical and mental disabilities, and events such as the Special Olympics.

Further, the Knights was the major movement supporting the addition of the phrase "under God" to the Pledge of Allegiance in 1954. It also successfully lobbied President Franklin Roosevelt to declare Columbus Day a national holiday in 1937.

The Knights of Columbus was an example of the religious principle of volunteerism that had grown among churches in the United States in the 19th century, including the more hierarchical Catholic churches. Even a sister Catholic organization called the Daughters of Isabella was created to advance among women the goals of the Knights of Columbus.

March 22, 1882—Congress passed the Edmunds Act declaring polygamy to be a felony. It also permitted prosecution for unlawful cohabitation, which was easier to prove than polygamy per se. The act was the first step of the response of Congress to the request of President Rutherford Hayes that "the right to vote, hold office and sit on juries in the Ter-

1885

ritory of Utah be confined to those who neither practice nor uphold polygamy."

The Mormons continued officially to treat the law as a joke, and it became a badge of honor to be arrested as a "cohab." However, Mormon leaders were becoming unofficially concerned. The Supreme Court had upheld the Morrill Act (see listing for 1862) in 1879, and the ruling made it clear that similar actions by Congress against the Mormons would also pass muster.

In the next decade, more than a thousand Mormons were convicted of unlawful cohabitation. The federal government continued to apply pressure to bring the Mormons into compliance with the laws of the nation.

1885, Taylor—A warrant was issued for the arrest of Mormon leader John Taylor on cohabitation charges. Taylor went into hiding, and he remained in hiding until his death in 1887. Regardless of what kind of spin Mormon leaders placed on events, the Mormon Church was in serious trouble and was about to face its most serious crisis since moving west.

1885, Strong—Congregationalist minister Josiah Strong published a widely read book titled *Our Country: Its Possible Future and Its Present Crisis*. Strong included much statistical material in the book reviewing the importance of money in a capitalist society and the problems this could cause. He saw America as the successor to ancient Egypt, Greece, Rome, and the Hebrews in showing the world new ways of living, and the United States was adding the love of liberty and a "pure spiritual Christianity."

However, after this somewhat calm beginning, Stone turned to the real essence of the book. The present crises he saw came from excessive immigration to the United States, and his specific villains were Roman Catholics and the Mormons. Stone feared that rather than the foreigners being "Americanized," the country was being "foreignized."

His prime complaint against Catholicism was its obedience to a foreign infallible pope. Stone feared Catholics would try to dominate the nation as they did in Italy and Spain, putting at risk America's system of free speech, free press, and free public education.

Stone's complaint against Mormonism was not polygamy per se, as that already seemed to be on its way out. To Stone, the basic problem with Mormonism was despotism. Rather than a religion, Mormonism was a

1886

state within a state, exercising total control over its people. The rapid growth of Mormonism was due to its extensive missionary work overseas, bringing more and more foreigners to the United States.

Thus, Stone's book, for all its extensive use of social data, essentially was a diatribe against immigrants who were different from mainstream America. One of the worst differences, in his view, was that the immigrants did not practice the pure Protestant religion he felt was the bedrock of the country. Almost a century after the promulgation of the First Amendment, there were still many religious leaders who felt it was understood that traditional Protestantism was the proper religion of the country.

1886, Abbelen—A Milwaukee priest of German ethnicity, P.M. Abbelen, protested to the Vatican that German parishes be "entirely Independent of Irish parishes" and that "the rectors of Irish parishes ... not be able to exercise any parochial jurisdiction over Germans enrolled in any German church."

Such issues were arising because Irish immigrants had come in huge floods in the 1840s because of the Irish famine. The Irish had become embedded in the hierarchy of the Catholic Church. In total numbers German immigrants roughly equaled the Irish flood that came to the United States in the later 1800s, but the Irish came a little earlier and tended to live in more concentrated areas.

The result was a near monopoly of Irish-born priests in the United States, and like all monopolies, this one was only reluctantly and very slowly given up. Complaints very similar to those of the Germans would be made in turn by Italians, Poles, Czechs, Portuguese, and Australians. Rome had little experience with the tremendous diversity of different nationalities found in one country as it was in the United States.

1886, Gladden— Congregationalist Washington Gladden wrote a book titled *Applied Christianity: Moral Aspects of Social Questions*. Gladden was one of the first churchmen to address the issue of churches using their resources to help people caught up in the problem of trying to achieve a healthy and moral life in the nation's cities.

Gladden wrote 38 other books attempting to raise both the consciousness and conscience of people on this issue. In 1900 (see listing) Gladden also ran for and was elected to the city council of Columbus, Ohio, to see what he could do from the inside to help solve the problems of people trying to cope with a newly urbanizing America.

1886, Huntington— Episcopal Bishop Frederick D. Huntington, writing in response to the Haymarket Riots of 1886, wrote that "Man has killed or maimed his fellow-man" because of an inability to see the common humanity that bound them. Taking up what he saw as the duty of the church to support the workers, he noted that in the New Testament "it is the rich and prosperous ... who are most severely denounced ... and most in need of a changed mind ... and a quickened conscience."

Huntington was joining those churchmen who believed the results of the Industrial Revolution were requiring churches to focus more on the needs of the poor than just focusing on the saving of souls of the population at large.

1887— James Cardinal Gibbons of Baltimore, in an ongoing dialogue with Rome concerning the support of Gibbons for unions in the United States, pointed out to the Vatican that to condemn the Knights of Labor would be to risk "losing the love of the children of the Church, and pushing them into an attitude of resistance against their Mother."

Cardinal Gibbons had supported the Knights of Labor since they were formed in 1869, both because the Knights had a large Catholic membership due to the surge of Catholic immigrants in the last five decades, and because Gibbons had decided to take the side of labor in general in the rich versus poor dispute going on in the nation.

Rome and European Catholics were not pleased with such actions. Unions seemed to be a radical element in the view of Europe, and unions led to socialism and communism in the view of conservative Catholics. Cardinal Gibbons said the workers had a right to pursue better working conditions, and further that associations and organizations are recognized as the most natural and just and most efficacious means to achieve any worthy public goal.

Gibbons added that even though Catholics may become associated with Protestants, atheists, or communists in the unions, Catholics in the United States must learn to associate with people not of their faith. "In a mixed people like ours, the separation of religious creeds in civil affairs is an impossibility."

1887

This view that unions met the needs of workers "to love the Church ... and save their souls ... but ... also earn their living" became a common theme of most churches as they moved to support workers in the new economic age.

March 1887—Congress passed the Edmunds-Tucker Act. This act was intended to be the final blow against the Mormon Church to bring it into compliance with the law. The act essentially unincorporated the Mormon Church and gave the federal government the right to seize all Mormon property with a value of $50,000 or more.

Mormon leader John Taylor, still in hiding (see listing for 1885), died in late summer, and was replaced by Wilford Woodruff, then 82 years old. Almost simultaneously federal lawyers initiated actions to implement the Edmunds-Tucker Act.

New leader Woodruff realized his only hope to avoid bending to the will of the federal government was to receive a reprieve from the Supreme Court. His hopes for such a reprieve were dashed in 1890 (see listing).

January 19, 1889—The Salvation Army officially split in two groups. One group simply renounced its allegiance to founder (in England) William Booth. A second group, headed by Booth's son Ballington and his wife Maud, would incorporate itself as a separate organization in America in 1896.

The Salvation Army was founded by Methodist minister William Booth in 1865 in London. Booth and his wife Catherine decided to work directly among the poorest and most needy people in London's East End. He had originally planned to send his converts to regular churches, but he soon found that the poor did not feel comfortable or welcome in the established churches. The congregations of such churches generally were appalled by the shabbily dressed, unwashed poor coming into their places of worship. Booth started a church especially for the poor that he called the East London Christian Mission.

In May 1878, when Booth was reviewing a proof copy of the annual report of the Christian Mission, his son Bramwell objected to a motto calling it "A Volunteer Army" on the basis that he was not just a volunteer but a person self-compelled to do God's work. Booth changed the wording to "Salvation Army," and the new name caught on.

1889

The organization that became the Salvation Army had been operating with a military flavor. "General" Booth had the support of "officers" who guided the "Army" in spreading the gospel of Christ and enlisting new "soldiers" in its work.

The Salvation Army endured taunts and ridicule, but it did really useful work among the poor, including soup kitchens, food depots, a day nursery, and a missionary hospital. It was serious about its work and bore the name the Hallelujah Army with pride.

The Salvation Army expanded to the United States in 1879 under Lieutenant Eliza Shirley, and its representatives met with President Grover Cleveland in 1886. The organization continued to grow across the United States thereafter. Today, over a half million people consider the Salvation Army their place of worship, and 3.5 million volunteers help the Salvation Army do its work.

Many people consider the Salvation Army to be a leading organization in terms of dispensing help where it is really needed. During World War II, the Salvation Army operated 3,000 service units for the armed forces, and its work was so successful that it led to the formation of the USO.

February 17, 1889—Billy Sunday, who would become a famous evangelist, held his first public crusade in Chicago. During his career as a popular religious speaker, it was estimated that more than 100 million Americans attended his events.

William Ashley Sunday was born on November 19, 1862. His parents were poor, and he spent some time in orphanages. He was an excellent athlete with great speed, and he became a professional baseball player. In the late 1880s he was wandering the streets of Chicago with some teammates on their day off, and he was captivated by the old gospel songs being performed by a street preaching team.

In short order, Sunday started attending the Jefferson Park Presbyterian Church, became a faithful Christian, and started speaking in churches and YMCAs. He developed an energetic evangelistic speaking style, and before long he was speaking around the Midwest and attracting attention around the nation.

His crusades encouraged listeners to come forward and accept Jesus Christ as their savior. It was estimated that more than a million did so

1889

during his career. Sunday's campaigns were managed by his wife, and the couple earned over a million dollars between 1908 and 1920. Some claimed Sunday was a charlatan as he moved within the higher levels of society. But his preaching seemed sincere and there was never a touch of scandal about him except for the escapades he had to bail his wayward three sons out of.

Sunday especially campaigned for Prohibition, and his exhortations to "Get on the Water Wagon" became famous. Even with the many undesirable effects of Prohibition, Sunday was quoted in the 1930s, after Prohibition had been repealed, that he would gladly lead the fight for it all over again.

Sunday's popularity declined after World War I (for which he sold numerous war bonds) as radio and movie theaters provided competing outlets for the thirst of the public for spectacle. But Billy Sunday and his success was a precursor for the radio and television evangelists later in the 20th century.

1889— Social worker Jane Addams founded her famous Hull House in Chicago. The Hull House was so successful and useful that it became the central core of what was called the Settlement House movement. Addams followed the principles of her Quaker father in pursuing social justice and civil rights for the poorest of the poor, but she and her followers felt such benefits were more readily supplied by an institution that was a full-time neighbor rather than by missionary-like activities that had an in-and-out visitor nature.

It was noted by one reformer that a nonpermanent presence in the slums would be like Jesus showing up each day, bringing his lunch, and "going home to heaven at night." The best neighborly love can only come from a neighbor.

The Hull House acted "as a school, a church, a library, a bathhouse, a theater, an art gallery, a bank, a hospital, a refuge, a hope. Whatever it needed to be, it became." And it was located right in the same neighborhood as the poor who needed its services so desperately. Addams believed that moral improvement must "come to all, or it would surely come to none." Her work began literally at ground level.

1890— Jacob Riis, an immigrant from Denmark who had arrived in New York City in 1870 and had gone on to establish the then new field of photo journalism, capped it off in 1890 with the publication of the book *How the Other Half Lives*.

The book was a searing indictment of life in the tenements of New York City for the immigrants who had been pouring into the city for several decades. The tenements, in which the poor lived, were "dark and deadly dens" Riis wrote, where children were "damned rather than born" into the world.

Riis asked where the churches were in such a neighborhood. He pointed out that the churches were outnumbered more than ten to one by the saloons. Riis added that "either the devil was on the ground first, or he has been doing a good deal more in the way of building." The congregations were much larger in the saloons than in the churches, Riis added, "and the contributions more liberal the week round."

Riis's book attracted much attention nationally as a shameful report on slum conditions, but certain church leaders were especially interested because a debate was going on in many churches at the time whether or not churches should expand their focus on saving souls to include social and political actions to assist people in the here and now.

The Industrial Revolution had resulted in the movement of people from the villages to the cities, and from working on farms to working in factories. Many religious leaders saw life in the cities as being inimical to the growth of families that were centered around religious values, and they saw Riis's book as a call to action.

October 6, 1890 — Leader of the Mormon Church, Wilford Woodruff, formally issued a Manifesto that Mormons should now "refrain from contracting any marriage forbidden by the law of the land." It was the official capitulation by the Mormons that they would specifically forgo polygamy and generally follow the laws of the United States.

Woodruff pointed out that appropriate laws had been enacted by Congress and "pronounce constitutional by the court of last resort," and it was his intent to "submit" to those laws and use his influence to have the Mormon Church do likewise.

Woodruff's last hope for a reprieve had been snuffed out by the Supreme Court's declaration the preceding May 19 that the Edmunds-Tucker Act (see listing for 1887) is constitutional and can be enforced.

The Manifesto was in some ways a sham in that polygamy among

1893

some members (including some leaders) continued secretly, but within a decade the Mormon Church would threaten polygamists with excommunication and cooperate with federal authorities in prosecuting them. The Manifesto helped Utah achieve statehood in January 1896, and the Church of the Latter-Day Saints slowly moved into the mainstream of the United States.

There was outrage among Mormons as well as outsiders when a report was published by the *Salt Lake Tribune* in 1910 that some surreptitious polygamy was still going on (see listing), but that was essentially the end of such duplicity. Some Mormon Fundamentalists, as they would call themselves, would continue to practice polygamy and create lurid headlines up to the present day. But their numbers are less than 1 percent of the present Church, which has always disowned them since the turn of the century.

1893, Toomy—In an article in the *Catholic World*, Alice T. Toomy stated that there was a legitimate place in public activities for Catholic women. A Women's Catholic Congress held in Chicago that same year gave consideration to such activities as "day nurseries and free kindergartens, protective and employment agencies for women, and clubs and homes for working girls."

Toomey noted that Catholic women were behind in such respects as "tens of thousands of our ablest Catholic women are working with the WCTU and other non–Catholic philanthropies because they find no organization in their own church as a field for these activities."

But in the same issue of the *Catholic World* to which Toomey had contributed, another Catholic female contributor stated that it was settled "beyond question that women, as women, can have no vocation in public life." The issue of women's rights in the Catholic Church was still a non issue.

1893, World Parliament—A gathering called the World's Parliament of Religions opened in Chicago. The exposition was the idea of Congregationalist John Henry Barrows. It was intended to serve as a platform for speakers representing religions from all over the world including Islam, Buddhism, and Hinduism.

In addition to such exotic religions, representatives came from the more conventional religions of Judaism and Catholicism, but from eastern as well as western versions. There were also representatives from American black religions, the concept of black denominations being operated by blacks still new to many Americans.

Noted church historian Philip Schaff spoke to the Parliament and pressed for greater harmony and unity among the many different denominations that had developed during the history of the 19th century in the United States. All denominations have some merit, he said, adding that "there is room for all these and many other churches and societies in the Kingdom of God." He concluded that this was a kingdom "whose height and depth and length and breadth, variety and beauty, surpass human comprehension."

The parliament by all accounts was very well organized, and its goal of being educational instead of exploitive was definitely achieved. The diversity of religions in the world matched what was going on in the United States at the time. The parliament supported what would be called the "varieties of religious experience" by noted philosopher and psychologist William James in his 1902 book with that title.

September 14, 1893— Pope Leo XIII appointed Archbishop Francesco Satolli to be the first apostolic delegate to the United States. The appointment was indicative of how the growing membership of Catholics in the United States was having a strong effect on the Catholic Church around the world.

December 31, 1894— As of the midpoint of the 1890s, the religious analyst, historian, and author Edwin Gaustad outlined the status of religious denominations in the United States in terms of their estimated memberships.

Roman Catholics were at the top with 8 million members, just over a third of all Christian denominations. Methodists were second at 5.5 million, Baptists third with 4 million, and Presbyterians and Lutherans next with about 1.5 million each, the Presbyterians leading slightly. The Disciples of Christ were sixth with about 1 million, and the Episcopalians and Congregationalists, once the leading denominations in the country, came in seventh and eighth respectively, with about 0.6 million each. The only religious group with a membership of such magnitude was the Jews at about 1 million.

1895

The population of the United States according to the 1900 census was 76 million. Religious denominations were counted at 26 million or about 34 percent of the total. By 1950 the total population would nearly double to 151 million, and the percentage of religious denominations would more than double to about 50 percent. This would put the total of religious denominations in 1950 at about 80 million, more than triple the 1900 number.

Repeating the denominations listed in 1894, the 1950 numbers were solidly increased but the order of leadership had changed. Catholics were still number one at over 25 million, but Baptists were the top Protestant denomination at more than 15 million. Methodists were now third at 11 million, with Lutherans fourth at more than 5 million. The Disciples of Christ had moved up to fifth with 4 million, and the Presbyterians had slid to sixth with over 3 million. The Episcopalians were seventh and the Congregationalist eighth with 3 and 2 million, respectively.

These selected eight denominations had grown from 22.7 million in 1894 to 68 million in 1950, but in 1950 there were other denominations with memberships close to or more than those on the selected list. The Mormons had grown from about a quarter million in 1894 to more than a half million in the state of Utah alone in 1950. The Mormons would grow to 13 million by the 21st century, but only half of their membership would be in the United States.

The numbers of Pentecostalists were hard to pin down because of the many name creations, changes, and mergers involved with their denominations, but by 1950 they were estimated to be in the millions. The Pentecostalists were on their way to becoming the largest Protestant denomination in the world, but typically only 5 percent of their membership is in the United States. Most of their original core growth in the United States came from the Methodists.

Jewish religious denominations in the United States grew to about five million by 1950, growing by a factor of five from 1900 to 1950. Thus, the mainstream religious dominations continued to lose influence in the first half of the 20th century, even as they continued to grow in absolute numbers.

1895, Nazarene— The denomination generally known as the Church of the Nazarene was founded in Los Angeles by Methodist Episcopal

1895

Church minister Phineas F. Bresee and Methodist layman Dr. Joseph Pomeroy Widney (a former president of the University of Southern California).

Bresee wanted to return more closely as he saw it to the preaching of John Wesley, founder of Methodism, and to emphasize reaching the poor and underprivileged as he felt Wesley had done. Widney, who supported the goals of Bresee, came up with the name of the new church after a night of prayer, using an original name for Jesus of Nazareth, i.e., the "Nazarene."

The church underwent mergers and a name modification (removing "Pentecostal" from the original title when the general meaning of that term changed), and to some the founding date became October 8, 1908, following a merger in Texas. But other mergers took place in later years as the church grew to its present size of about 1.7 million members worldwide.

1895, Stanton— Feminist Elizabeth Cady Stanton played the key role in the issuance of what came to known as *The Woman's Bible*. It was issued in two volumes, one in 1895 and the second in 1898.

Stanton believed that present interpretations of the Bible relegated women to a permanent subservient position to men in all areas of life. What was needed was a new understanding, essentially a new translation. To those shocked and offended by the thought that scripture could be so revised, Stanton wrote: "Come, come, my conservative friend, wipe the dew off your spectacles, and see that the world is moving."

The world in fact was moving towards gender equality in nearly all areas, but it moved extremely slowly in the field of religion, in spite of Stanton's championing *The Woman's Bible*.

1895, Russell— Following the founding of the Anti-Saloon League as a state organization in Ohio in 1893, minister Howard H. Russell, a lawyer who converted to a life in religion, took it to a national level in 1895. The Anti-Saloon League was aligned in its goals with the general temperance movement in the United States, which included the well-known Woman's Christian Temperance Union (WCTU), but the Anti-Saloon League focused specifically on achieving political action.

Russell raised funds to nurture the league through its early years, and mentored its future leaders. His title as superintendent of the League was

1896

passed on to previous field secretary of the league Wayne B. Wheeler in 1902. It was Wheeler who led a successful fight in 1906 to prevent the reelection of Governor Myron T. Herrick, giving the league considerable notice in the political area.

The league did not make an issue of whether individual politicians drank or not. It simply focused on how they voted on legislation affecting their cause. As a result, the Anti-Saloon League was given most of the credit, over the more well-known organizations in the temperance movement such as the WCTU, for the passage of the 18th Amendment in 1918 that created prohibition.

July 9, 1896—William Jennings Bryan delivered what became known as his "Cross of Gold" speech. Bryan was a famous fundamentalist Protestant preacher who had been nominated by the Democratic Party to run for president of the United States against Republican William McKinley.

The speech had nothing to do with religion per se. The subject was essentially about economic policy and the use of the gold standard, but Bryan's fame as a preacher made his statements about common people being "crucified" on a "cross of gold" stand out in everyone's memory.

However, in spite of his excellent rhetoric on the campaign trail, Bryan lost the election to McKinley in November. Bryan was nominated two more times by the Democrats to be their presidential standard bearer, but never was a winner. He became a very successful speaker on religious themes, and then died famously at the age of 65 in 1925 just after his appearance in the notorious Scopes Monkey Trial about the teaching of evolution (see listing).

1896, Love—Black pastor E. K. Love said, following the founding in 1895 of the black National Baptist Convention, "It never was true anywhere, and perhaps never will be, that a Negro can enjoy every right in an institution controlled by white men that a white man can enjoy." The point was being made once again that the best religious organization for blacks was one operated by blacks for blacks.

By 1900 the new black denomination had two million members, its own publishing house, and was educating missionaries to work in Africa. By 1915 the black National Baptist Convention would follow the trend of nearly all Protestant churches in the United States and split into two factions. But each part would continue growing rapidly.

1896, Herzl — A Jewish immigrant from Hungary, Theodor Herzl, published a book called *The Jewish State*. Herzl argued that Jews would have no peace and no freedom from harassment and persecution until they had a land of their own. He was seen as a leader of Zionism, the program for a Jewish homeland.

Herzl pleaded for sovereignty over any portion of the globe suitable for Jewish national requirements, and granted such "we will attend to the rest." Then the Jews could reverse in the 20th century their history of the last 2,000 years.

Herzl could not know it at the time, but his dream would become a reality a half century later when the state of Israel was created May 14, 1948 (see listing).

1897, Church of God — Two black Baptists founded the Church of God in Christ in Lexington, Mississippi. This was a church involved in the Pentecostal movement, and it ultimately became the largest black Pentecostal church in the world.

This church moved beyond the borders of the United States, expanding first to the Caribbean, and then moving to Central and South America and ultimately to Africa as well. But there was much more to the Pentecostal story, and the Pentecostal Church in a dizzying number of names and variations is now estimated to have 500 million members worldwide, second only to the Roman Catholic Church among Christian groups.

The basic story and history of Pentecostalism in the United States begins with the entry for January 1, 1901.

1897, Sheldon — A Congregationalist pastor in Topeka, Kansas, named Charles M. Sheldon, wrote a novel called *In His Steps* that was first published this year. The book would be reprinted or serialized many times thereafter and become an all-time best seller.

The basically simple story encouraged city dwellers to consistently ask themselves "What would Jesus do?" Sheldon addressed the problems of the increasing distance between rich and poor, the irrelevance of religion for those whose basic needs for food and housing were unmet, and the unwillingness of decent church people to directly address the problems in their own neighborhoods.

The phrase "what would Jesus do?" became a catchphrase that is used

1897

even today to direct the attention of well-minded people to real problems needing solutions that are basically simple but effective and reflective of the moral standards of the concerned person.

1897, Solomon—Jewish activist Hannah Solomon, speaking in support of the National Council of Jewish Women, said that the persecution that any woman may receive by placing herself in public roles working for the good of her religion and humanity is only a "sting" that lasts for a short time.

Solomon added that a woman could bear stronger burdens than a man because rather than being created merely out of dust, "the Lord waited until he could build her out of a strong, healthy, germproof bone."

Thus, the National Council of Jewish Women was more than capable of establishing schools, providing manual and vocational training, providing summer camps, encouraging philanthropy, and taking part in a host of activities that put them in the public eye.

April 24, 1898—The United States declared war on Spain. There were many political issues involved, but with the end of the relatively brief war (a peace treaty was signed less than 10 months later), new religious issues arose as well.

The United States took possession of the Philippines, Puerto Rico, and Guam at the end of the war. The initial focus of the war, Cuba, was granted in a few years the full independence it had been seeking from Spain. But with its new possessions and its annexation of Hawaii in July 1898, the United States at the end of the war had an overseas empire. However, it was an empire of decidedly mixed ethnic groups and religions.

The war of 1898 marked a new tipping point in many ways in the approach the United States took in considering religious issues. A little more than a century after the adoption of the First Amendment in 1791, the government had to decide if after it sent its military forces ashore in a foreign political conquest it should send missionary forces ashore for a religious conquest as well. Or did the concept of freedom from and of religion apply to new foreign conquests also? The year of 1898 marked the first such conquest in the nation's history.

The people of the Philippines were essentially Catholic following their rule by Catholic Spain. Many in the United States saw the Filipinos as barbaric heathens in need of salvation and political direction by the United States. The Filipinos, who had been fighting with Spain for their independence, were dismayed to learn that they had effectively just exchanged one foreign ruler, Spain, for another, the United States. An armed insurrection once directed against Spain now went on for several more years against the United States.

President McKinley declared the Filipinos too uncivilized to rule themselves, and he said he saw the need to "Christianize" them (from the Protestant point of view) as well. But Catholic Church leaders strongly objected to this line of thought.

Bishop John Lancaster Spaulding noted that the American people had realized great blessings from our "articles of faith" derived from the Declaration of Independence and the Constitution, "but we have never dreamed that they were articles to be exported and thrust down unwilling throats at the point of the bayonet."

Archbishop John Ireland objected on similar grounds to the thoughts of some Protestants to send missionaries en masse to the Philippines to rescue the Filipinos from the Catholicism imposed on them by Spain. He pointed out that there would be a great outcry from Protestants if the situation were reversed. Strategically it would be a bad move if other nations saw that the United States followed its military victory with an effort to throw out the old religions with one preferred by the United States. In such an event Ireland said our flag would become a symbol of "cruel oppression and religious tyranny."

The religious issues became moot when political movements in the United States turned in the direction of ultimately granting the Philippines independence (which finally happened just after World War II). Similar issues in Puerto Rico were basically avoided because, in this case, political movements in the United States took the direction of making Puerto Rico a commonwealth of the United States (essentially one step below being a state).

Hawaii presented yet another situation. Legislation in 1900 made all citizens of the Republic of Hawaii as of August 12, 1898, citizens of the United States. The population of Hawaii was about 150,000 at the time, with more than half being Japanese and about one-quarter being Chinese. Few of these were citizens of the Republic of Hawaii, but they were still

1899

treated much more favorably than most Asians, who faced many restrictions because of the rampant anti–Asian bias in the United States, especially in California.

Most members of the minority Republic of Hawaii were Christians because of the efforts of the New England Congregationalist missionaries who had been coming to Hawaii since the 1820s. But the majority of Japanese and Chinese were practicing Buddhism, Confucianism, and Shinto. Thus, Hawaii provided an entryway for these religions to gain a significant foothold into the mainland United States as well as into the new territory of Hawaii.

Anti-Asian bias would keep Hawaii from becoming a state until 1959 (after more than 18 attempts to do so since 1903). However, in spite of this bias, tens of thousands of Asians ultimately would become citizens of the United States as an unexpected consequence of the annexation. Further, no federal attempt would be made to keep them from practicing their religions.

Thus, 1898 would mark a fundamental policy decision by the United States concerning religion, even if it was primarily brought about by a simple lack of action rather than a policy statement. After 1898, whatever foray the nation would make militarily into the outside world would not be accompanied by any attempt to modify the religious beliefs of any other country. Freedom of and from religion everywhere would remain a basic tenet of the United States.

January 1899— In his apostolic letter called Testem benevolentiae, Pope Leo XIII condemned what he saw as the "heresy" of "Americanism." He felt American Catholic clergy were improperly trying to reconcile basic Catholic teachings with modern thought and liberties.

It was not the first time, nor would it be the last, that Rome, used to tying church and state very much together, would have theological difficulties with priests in the United States who found themselves caught between the requirements of separation of church and state in the United States and total unquestioning obedience to Rome.

December 27, 1899— Carrie Nation, a leader of the American Christian temperance movement, raided and partly wrecked her first saloon in Medicine Lodge, Kansas. Nation would become notorious for her attacks, but local bar owners and authorities were not amused by her clearly illegal actions. In some communities she was simply shown the way out of town and told not to return upon threat of jail.

Nation was primarily interested in publicity, of which she obtained a great deal. She knew she would need lots of income to pay her various fines, legal expenses, and damage claims while she went about creating her unique way of keeping her cause before the public. She would, for example, create small hatchets from wood fragments of her bar attacks and sell them as souvenirs to her followers to raise funds.

Nation essentially got the last laugh on her many critics when Prohibition became the law in 1919, but the results of Prohibition were so devastating in so many unexpected ways that the American Christian temperance movement could hardly celebrate its success.

March 21, 1900—The Bible Institute for Home and Foreign Missions located in Chicago changed its name to the Moody Bible Institute after the death of its founder Dwight L. Moody in 1899 (see listing for 1875/Moody).

As the Moody Bible Institute, the organization gained international fame.

1900—Congregationalist minister Washington Gladden (see listing for 1886) ran for a position on the city council of Columbus, Ohio. Gladden admitted he had "no special fitness" for the office, but he was elected nonetheless. As a man who would write 39 books focusing on the special needs of people in the growing cities of America, Gladden recognized that a voice from inside might be more effective than a voice from the pulpit or the written page.

Gladden served a term of two years on the city council, and he learned firsthand how difficult it was for even men of the best intentions to correct problems within the municipalities of the United States. He stated that the first problem is that responsible citizens "think it bad form" to go into local politics. This leads to a second problem that local (and many state) politicians are not so much corrupt as incompetent.

Gladden added that major policy decisions "are generally in the hands of men who have no fitness to deal with them; and this is mainly because

1901

the men who have the necessary equipment for such work almost uniformly refuse to undertake it." There was not much church leaders could do to address the problems of cities without a larger percentage of good citizens getting involved as well.

January 1, 1901—In Topeka, Kansas, Charles F. Parham gathered together some of his students at the Bethel Bible College to discuss events they had been undergoing as part of the research into Pentecostalism Parham had assigned them. Parham had been a pastor in the Methodist Episcopal Church before he left the church to found the Bethel Bible College.

The students reported events involved with the Holy Spirit giving them his blessing and baptism and other gifts, the most prominent of which were that they began speaking in tongues, i.e., speaking in other languages without actually having been taught the language.

This event, along with the Azusa Street meetings in Los Angeles starting five years later in 1906 (see listing for April 1906), is taken by many Pentecostals as the founding of their denomination in the United States. However, the founding of the Church of God in Christ in 1897 (see listing) preceded these events, although the Church of God in Christ was founded primarily for blacks. The Pentecostal movement as a whole involves members of all races.

Pentecostalism is based on the story in the Bible in the book of Acts when on Pentecost the Holy Spirit (Holy Ghost in some denominations) descended on the Apostles and most notably caused them to speak in tongues. The apostles also received a baptism blessing from the Holy Spirit. The practice of Pentecostalism also involves vigorous preaching (from either sex) and vigorous congregations as well. Shouting and hand-clapping accompany the services, and as much attention is given to the manner of the service as to doctrine. There were Pentecostal movements in England in the 1830s and over 100,000 people were said to convert to Christianity at a huge revival in Wales in 1904. There were many such activities in the world before the Pentecostals became established in the United States.

Pentecostalism at the beginning was closely allied with the "Holiness" movement. The Holiness movement came directly out of Methodism where its founder John Wesley stressed the biblical text in Matthew

5:48 for followers "to be perfect as your Heavenly is perfect." The Holiness movement quickly grew to include the emotional, passionate shouting and hand clapping typical of Pentecostalism. There were several new denominations established after the Civil War. Examples include D. S. Warner's Church of God in 1880, A. B. Simpson's Christian and Missionary Alliance in 1887, J. H. King's Fire Baptized Holiness Church in 1895, and The Pilgrim's Holiness Church in 1897.

The founding of the Holiness/Pentecostal Church of God in Christ also in 1897 (that became the largest black Pentecostal Church in the world — see listing for 1897) flowed out of this activity, and the two movements were closely entwined for a number of years. But new denominations arose regularly in both movements and their names were literally impossible to keep track of. Present estimates are that there are about 11,000 denominations worldwide among the 500 million people that make up Pentecostal or related churches around the globe.

1902 — Rabbi Solomon Schechter arrived in the United States. Schechter became the president of the Jewish Theological Seminary in New York. He defended what became known as the Conservative Jewish approach. Reformed Jews urged great changes in Jewish culture to concentrate on becoming American and fitting in with the "new country that offered great freedom of religion." Orthodox Jews argued for no change because they no longer had to change their customs to hide from authorities in this "new country that offered great freedom of religion."

The conservative approach, championed by Schechter, argued that an in-between approach was better. Some change, but only as Judaism desired it, was the delightful flexibility offered to Jews in this "new country that offered such freedom of religion."

The issue arose because after the Civil War, Jewish immigration changed from one dominated by German Jews to one dominated by Eastern European and Russian Jews. Each group had its own history of persecution in the old country and thus its own expectation of how best to proceed in the new country, the United States.

Schechter wrote, "There is nothing in American citizenship which is incompatible with our observing the dietary laws, our sanctifying the Sabbath, ... or our perpetuating any other law essential to the preservation of Judaism." In Europe, he added, compromises were forced upon us. Here

1904

they are not. In short, for perhaps the first time in their long history, Jews were free to practice their religion (or not) exactly as they pleased.

1904— Evangeline Booth, daughter of the founder of the Salvation Army in Britain (see listing for January 19, 1889), began a thirty-year stint until 1934 as the field commissioner of the Salvation Army in the United States before ultimately moving up to general of the whole international movement afterwards (the Salvation Army used military designations for its leaders).

The Salvation Army gained a reputation here as elsewhere for providing social services to the poor, "the lowest fallen, the most depraved, and the most neglected." Revivals were fine, one leader said, but they appealed to the middle-class churchgoer, while "the godless multitudes drifted past their doors."

The Salvation Army easily moved women into their leadership ranks. One leader noted that "problems that statesmanship and philanthropy have failed to solve have yielded to the gentle magic of these heroines of slumdom." The words and deeds of these heroines, "powerful in their simplicity, go straight to the hearts of their hearers and result is wonderful reformations."

April 14, 1906— A revival being conducted in Los Angeles by black evangelist William J. Seymour moved into the unused and vacant African Methodist Episcopal Church at 312 Azusa Street. Following that move the revival expanded and continued for almost a decade. It became the legendary Azusa Street Revival that many consider the true establishing act of the Pentecostal movement in the United States, even though some other basic Pentecostal events took place a few years earlier as noted in this chronology (see the listing for The Church of God in Christ in 1897 and the January 1, 2001, listing about Charles Parham in Topeka, Kansas).

William J. Seymour in 1906 was 34 years old, the son of former slaves. He had been a student of Pentecostal preacher Charles Parham as well as an interim preacher in a small Holiness Church in Houston, Texas. With Parham's blessing and financial assistance, Seymour accepted an offer to preach in Los Angeles for a planned stay of about a month. But Seymour never left Los Angeles again, as his preaching stay extended to 1922 when he died of a heart attack at the age of 50.

Seymour arrived in Los Angeles on February 22, 1906, and began preaching at Julia Hutchins' Holiness Church. When he returned the next Sunday he found the church door padlocked. Hutchins and the elders of the church did not like his message. However, some members did approve and Seymour spent the next five weeks holding prayer meetings in the homes of several of those members. Word began to spread and members of other local Holiness churches began to attend, as well as neighborhood and then city members from black, white, and Latino areas.

As it became known Seymour and others were speaking in tongues, even Hutchins and members of her congregation began to swell the crowd until the front porch of one of the homes being used collapsed from the weight. At that point, the semi-abandoned church at 312 Azusa Street was pressed into service. By mid–May anywhere from 300 to 1,500 people were attempting to squeeze into the building, and services were being led spontaneously by persons of all persuasions, including women. Services were going almost around the clock, and news of the activities spread outside Los Angeles. All races and income levels were represented among the attendees, some skeptical, some wanting to take part in such unusual services, some wanting to see what the fuss was about. The revival went on in this way for several years.

By 1913, the revival flavor of the event had begun to wind down, and by 1915 most of the media attention and crowds had left. People had marveled at the revivals of the past that had gone on for as long as several weeks. But Azusa Street went on for several years. No wonder it was taken as the basic establishment of Pentecostalism in the United States.

Many of the 1906 attendees left to form their own congregations. Soon many of these would join to form the Assembly of God (see listing for April 1914) which would grow to 57 million members around the world. But splits and reformations would continue indefinitely among Pentecostal churches. As previously noted, the Pentecostal Church in all its variations is today the largest Protestant Church in the world with about 500 million members. Only the Roman Catholic Church is larger. The Pentecostal Church remains the most rapidly growing church in the world.

1907—A Baptist seminary professor from Rochester, New York, named Walter Rauschenbusch, who had taken up the cause of unionism, wrote that it was time to turn the spiritual force of Christianity "against the materialism and mammonism of our industrial and social order."

1908

Rauschenbusch felt churches were not doing enough to accomplish what he saw as social justice, and he was scornful of modern revivalism. He wrote that it produced only "skin deep changes. Things have simmered down to signing a card, shaking hands, or being introduced to the evangelist."

Rauschenbusch added that we have been taught that "man does not live by bread alone," and thus Christians should have the courage of their convictions and support unions against the excesses of the Industrial Revolution.

1908 — About 12 million Protestant Church members were represented by the formation of the Federal Council of Churches. One of the first orders of business for the group was to develop a Social Creed to put "conscience and justice and love" into our "Christian civilization."

The council urged such then-radical steps as the abolition of child labor, more careful regulation of women's work, at least one day in seven off from work, and "the principle of conciliation and arbitration in industrial dissensions." All of these "radical" ideas eventually became commonplace.

June 29, 1908 — Pope Pius X published the apostolic constitution Sapienti consilio that caused the American Catholic Church to stop being considered a missionary church. From now on the Catholic Church was a full-fledged member of the Roman Catholic Church rather than coming under the control of the Congregation de Propaganda Fide.

1910 — The National Conference of Catholic Charities was formed to coordinate the activities of a number of Catholic organizations offering many social functions. These organizations included the Catholic Young Men's National Union, the Sisters of Charity, the Sisters of Mercy, and the Sisters of St. Joseph, among others.

Once again, the National Conference of Catholic Charities demonstrated the commitment of the Catholic Church, as well as their Protestant and Jewish counterparts, to play a key role in offering social and economic assistance to the population at large in addition to providing religious services to their congregations.

July 20, 1910—The Christian Endeavour Society of Missouri began a campaign to ban movies that showed kissing between nonrelatives. The Missouri group was a forerunner of what would become known as the Religious Right in the United States.

October 1910—The *Salt Lake Tribune*, originally established as an anti–Mormon newspaper to balance the views of *The Deseret News*, which was owned by the Mormons, published the names of about 200 Mormons who had taken plural wives after the publication of leader Wilford Woodruff's 1890 Manifesto (see listing) pledging to stop the practice of polygamy.

But perhaps the most notable reaction to the newspaper story was that a number of prominent Mormons shared the outrage of outsiders. The Mormon Church as a whole undertook actions to finally eradicate polygamy and make the Manifesto a reality. Within a decade the Mormons, including their leaders, were actively encouraging the prosecution of "cohabs."

From the 1920s onward the Mormon Church headquartered in Salt Lake City was essentially in full compliance with the laws of the nation. Only various splinter groups in other locations refused to give up the practice of polygamy. They are a tiny (less than 1 percent of all Mormons worldwide) but notorious group that even today make headlines as they are legally prosecuted by state and federal agencies. They have long been disavowed by the Salt Lake City church.

1912—Jewish activist Henrietta Szold founded the Women's Zionist Organization of America to pursue the idea of a Jewish state. Six years later in 1918, the Jewish Theological Seminary in New York City became a major recruiting and training center for American Zionists. The movement would continue to grow until the dream of a Jewish state was realized on May 11, 1948 (see listing).

1913—The Anti-Defamation League was created by Jewish activists. Prejudice was increasing against Jewish groups in direct proportion to the growing number of Jews that were coming to the United States in the record high immigration levels of the first part of the 20th century (a level that would decrease sharply in the coming decades due to the restrictive immigration laws passed by the 1920s).

1914

The Anti-Defamation League had the very reasonable goals of trying to identify sources of religious and racial prejudice and then trying to eliminate that prejudice through programs of education and persuasion. But popular and powerful public voices such as that of Henry Ford made it very hard to counter anti–Semitism. Bias against Jews was evident everywhere in the next several decades in such areas as housing restrictions and quotas being enforced to limit the number of Jews who could enroll in institutions of higher education.

April 1914— The World Assemblies of God Fellowship, commonly known as the Assemblies of God, was founded during an eleven-day conference in Hot Springs, Arkansas. The conference was arranged by about 300 preachers and laymen to consolidate the many churches and groups that had sprung from the April 1906 Azusa Street multiyear revival in Los Angeles (see listing) and its immediate predecessors.

The resulting organization was incorporated under the title of the General Council of the Assemblies of God, which evolved into the Assemblies of God. Many branches and sub-branches grew out of this organization and spread all over the world. They are generally known as Pentecostal churches containing believers who consider themselves "Spirit baptized" through action of the Holy Spirit. Although some congregations have varying views on the nature of this baptism, all practice speaking in tongues and vigorous worship services full of shouting and clapping and body movements.

The Assemblies of God grew into a denomination (cooperative fellowship) with a present membership of 57 million around the world in almost 300,000 congregations (about 5 percent of which are in the United States). It is considered the largest single denomination among the 500 million members that make up the Pentecostal churches operating under numerous names in over two hundred countries worldwide.

1915— Disturbed by what he saw as a gradual shift from neutrality to siding with Great Britain and her allies in the battle in Europe that had started in 1914 and became World War I, Unitarian minister John Hayes Holmes spoke out against the idea that war is justified if it has a noble purpose.

Holmes stated that "No man is wise enough, no nation is important

1917

enough, no human interest is precious enough, to justify the wholesale destruction and murder which constitutes the essence of war."

Rabbi Stephen Wise of New York agreed with Holmes and wrote a letter to President Woodrow Wilson (a staunch Presbyterian) to protest what he also saw as a steady building of a war mentality. In his letter, Wise stated, "I should not, my dear President, have written in this way, nor would I burden you with my thoughts on this question if I did not feel conscience bound to dissent in my pulpit and on platform from your position."

But other religious leaders took the position that pacifism did not include failing to defend yourself when attacked. Taking a position that "war is a bad thing" is self-evident, and this position is not enough when other countries decide to go to war and you must choose to acquiesce or to fight back. President Wilson had little trouble in getting the backing of the nation when he decided to join the war effort in 1917.

1917—A National Catholic War Council was formed to respond to the many needs caused by the entrance of the United States into World War I. The organization proved so useful that it was continued after the war ended at the end of 1918, and it was eventually renamed the National Catholic Welfare Conference.

In 1919, the conference adopted the Bishops' Program of Social Reconstruction that called for "a reform in the spirit of both labor and capital." Guided by Monsignor John A. Ryan, the bishops called for a number of reforms that would combine a "Christian view of work and wealth" to address many problems resulting from the Industrial Revolution.

December 18, 1917—The 18th Amendment, the Prohibition amendment, was approved by Congress and started the ratification process. It was ratified on January 16, 1919 (all states ultimately ratified it except Rhode Island). Prohibition turned out to trigger more than a decade of lawlessness and violence until it was repealed by the 21st Amendment in 1933.

When it began, Prohibition marked the successful culmination of a drive towards temperance that religious groups had officially organized to achieve almost a century ago (see listing for February 13, 1826). The most notable groups pursuing the Prohibition amendment to its successful conclusion were the Women's Christian Temperance Union (WCTU—see

1918

listing for August 1874) and the Anti-Saloon League (see listing for 1895/Russell).

The WCTU continued its operations after the 18th Amendment was passed (and after it was repealed), concentrating on women's issues of all kinds. The achievement of prohibition was only one of the many activities it engaged in after its founding. The WCTU is today the oldest voluntary, nonsectarian, women's organization in continuous existence in the world.

1918—The Central Conference of American Rabbis (Reform Judaism) added its voice to the growing chorus of religious groups calling for economic reform in terms of how workers are treated. The rabbis called for the almost now-standard abolition of child labor, but they added a request for reviewing the age limit defining child labor to be sure it was "consistent with moral and physical health."

The rabbis then upped the ante by calling for something new named "workmen's compensation" in the case of "industrial accidents and occupational diseases." They added that labor's right to "organize and bargain collectively" must be recognized, a "minimum wage" must be established, and some sort of "social insurance" be created for "meeting the contingencies of unemployment and old age."

In many ways the rabbis were well ahead of their time, but all of these radical ideas ultimately came to fruition in the United States.

June 4, 1919—The 19th Amendment, known as women's suffrage because it gave women the right to vote, was approved by Congress to begin the ratification process. The amendment was ratified on August 18, 1920.

A long list of women's rights groups and women's religious groups had long been active in obtaining the right of women to vote. The religious groups tied their activities in this area to the right of women to take leadership roles in their churches and synagogues. Among the leading religious groups in this area was the Woman's Christian Temperance Union (WCTU), perhaps better known for its efforts in achieving Prohibition (see listing for December 18, 1917), but the WCTU was active in a broad role of women's issues (and still is).

The 19th Amendment has been used as the linchpin for supporting the right of women to take full part in many religious activities. Actually, the text of the body of the amendment is extremely brief. It reads "The right of citizens of the United States to vote shall not be denied or abridged by the United States or any state on account of sex." But this simple sentence ultimately brought a revolution in the role of women in all facets of life in the United States.

It similarly supported a dramatic increase in the roles of women in their religious lives, but some churches (notably the Catholic Church) refused then and still refuse now to expand what they see as the historical role of women in the church (and in other aspects of life for that matter).

May 21, 1922 — Harry Emerson Fosdick, a noted liberal Protestant preacher of the early decades of the 20th century, delivered a sermon titled "Shall the Fundamentalists Win?" In this sermon, Fosdick took the modernist position. He saw the Bible as a description of the development of God's will, not necessarily a record of the literal word of God.

Fosdick was calling for an intellectual, open-minded, and tolerant "Fellowship of God." In his view, the tenets of Christianity were open to change over time. But his was a minority view.

Fundamentalists were outraged. Fosdick was investigated by his local church, the First Presbyterian Church in New York City, and he probably escaped censure only by resigning in 1924. However, he was immediately hired as pastor of John D. Rockefeller's famous new Riverside Church, also located in New York City.

Fosdick's new church distributed his sermon nationwide, although the church used the somewhat less militant title "The New Knowledge and the Christian Faith." Fosdick won wide recognition for his sermons, radio broadcasts, and books.

January 1, 1923 — Noted female evangelist Aimee Semple McPherson presided over the opening and dedication of the huge domed church named the Angelus Temple in the Echo Park area of Los Angeles. The church would become the center of the incredible fund-raising skills demonstrated by McPherson, and would launch a new religious denomination called the International Church of the Foursquare Gospel (see listing for 1927). It was commonly known as the Foursquare Church.

McPherson was an extremely controversial (and for some years an

1923

extremely popular) figure. When she was 25 years old in 1915, she embarked on a series of revival meetings in Canada and the eastern part of the United States. She was actually as a Pentecostal preacher, but her revival tour was intended to fulfill a promise she had made to God when she was trying to recover from an illness.

McPherson's revivals were emotional in the Pentecostal style, and she was soon preaching to capacity crowds across the United States. By 1921 her husband was so frustrated by her continual touring that he successfully sued her for divorce on the grounds of abandonment. McPherson finally arrived in Los Angeles and began looking for a place to settle and raise her family. This led to the construction of the Angelus Temple in 1923.

McPherson was such a popular preacher and effective fund-raiser that she had raised the $1.5 million to build the temple from private donations, and then she turned the church (with a seating capacity of 5,300) into a gigantic money machine. She preached there to a capacity crowd three times a day, seven days a week. In the beginning she handled every service herself, and often collections were taken with the admonishment of "no coins, please."

Pentecostalism was just beginning to expand widely in the 1920s and was still unpopular in some parts of the public. So McPherson toned down her sermons accordingly, although she still practiced speaking in tongues and faith healing as she found it appropriate. Her sermons were illustrated featuring stage demonstrations and attracted people from the entertainment industry looking for a "show." She entered floats in the Rose Bowl parade and generally pursued publicity avidly. She was the first woman to preach a sermon over the radio, and ultimately operated a radio station of her own (KSFG).

With McPherson it was hard to tell where entertainment stopped and religion began. She lost her favorable position with the press in 1926 when she claimed to have been kidnapped after disappearing for 35 days in what seemed to be part of a romantic affair with a married engineer from her radio station. Her influence slowly declined, and she was involved with some other scandals until she died of an accidental drug overdose in 1944.

McPherson lived on a big stage, but finally faded away. Still, her legacy includes the Foursquare Gospel Church, which today has about 5

1925

million members worldwide (over 90 percent of which are outside the United States which is typical of churches having Pentecostal roots).

June 4, 1923— The United States Supreme Court ruled that a Nebraska law used to prosecute a man teaching German in a Lutheran school at the request of parents was unconstitutional. The probable but unspoken purpose of the Nebraska law was to prevent the teaching of German while anti–German feelings still ran high after World War I.

The stated purpose of the law was to promote "assimilation and civic" development. But the Supreme Court ruled that "in a time of peace and tranquility" the law violated the due process clause of the Fourteenth Amendment. The Supreme Court thus avoided any emotional reaction to a situation that seemed relatively harmless on its surface.

September 15, 1923— In an attempt to control the activities of the Ku Klux Klan, the governor of Oklahoma, John Walton, placed the state under martial law. The Ku Klux Klan, formed in the 19th century, would be a problem for a good part of the first half of the 20th century as well with its antiblack, anti–Catholic, and anti–Semitic activities.

May 27, 1924— Meeting in Maryland, the General Conference of the Methodist Episcopal Church repealed its ban on dancing and theater attendance by church members. This was an attempt to make the Methodist Church more relevant to the life styles of its members, but as the century progressed many "mainstream" denominations would find their memberships declining as other denominations became more attractive.

October 8, 1924— The National Lutheran Conference, meeting in New York, banned the playing of jazz music in the local churches.

May 13, 1925— The state of Florida passed a law requiring daily readings from the Bible in all public schools. This would be a daily occurrence in many public schools across the nation until the Supreme Court would recognize in the 1950s that such laws were a clear violation of the First Amendment of the Constitution.

June 1, 1925— The United States Supreme Court ruled that an Oregon law requiring parents to send their children between the ages of 8 and 16

1925

only to public schools in the district in which they resided, was unconstitutional.

The law had been challenged by the Sisters of the Holy Names of Jesus and Mary, who operated a parochial school. The court ruled unanimously that the law was unconstitutional because "the fundamental liberty upon which all governments repose in this Union excludes any general power of the state to standardize its children by forcing them to accept instruction from public teachers only."

This decision was a major victory for parochial schools throughout the United States because it upheld their right to establish and maintain such school systems.

July 10, 1925— The trial of biology teacher John Scopes, who had been formally arrested three months earlier in May for teaching evolution to his high school class, began in Dayton, Tennessee. The so-called Scopes Monkey Trial became a carnival, even though it appeared on the surface that serious issues were at stake. Some saw the trial as a battle between religious fundamentalists and the more liberal version of religion that had developed in the six decades since the Civil War.

The trial was actually created as a publicity stunt by the powers that be in the city of Dayton. The population of Dayton had fallen to 1,800 from 3,000 over the past three decades, and it was hoped the trial and resulting publicly would reverse the trend.

The impetus for staging the trial as a publicity stunt was that the state of Tennessee had enacted legislation in February 1925 to ban the teaching of evolution in schools. The American Civil Liberties Union (ACLU) had advertised that it would offer its services free to anyone challenging the Tennessee law. Several town leaders, including the superintendent of schools, got teacher Scopes to agree to be arrested for teaching evolution. The group actually hoped to overturn the new law, but their primary purpose was to attract attention (and visitors) to Dayton. They succeeded beyond their wildest dreams.

Fundamentalist Williams Jennings Bryan (see listing for July 9, 1896), who had led the battle to get a ban on teaching evolution passed in 15 states, offered his services to help the prosecution when he heard about the trial and the involvement of the ACLU. In turn, famous defense attorney Clarence Darrow (now retired) offered his services to the defense. An incredible carnival atmosphere with banners and lemonade stands developed in Dayton as the media descended on tiny Dayton to watch the famous men do battle.

The trial featured Darrow calling Bryan to the stand as an expert on the Bible. The press reported that Darrow won the debate by finally making Bryan look unsure and foolish. But Darrow ended the trial by asking the judge to declare Scopes guilty. Darrow hoped to appeal the verdict to the Tennessee Supreme Court and get a reversal on constitutional grounds.

The jury issued a guilty verdict after eight minutes of deliberation, and the judge fined Scopes $100, the minimum permitted. The Tennessee Supreme Court did take up the case 18 months later, but it simply reversed the verdict on the technical grounds that the jury, not the judge, should have set the fine. Then the Tennessee Supreme Court dismissed the case.

It would not be until 43 years later in 1968, that the United States Supreme Court would find such laws unconstitutional. But even then, as is often the case in such emotional issues, the question would continue to appear again and again in the courts under slightly different guises. It still does so today.

1926, Klan— With the substantial reduction of immigration following the restrictive laws put in place in 1924, some groups in America tried to return to the days when white Protestants ruled the land. The most visible among them was probably the Ku Klux Klan.

The Klan was formed after the Civil War essentially to terrorize blacks, but they easily evolved to a position of being anti-everything except white Protestants. The Klan had something of a revival in the early 20th century, and in 1926 their Imperial Wizard made their desires quite clear.

"America must remain Protestant," he declared, adding that the nation's destiny would be fatally damaged "if we become priest-ridden, if we had to submit our consciences and limit our activities and suppress our thoughts at the command of any man, much less of a man sitting upon Seven Hills thousands of miles away." The Klan could be as anti–Catholic as it was antiblack.

Many religious leaders decried the views of the Klan, and the rabbi of Temple Emmanu-El in New York City asked, "What justification is there for this 20th century religious persecution on American soil?" The

1927

rabbi said that the Americanism of the Klan was the most un-American feature to be seen in all the land.

1927 — Famous (or notorious) female evangelist Aimee Semple McPherson (see listing for January 1, 1923) founded the International Church of the Foursquare Gospel, commonly known as the Foursquare Church. McPherson was basically a Pentecostal preacher, and her new church followed those teachings.

The center of the Foursquare Church was the domed Angelus Temple (with a seating capacity of 5,300) McPherson had built in 1923 in Los Angeles. McPherson was a true celebrity in Los Angeles, leading a parade including such people as the mayor and various movie stars through the streets of Los Angeles to services at the Angelus Temple.

Various scandals dimmed the light of McPherson's celebrity status, but the Foursquare Church prospered. After McPherson's death in 1944, her son led the church to ever greater growth and prosperity. By 2000, the church had a membership of over 200,000 in over 1,800 churches in the United States.

But as with nearly all Pentecostal denominations, splits and mergers over the years make the core membership of any denomination hard to discern. In 1948, together with other Pentecostal churches, the Foursquare Church formed the Pentecostal Fellowship of North America. In 1994, this fellowship reorganized as the Pentecostal/Charismatic Churches of North America after consolidating with blacks from the Church of God in Christ.

However the various pieces are defined, some sources today credit the Foursquare Church with 5 million members worldwide in 30,000 congregations, with most of them overseas.

1928 — The presidential election campaign of 1928 brought out a surge of anti-Catholic bias across the entire United States. The Republicans nominated Herbert Hoover to continue the Republican domination of the 1920s, but the Democrats nominated Catholic Alfred E. Smith of New York. It was the first time in the nation's history that a major political party had nominated a Catholic to run for the office of the presidency.

Smith had a substantial political record, having been a member of the New York legislature for many years and having served as the governor of the state for four terms. But on a nationwide basis, the prime factor in Smith's background was that he was a Roman Catholic. All of the old statements about the dangers to American liberty that followers of a foreign pope represented were a big part of the campaign rhetoric.

Smith lost to Hoover by a wide margin. There were a number of other factors involved including the substantial prosperity of the nation in the 1920s before the stock market crash of 1929, but the single biggest problem for Smith was the fact that he was a Catholic. It would be another 32 years before the United States would accept a Catholic as president with the election of John F. Kennedy in 1960.

1929 — Noted journalist and author Walter Lippman published *A Preface to Morals*, which stated in essence that traditional religion was outmoded and could no longer serve as the basis for which people could make moral choices.

John Dewey, another noted writer and social philosopher of the time, wrote along the same lines in 1934 saying that "Anthropology, history, and literary criticism have furnished a radically different version of the historic events and personages upon which Christian religions have built." He noted that ancient texts are not the way to truth but that experimentation, investigation, and inquiry are the proper methods.

Men such as Dewey and Lippman were the leaders of a general movement questioning the validity of established religions and all of their creeds and protocols carried forward from ancient times when mankind knew much less than it did now.

April 28, 1930 — The United States Supreme Court upheld a lower court ruling that the state of Louisiana violated no constitutional law by enacting a tax to supply free textbooks to the children of the state. Opponents had argued the tax was improper because some children used the textbooks in religious and other sectarian schools.

The Court ruled that the true beneficiaries of the law were the children of the state. No special schools were identified as recipients, and all children benefited without any form of discrimination based on race, color, ethnic origin, or religion. The schools in which the textbooks were used were irrelevant to the intent of the process, which was to provide free textbooks to all children. Thus, no constitutional law was being violated.

1931

1931, Council of Churches — The Federal Council of Churches, the National Catholic Welfare Conference, and the Central Conference of American Rabbis came together to try to find "Permanent Preventives of Unemployment."

In the same year, Pope Pius XI issued the encyclical "Quadragesimo Anno" (Fortieth Year) referencing to the socially progressive document issued by Pope Leo XIII in 1891. The pope urged everyone to address the needs of social justice as the depression deepened in the world as well as the United States.

But however well meaning, pronouncements by religious leaders failed to avoid or ameliorate the huge depression that was threatening social order everywhere. It would take dramatic action by new President Franklin Roosevelt to establish some glimmers of hope in the United States, and even at that most historians agree that it wasn't until the end of the decade and the building of armaments in preparation for World War II that the country was pulled out of the depression.

1931, Witnesses — Joseph F. Rutherford, current president of the denomination originated by Charles Taze Russell in 1872 (see listing), changed the name of the denomination to the Jehovah's Witnesses. Rutherford also later presided in March 1940 over the final name change of the main publication of the denomination, settling on the title of *The Watchtower Announcing Jehovah's Kingdom*.

1933 — Catholic activist Dorothy Day led the founding of the Catholic Worker movement. Day stated the objective of her activities very simply. "We just went out and did things." She didn't wait for pronouncements and the formation of committees and so forth. She and her followers just took action.

Day had led a rather Bohemian lifestyle early in life, but following the birth of her daughter she began a spiritual conversion that led her to join the Catholic Church in 1927 when she was 30 years old. She had experience as a writer, and with fellow Catholic activist Peter Maurin, she founded the newspaper *The Catholic Worker*, which was the core of the Catholic Worker movement. The goal of the movement was to help the poorest of the poor and to espouse a pacifist attitude among the warlike issues developing in the 1930s.

1936

Her movement and its Hospitality Houses simply fed those who were hungry and offered shelter and clothing to the poor. The Hospitality House concept spread into the United States and even other countries, although their pacifist theme was a problem when World War II broke out. The issue of helping the poor in the Depression was taken up by many other religious organizations, but the need for help during that time tended to overwhelm the resources of these organizations.

June 10, 1935— Alcoholics Anonymous (AA) was founded in Akron, Ohio. A recovering alcoholic executive named Bill Wilson and a Dr. Bob Smith, who took his last drink on that day, are recognized as the cofounders of the organization.

Later, the Reverend Dr. Sam Shoemaker, rector of the Calvary Church in New York City, was given credit by Bill Wilson as a cofounder. Shoemaker's church was the American headquarters of a loose Christian organization called the Oxford Group, which stressed Christian principles but insisted it was not a church or a denomination, but just a group of like-minded people. Shoemaker helped Wilson write the book *Alcoholics Anonymous*, which described the program and used many principles from the Oxford Group.

One of the keys to success of AA was to get members to realize their need of the help of whatever God an alcoholic believed in overcoming alcoholism. The AA listed "Twelve Steps" to follow to achieve success. The AA was one of the few groups to make a positive impact on a disease many doctors in the 1930s described as incurable and ultimately fatal. The AA program has since been used in countries around the world.

However, the AA found that trying to include drug addicts, for example, in its meetings was not successful because people who attended AA needed to be among people having exactly the same problem. Thus, other such groups seeking addictive cures have tried to adopt the "Twelve Steps" of the AA to the specific addiction needing a cure. The AA has found also that its goals generally cannot be realized unless there is a spiritual conversion or spiritual awakening ultimately reached independently by the member seeking help.

November 1936— Controversial Catholic "Radio Priest" Father Charles E. Coughlin temporarily stopped broadcasting making good on his prom-

1936

ise to retire if the candidate of the new Union Party Coughlin help found did not get at least nine million votes in the presidential election of 1936. When Coughlin's candidate, William Lemke, got only one-tenth of that number, Coughlin was silenced for a few months. But when he came right back in 1937, his diatribes turned especially nasty.

In 1923, Father Coughlin became a priest at the National Shrine of the Little Flower Church in Royal Oak, Michigan, a suburb of Detroit. He began regularly broadcasting sermons on Detroit station WJR in 1926, when radio was still a novelty. In 1931 CBS dropped its free sponsorship of his program, so Coughlin raised enough money to create his own radio station. He soon claimed millions of listeners, and was an ardent backer of Franklin Roosevelt and the New Deal in the 1932 elections.

However, by 1934, Coughlin was attacking the New Deal and calling Roosevelt a tool of Wall Street and "international bankers," a term then used in a distinctly anti–Semitic way. When his new party failed in 1936, Coughlin turned to vicious attacks on "Jewish conspirators" and he began to speak favorably of Hitler and Mussolini. Coughlin began publication of a newspaper called *Social Justice* in which he printed excerpts from speeches by Joseph Goebbels, Hitler's chief of propaganda.

Members of the Catholic Church hierarchy in the United States tried to have Coughlin forced off the air, but the Vatican in Rome took the position that only the bishop of Detroit, Michael Gallagher, had the proper authority to do so, and as Gallagher supported Coughlin, Rome could do nothing. This was one of a number of issues in the 1930s and 1940s concerning anti–Semitism on which the Catholic leadership in Rome practiced studious inaction and left the Catholic Church open to claims of an anti–Semitic attitude.

Coughlin's active support of Nazi Germany (he gave the Nazi salute at a rally in 1938) soon caused the government to deny his broadcasting permit. It was noted that First Amendment free speech rights did not necessarily apply to broadcasts because the airwaves were a commonly owned national resource and subject to regulation.

Coughlin tried to get around the problem by purchasing airtime on other radio stations to broadcast recordings of his speeches, but only a few stations were interested. Then in October 1939 (one month after Hitler's invasion of Poland), the National Association of Broadcasters (NAB) passed new restrictions on the sale of radio time on controversial issues. Among other things, manuscripts had to be submitted in advance. Coughlin wrote in his newspaper that he had been forced off the air.

During these episodes, newspapers in Germany, where Coughlin was a hero, ran headlines screaming that "America is Not Allowed to Hear the Truth." Coughlin appeared to be equally divided between spreading anti-Semitic information and supporting Nazi Germany, although it could be difficult to separate one from the other.

The final blow to Coughlin's reach came when the Roosevelt administration decided that although Coughlin did have a First Amendment right to publish whatever he wanted to publish in his newspaper, he had no such right to require the United States Post Office to deliver it. The administration thus revoked his mailing privileges.

Coughlin's influence fell rapidly, and after the December 1941 declaration of war, Coughlin's views were seen as supporting the enemy. In 1942, a new bishop arrived in Detroit and told Coughlin to cease his controversial political activities and confine himself to the duties of a parish priest. Coughlin remained as the priest of the Shrine of the Little Flower until he retired in 1966. He continued to write pamphlets denouncing communism until his death in 1979 at the age of 88.

May 10, 1939—After a separation of nearly a century, the Methodist Episcopal Church in the United States was formally reunited with the Methodist Episcopal Church, South. The southern branch had broken off due to disagreements in policy over the issue of slavery (see listing for May 1, 1845).

However, even though the Methodist Church was reassembling some lost pieces, new religious denominations such as Pentecostalism and Adventalism were continuing to grow in the United States, and the old mainline denominations such as Methodists, Baptists, and Presbyterians would continue to lose their relative influence. Protestantism per se would continue to grow rapidly as the population of the United States doubled between 1900 and 1950, but the number of denominations into which Protestantism was split would continue to grow even more rapidly.

1940—As part of determining a case regarding a religious issue, the Supreme Court of the United States decided that the First Amendment applied to the states as well as the federal government. This decision con-

1948

firmed that each individual state must observe the requirement to offer freedom of and from religion. No state law or state constitution could be in violation of this requirement.

This decision was part of the reason that in a growing pluralistic society like that of the United States, more and more individuals and organizations turned to the courts to settle differences in their views of what the First Amendment did and did not permit.

The result was that in a single decade such as the 1970s or 1980s, the Supreme Court would hear more cases concerning religious issues than it had heard in total between 1790 and 1940. This was partly a reflection of the fact that a case heard today could reappear tomorrow in a slightly different form (and possibly obtain a different result), and partly a reflection that in a rapidly changing world, the Constitution was viewed as a rock of stability.

March 8, 1948 — The Supreme Court of the United States decided that the use of public school system resources in Champaign, Illinois, to support classes in religion violated the establishment clause of the First Amendment and was unconstitutional.

The classes were offered by various religious groups, and the fact that students were released for a time from their duty to attend school if they opted to take the various religious courses, clearly violated the First Amendment, in the opinion of the court.

After this opinion, the rest of the century would find the Court often being asked to rule in similar cases, and except for some very narrow circumstances, the Court would find in favor of those requesting practices involving religion in almost any way to be barred from public schools.

May 14, 1948 — Israel was formally established as an independent state. The dream of Theodor Herzl (see listing for 1896) and the Zionists who followed finally came true. However, the declaration by Israel was immediately followed by war with its Arab neighbors, a war that in various degrees of intensity has been going on ever since.

The new state promised to be operated on the basis of religious freedom for all regardless of race or sex. The United States recognized the new state 11 minutes after its founding, and the other super power, the USSR

1951

(which had previously supported some crucial resolutions in the United Nations), followed with its recognition in three days.

The recognition of Israel by the United States followed an internal battle between President Harry Truman and members of a group of privileged liberals known as the "wise men" (called later by some critics the "naïve boys") who were trying to shape the foreign policy of the nation at the time. They felt Israel was hopelessly outnumbered by its Arab opponents, and that Truman was primarily trying to build Jewish support for the fall elections.

At any rate, Truman won the internal battle, and to the surprise of much of the world the Israelis won the war that followed its announcement of statehood. Truman insisted later that his actions were guided by a determination to do "the right thing," and to the surprise of much of the United States, he also won the 1948 election.

1951—A new Catholic bishop named Fulton J. Sheen began appearing on the relatively small DuMont network at 8:00 P.M. on Tuesday nights. The time was selected because the famous entertainers Milton Berle and Frank Sinatra were on competing networks at that time, and DuMont was trying to find anything that could give them a chance to cut into the ratings of Berle and Sinatra.

To the surprise of most observers, Sheen, simply preaching to a live audience in a show titled *Life Is Worth Living*, held his own in the ratings. The show eventually won an Emmy Award in 1952 for its performance in 1951. The show ran until 1957, drawing as many as 30 million viewers on a weekly basis.

Probably the most known episode came in February 1953 when Sheen especially criticized communist Russia (a favorite target) and said Soviet leader Joseph Stalin "must one day meet his judgment." Shortly after, Stalin died, on March 5, 1953. Many viewers felt Sheen had amazingly predicted Stalin's demise.

Sheen was well prepared for his emergence as an unlikely television star. He was 56 years old in 1951, and had been an active writer and teacher since his ordination in 1919 (he eventually wrote 73 books starting in 1925).

Sheen began a weekly Sunday night radio broadcast called *The Catholic Hour* in 1930. By 1950 the program had a listening audience of

1951

four million people, and was receiving between three and six thousand letters weekly from listeners. *Time* magazine ran an item on Sheen in 1946 calling him "the golden-voiced Msgr. Fulton J. Sheen, U.S. Catholicism's famed proselytizer."

Sheen moved easily into his television role in 1951, and then later hosted a nationally syndicated series called the *Fulton Sheen Program* from 1961 to 1968. Sheen spent most of his final years writing (he died in 1979 at age 84). Shortly before his death he was embraced by Pope John Paul II at St. Patrick's Cathedral in New York as "a loyal son of the Church" for Sheen's lifetime of writing and speaking about the Church.

September 30, 1951— The Reverend Billy Graham and his *Hour of Decision* program was first aired on television on the American Broadcasting Company (ABC). Popular evangelists of the past like Billy Sunday (see listing for February 17, 1889) barely reached in his entire career the number of people who watched the performance of Billy Graham on a single program. Graham's reach would ultimately span the whole globe. It has been estimated that in his lifetime he preached to over two **billion** people via television and radio.

In his career, Graham would become involved with 11 presidents, starting with Harry Truman. Some relationships would be more rewarding than others, but each was a reflection of the fact that Graham was a national figure. In this way, Graham was probably the most famous of the televangelists in the United States during the second half of the 20th century, a time when a considerable number of such evangelists appeared on the scene.

Graham was an ordained Baptist preacher who became interested in modern revival meetings. At the age of 31, he started a crusade in Los Angeles in 1949 that made him a national figure. In his career, has appeared in more than 40 such crusades around the world.

He founded the Billy Graham Evangelistic Association in 1950, an organization that includes his weekly radio program, his television specials, movies, magazines, a Web site, and a newspaper column.

Graham was noted for refusing to appear in segregated venues, for putting up bail to secure the release of Martin Luther King, Jr., from jail, and refusing to appear in South Africa until the country modified its apartheid policy. But although he was easily the most revered evangelist of his

1952

time, Graham was cool to Catholics and Jews. His was a clearly fundamentalist Baptist religion.

1952 — Minister Dr. Norman Vincent Peale published his book *The Power of Positive Thinking*. The book was an instant success. It stayed on the bestseller list for 186 consecutive weeks after publication (heading the list for over two years), and sold two million copies in the 1950s. Total sales to date number some seven million copies.

The book was sort of a capstone for Peale's career, although he was only 54 when the book was published in 1952, and Peale lived a very active life as a preacher and writer afterwards until he died at the age of 95 in 1993. The book was criticized by Peale's churchly counterparts for its loose interpretation of scripture (Peale seemed to present God as a benign power trying to help the individual rather than the great creator and judge), and by mental health experts for its seemingly simplistic approach to curing anxieties by utilizing positive thinking. Many others found too much emphasis on material success.

But as happens in so many similar cases, as many critics found reasons to dislike the book, the public for whom it was intended loved it. People involved in direct selling activities, such as Tupperware and related home products, and insurance salesmen, recognized and used *The Power of Positive Thinking* as their new Bible, being especially pleased that it recognized their striving for individual success as an effort blessed by God.

In spite of his critics, Peale had an impressive resume to support his writings. Peale started out as a Methodist minister in 1922, switched his allegiance to the Reformed Church in America in 1932, and began a 52-year stint as pastor of the famous Marble Collegiate Church in Manhattan. He became one of the most popular preachers in New York City, and oversaw an increase in the membership of the church from 600 to over 5,000.

Peale started a radio program called the *Art of Living* in 1935, and the program ran for over 54 years. Under the sponsorship of the National Council of Churches, Peale moved into television when that medium arrived in force after World War II.

In the meantime, Peale began to edit a nondenominational inspirational magazine called *Guideposts* (which is still in circulation). He started to write books, and his sermons were mailed monthly. With other famous

1953

businessmen during the Great Depression, Peale helped found an organization called 40Plus to assist managers and executives to find new employment.

Peale teamed with a psychoanalyst named Smiley Blanton to form a "religio-psychiatric" outpatient clinic next to his church. The two wrote books together, alternating the writing of chapters with Peale writing from a religious viewpoint and Blanton from a psychiatric viewpoint. Their best-known book (published in 1940) was *Faith is the Answer: A Psychiatrist and a Pastor Discuss Your Problems*.

Peale was essentially a living example of the power of positive thinking. That is what many readers said about their very positive response to his book. They found the book directly applicable to what they were doing in their lives. It wasn't a philosophical treatise filled with lofty ideas. It was an instruction manual about how to take control of their lives. The critics could nitpick as much as they wanted, but Peale dug deeply into his background and provided a message that resonated with his readers.

July 21, 1953— Methodist Bishop G. Bromley Oxnam, a leader of the National Council of Churches, appeared before the House Un-American Activities Committee (HUAC), the notorious committee assisting equally notorious Senator Joseph McCarthy in his witch hunt for communists in all areas of American life.

Bishop Oxnam had vigorously pursued such a hearing to refute charges HUAC had made in its normal reckless manner about communist sympathizers in the National Council of Churches and other such church groups. The result of the hearing was best summarized by *Time* magazine in its subsequent issue carrying the date of Monday, August 3, 1953. The magazine started its coverage by saying simply "The Winner: The Bishop."

HUAC and Oxnam had been conducting a war of words for some months. Among other things Oxnam had dubbed the members of the HUAC as "vermillion vigilantes." Oxnam explained that the HUAC was creating as much national distrust as the "Reds" the HUAC was supposedly hunting, but had so much "yellow in their makeup" that another color was needed to describe them.

During the six-hour hearing, the feisty 62-year-old Oxnam engaged the members of the HUAC in face-to-face verbal duels, at one point saying the committee's methods gave rise to a "new ... Ku-Kluxism." Before

1954

hundreds of applauding churchmen in the audience, Oxnam refuted specific charges by the HUAC and denied belonging to a long list of communist front organizations the committee questioned him about.

When Oxnam stepped down from the stand, it appeared that for once it was the HUAC who breathed a sigh of relief rather than its witness. Afterwards, the HUAC unanimously announced that it had no record of communist membership by Bishop Oxnam. Later some members of the committee lamely grumbled that they had never actually called Oxnam a communist but only a communist dupe. The statements smacked of sour grapes from a clear loser.

1954—Pulp science fiction writer L. Ron Hubbard founded Scientology, a religion that has been the center of controversy ever since it was founded. Hubbard died in 1986, but Scientology and the surrounding controversy continue to this day.

Cynics who question the motives of Scientology cite statements supposedly made by Hubbard in the late 1940s when he was a struggling writer working for the standard pulp fiction price of a penny a word. Hubbard was quoted in a July 28, 1977, *New York Times* article as having told a meeting of authors, "Writing for a penny a word is ridiculous. If a man really wanted to make a million dollars, the best way would be to start his own religion."

Hubbard took a step in that direction by publishing a book titled *Dianetics: The Modern Science of Mental Health* in 1950. The book was based on studies Hubbard had been doing in the areas of magic, the occult, hypnosis, Buddhism, and related areas. Hubbard had previously told his literary agent he was working on a new therapy system that had tremendous promotional and sales potential.

Hubbard started the Dianetic Research Foundation in 1951 (selling instruction in his new therapy), and from work carried out in this area established the philosophy of Scientology which led to a 1952 book titled *Scientology: A History of Man*. In 1954 the Church of Scientology was founded. Hubbard claimed that whereas Dianetics had addressed the body, Scientology addressed the soul.

The history of Scientology since has been battles with the IRS to maintain the tax-exempt status of a church, and battles with cynics who

1954

claim Scientology has a profit motive. Large sums of money have been involved as followers have included movie stars and other celebrities who have spent hundreds of thousands of dollars to complete courses in Scientology.

The controversy over Scientology's legitimacy as a religion raises a basic question, especially in the United States with its careful protections of freedom of religion: What exactly is a religion? Anybody can start one, and quite literally anyone who starts a religion will attract followers who will attest to its benefits and insights.

Scientology has many high-level followers who find in it something of value. Scientology has a high profile, but there are certainly other religions that attract followers. And if some of those followers happen to be wealthy, their participation can appear to support the declaration attributed to Hubbard that starting a new religion is the easiest way to making a million dollars.

May 17, 1954—In a truly landmark decision, the United States Supreme Court announced that the separate-but-equal doctrine used to establish segregation in public schools was unconstitutional. This decision meant that segregation by race was now illegal and all public school systems in the United States would have to assign students and resources to public schools on a "color-blind" basis.

This was not a religious issue per se, although it might mean some churches in some areas could get a fairer share of resources simply given to religious institutions by states where a separate-but-equal process was used to distribute the resources. If government entities were simply going to give away their resources, they would have to treat all institutions equally.

Ironically, where religious institutions were concerned, the separate-but-equal concept was one that the institutions preferred. For example, it has been noted several times in this chronology that black congregations wanted churches operated by black preachers. Similarly, Polish Catholics wanted their parishes operated by priests who were Polish, and so forth. Religious groups wanted racial and ethnic consistency in their leaders, and if they didn't get it would form new congregations that offered it. Segregation, in essence, was just what they wanted.

Freedom of religion was just fine, but many, if not most, congregations wanted it on their terms. They did not mind, even preferred, segregation as long as they were the ones controlling it.

June 19, 1956—Evangelist Jerry Falwell broke away from the church where he was first "saved" and founded the Thomas Road Baptist Church in Lynchburg, Virginia. The Thomas Road church would be the core of his operations for the next half century.

Falwell was only 23-years-old at the time and a recent graduate of the Baptist Bible College in Springfield, Missouri. Falwell believed that church and state were inseparable, regardless of what the First Amendment said. He believed the teachings of the church should be an integral part of everyone's life.

Falwell would become embroiled in many controversies because of his strict religious views and his intention to spread them widely (see listing for 1967).

November 26, 1956—A student named Ellery Schempp read passages from the *Koran* rather than from the Bible during the time set aside in his public school in Pennsylvania for mandatory readings from the Bible. Schempp was sent to the principal's office, but his family requested help from the American Civil Liberties Union (ACLU). The case ultimately entered the courts and grew into the fundamental question of whether the local government, in the form of its school boards, could constitutionally mandate readings from the Bible in the public schools.

Taking the normal glacial path through the courts with such issues, it wasn't until June 17, 1963 (see listing), that the Supreme Court issued a decision that such mandatory devotional Bible readings in public schools were clearly a violation of the First Amendment and thus unconstitutional. Even if students were given permission with parental consent to opt out of such issues, the practice was unconstitutional. The judges added in their ruling that peer pressures, especially at the public school level, would make a truly "free" decision to opt out nearly impossible. Besides, such a mandatory religious practice by any government entity was obviously a violation of the First Amendment.

The Supreme Court combined the case with a similar one from Maryland (see listing for December 8, 1960), and amid headlines that shouted that the decision "kicked God and prayer out of the schools," the Court

1957

made it clear that the First Amendment, written over 170 years ago, really meant what it said.

However, as has been consistently the case in issues of this type, people tried over the years to find ways to make religious practices consistent with the Constitution, and in 1993 a ruling would be made that "student-led and student-initiated" prayer of a "non-sectarian and non-proselytizing" nature would be permitted at graduation ceremonies.

The Supreme Court continues to attempt to carefully consider "both sides" of the First Amendment, i.e., freedom of religion and freedom from religion. This even-handed approach, however, ensures that the Supreme Court will have to continue to hear such cases indefinitely.

June 25, 1957—The Congregational Christian Church and the Evangelical and Reformed Church merged, thus creating the United Church of Christ.

March 3, 1959—The Unitarian Church and the Universalist Church voted to merge into a single denomination. The process of merging and splitting apart continued to be a standard operating procedure of Protestant churches in the 20th and 21st centuries.

April 28, 1960—The Southern Presbyterian Church (PCUS), at its 100th General Assembly, passed a resolution stating that sexual relationships in the context of marriage, even without the intention to conceive children, were not sinful.

September 12, 1960—John F. Kennedy, the nominee of the Democratic Party for president of the United States, made a speech before the Greater Houston Ministerial Association, a group of Protestant ministers, to clarify issues regarding his Catholic faith and its effect, if any, on his ability to properly carry out his duties as president without interference from Rome.

Most observers felt Kennedy did a "presidential" job delivering his speech and responding to questions afterward. The event was televised, and as Kennedy would show in the first presidential debate two weeks later, his mannerisms were extremely well suited to television. The clergy, however, only realized after the fact how poorly they looked on television, often appearing hostile and bigoted.

1961

In the opinion of many analysts, Kennedy's appearance in Houston went a long way towards defusing the religious issue, and played a significant role in his eventual election as president (see listing for November 1960).

November 1960— In a very close election, Catholic John F. Kennedy was elected president of the United States over ex–Vice President Richard M. Nixon. In fact, the election was so close that some analysts felt voting irregularities in Illinois and Texas swung the election to Kennedy. But Nixon made no formal complaint and the election stood.

Kennedy was the first (and so far only) Catholic to be elected president of the United States. In spite of the very close election, Kennedy became a very popular president. After 184 years as a nation, Catholics could now be said to have entered the mainstream of American religious institutions.

Kennedy's subsequent assassination in 1963 had no religious overtones at all, and the outbreak of grief following the event was widespread and intense.

December 8, 1960— Madalyn Murray (later O'Hair), a dedicated atheist activist who would make many headlines in the second half of the 20th century, filed a lawsuit in Baltimore to end the practice of required daily Bible readings and recitations of the Lord's Prayer in public schools.

This case was the one the Supreme Court combined with a similar Pennsylvania case (see listings for November 26, 1956, and June 17, 1963) when making its June 1963 ruling that such practices were unconstitutional. It was activists like Murray/O'Hair that brought such issues to a head in the 1950s and after. This forced the Supreme Court to rule such practices unconstitutional and essentially reject the unstated concept that the United States was a Protestant Christian nation no matter what the First Amendment had to say.

1961— The American Unitarian Association (AUA) and the Universalist Church of America (UCA) merged into one organization, called the Unitarian-Universalist Association. Both the AUA and the UCA had been declining in membership for years, and they hoped for a reversal of this trend by merging.

1961

The AUA had been founded in 1825 (see listing for July 19, 1825), and the UCA grew out of the same activities. In 1833 (see listing) the AUA had replaced the Congregationalist Church as the denomination with the most members in Massachusetts. But now both churches were only on the fringes of organized religion.

A few years after the merger, the Unitarian Christian Fellowship (UCF), formed relatively recently in 1945 to maintain a stronger Christian flavor to the almost non–Christian services of the AUA, became the Unitarian-Universalist Christian Fellowship. There was no assurance of the long-term survival of these groups.

October 1, 1961— The Christian Broadcasting Network, founded and run by evangelist Pat Robertson, began broadcasting over television. Robertson's radio broadcasts had begun just two months earlier in August 1961.

The growth of the number of television sets in homes since the end of World War II made television a prime target for evangelists such as Robertson. Radio was considered "old hat" by now, and although widely used by evangelists, it did not have nearly the impact of television.

Exactly 26 years later, on October 1, 1987 (see listing), Robertson would announce he was planning to run for president of the United States. Such was the degree of power felt by the television evangelists of the second half of the 20th century.

1962— One of the earliest rulings of the Supreme Court concerning required prayer in public schools (see also the listing for June 17, 1963) that inflamed passions everywhere came when the Court issued a verdict on prayer required in public schools by the New York State Board of Regents.

The prayer, written by the regents, was required to be recited every day by every child. The requirement obviously violated the clause of the First Amendment forbidding the establishment of any religion by a government entity, but the outrage by many citizens that greeted the decision has continued up to the present time. This chronology notes many instances in which individuals and states have attempted to get around the ruling.

No one has succeeded to date in making an end run around the First

1963

Amendment, but attempts continue to be made. Present indications are that the attempts will never cease, but few people are willing to concede that attempts on behalf of their religion are the only ones they are willing to support.

March 27, 1962 — Archbishop Joseph F. Rummel of Louisiana directed all Roman Catholic schools in the New Orleans diocese to end their policies of racial segregation. The adoption of the elimination of racial segregation by Catholic schools was an important step in extending the reach of the Supreme Court decision eliminating racial segregation in all public schools (see listing for May 17, 1954).

Because many Catholic schools were defined as private, not public, schools, they could stand outside the reach of the Court ruling. Further, before the ruling, Catholic schools could run afoul of state laws in the South if the Catholic schools tried to operate as integrated schools. The Court ruling supported those Catholic schools that chose to integrate, no matter where they were located.

May 21, 1963 — The governing body of the United Presbyterian Church stated for the record that it was opposed to mandatory prayer in public schools, Sunday closing laws, and special tax treatment for churches and the clergy.

This statement came almost exactly one month before the Supreme Court issued its ruling finding mandatory Bible reading and prayers in public schools to be unconstitutional (see listings for June 17, 1963, and November 26, 1956).

June 17, 1963 — The United States Supreme Court ruled that a Pennsylvania state law mandating devotional Bible reading in public schools (see listing for November 26, 1956) was unconstitutional, even if the law was amended to permit students to opt out (with parental consent).

The Pennsylvania case was combined in this ruling with a similar Maryland case (see listing for December 8, 1960). The Court ruling specified that any such religious exercise with a mandatory component was clearly unconstitutional. A prior ruling made in 1962 in the case of the required reading by students of a prayer written by the New York State Board of Regents (see listing for 1962) contained the same elements.

1965

Newspaper headlines concerning the ruling characterized it as one that "kicked God and prayer out of the schools." However, three decades later the Court would rule that "student-led and student-initiated prayer" of a "non-sectarian and non-proselytizing" nature would be permitted at graduation ceremonies (see listing for June 7, 1993). The issue of prayer in public schools would continue to be a fluctuating and contentious issue.

1965 — A 36-year-old theologian named Harvey Cox published a book called *The Secular City*. It was a book that encouraged modern men and women to find meaning in the world that they were in rather than some unknown world beyond this one.

Cox wrote that the world "does not come to man already finished and ordered. It comes in part confused and formless and receives its significance from man." In its way, the book was part of the "death of God" movement that had its impetus in the 1960s.

March 9, 1965 — Three white Unitarian ministers, who were participating in a street march supporting civil rights in Selma, Alabama, were among those beaten by a mob protesting against the march. One minister, Reverend James J. Reed, died later in a Birmingham, Alabama, hospital.

Three months later in June 14, 1965, an editorial signed by 16 prominent Protestant clergy men appeared in the journal *Christianity and Crisis*, protesting that American policies in Vietnam threatened "our chance to cooperate with the Soviet Union for peace in Asia."

Although the clergymen in both instances felt they were following their Christian consciences, analysts pointed out that not all members of Christian congregations were pleased to find their church members embroiled in matters of civil rights and foreign policy. These members felt that such issues were not the proper place for the application of church resources.

The question of what were the proper places for churches to direct their attention to had been an issue in many churches since well before the Civil War and through the depression of the 1930s, and the civil rights revolution of the 1960s. The war in Vietnam rekindled old arguments.

November 18, 1966 — Because of a decree made by Pope Paul VI earlier in the year, today was the last Friday in the history of the Roman

Catholic Church in America that Catholics were required to abstain from eating meat.

1967— Evangelist Jerry Falwell (see listing for June 19, 1956) created the Lynchberg Christian Academy, a fully accredited Christian day school offering K–12 education. As a private school, the new academy was fully segregated at its inception.

In 1971, Falwell launched the Liberty Baptist University. Falwell was sued by the Securities and Exchange Commission (SEC) for fraud and deceit in 1972 in connection with issuance of bonds to build the school. The school won its case in 1973, but was forced to reorganize under the bankruptcy laws. Millions of dollars of investors' money were lost, but Falwell was still regarded as an aggressive fundamentalist evangelist and he was asked to form the Moral Majority organization in 1979 (see listing for June 1979).

April 23, 1968— The Methodist Church and the Evangelical United Brethren churches merged in Dallas, Texas, to form the United Methodist Church. The combination was the second largest Protestant denomination in the United States (behind the Baptists).

November 12, 1968— The United States Supreme Court overturned a ruling by the Arkansas Supreme Court concerning the "anti-evolution" statute of the state. The higher court found that the statute was unconstitutional because it did not forbid teaching all versions of the origin of man, but only those versions in conflict with the Bible. This ruling reversed the lower court ruling that found simply that the state had power to specify the public school curriculum.

June 28, 1971— Chief Justice Warren Burger articulated a three-part test for laws dealing with the question of the establishment of religion clause of the First Amendment. This test would be used in such cases that came before the Supreme Court in the future.

The specific case in question was known as *Lemon v. Kuraman* and dealt with the question of state aid provided to "church-related educational institutions" in Rhode Island and Pennsylvania. Burger stated that establishment laws, to be constitutional, must have a "secular legislative purpose," must have principal effects which neither advance or inhibit

1972

religion, and must not foster an "excessive government entanglement with religion."

The Court found that the laws in question, by subsidizing parochial schools, furthered a process of religious inculcation. Also, the continuing state surveillance necessary to enforce the specific provisions of the laws would inevitably entangle the state in religious affairs. Finally, the Court found that there was "an unhealthy divisive political potential" concerning legislation that appropriates support to religious schools.

The laws in question were found unconstitutional.

May 15, 1972—The United States Supreme Court found in favor of certain Amish and Mennonite parents in Wisconsin who did not want to send their children to public school through age 16 as required by Wisconsin law. The parents argued that requiring their children to attend school beyond the eighth grade violated their religious beliefs.

The Court held that an individual's interest in the free exercise of religion outweighed the state's interest in compelling school attendance beyond the eighth grade. The Court found that the values and programs of secondary school were "in sharp conflict with the fundamental mode of life mandated by the Amish religion," and that an additional one or two years of high school would not produce the benefits of public education cited by the Wisconsin law.

February 13, 1973—The National Council of Catholic Bishops in the United States stated that any person undergoing or performing an abortion would be excommunicated from the Roman Catholic Church. This announcement came 22 days after the Supreme Court ruled that the Court had discovered a right to privacy in the Constitution that gave women a constitutional right to have an abortion.

The Catholic Church decided that a legal right to an abortion in the United States was irrelevant to the teachings of the church, and that abortion in any form was a sin in the eyes of the church.

September 4, 1973—The Pentecostal Denomination the Assemblies of God (see listing for April 1914) opened its first theological graduate school in Springfield, Missouri. This was the second school of theology in the widely splintered Pentecostal denomination opened in the United States.

1978

Television evangelist Oral Roberts had opened the first such school earlier in Tulsa, Oklahoma. He had founded Oral Roberts University in 1963. Roberts himself, however, would become the target of much ridicule in 1987 when he seemed to overstep the bounds of reason (see listing for January 1987).

January 13, 1974—Evangelist Jim Bakker led the beginning of the broadcasting of the *Praise the Lord* (PTL) *Club* in the United States.

Over the years many television evangelists would be accused of fraud in connection with the many millions of dollars they would raise with their television programs, but Bakker (and his wife Tammy Faye) would become one of the most notorious of all (see listing for June 1979 concerning Jerry Falwell). In spite of these frauds, there was no end of new members anxious to join new ventures and continue to contribute new millions. One estimate was that by the 1980s over a billion dollars had flowed to television evangelists.

September 16, 1976—The Episcopal Church officially approved of the ordination of women as priests and bishops. Although many Pentecostal-derived denominations already included women among its preachers and leaders, the Episcopal Church was a leader among mainstream denominations in essentially granting full equality to women in the leadership of the church.

November 10, 1977—Pope Paul VI abolished the automatic excommunication that had been imposed on divorced Catholics who remarry. This excommunication had first been imposed by the Plenary Council of American Bishops 93 years ago in 1884. The abolishment represented a slight easing of Catholic edicts, but any additional easings would come only at a very glacial pace.

June 8, 1978—The Mormon Church officially ended its policy of discrimination against blacks after a period of 148 years. The church announced that blacks could now serve as spiritual leaders, and three days later, a black named Joseph Freeman, Jr., was ordained as the first black Mormon priest.

1978

October 16, 1978 — John Paul II was elected as the new pope. The election was first notable only in the sense that John Paul was the first pope originating from Poland. But John Paul would become an immensely popular pope around the world because of his intensive travels and his sensitivity to improving relations with other religious denominations and his attempts to liberalize Catholic dogmas.

November 18, 1978 — Over 900 followers of a religious cult leader named James (Jim) W. Jones joined their leader in a mass suicide in the jungles of Guyana, South America. The mass suicide followed the murders of five people (11 others were shot but survived) of a group led by Congressman Leo Ryan of California (who was among those killed) to investigate conditions at Jonestown.

Although Jim Jones appeared to be a reasonably conventional religious leader for most of his life (he was 47 when he died at Jonestown), the events of Jonestown marked a sort of dividing line between the toleration of religious freedom in all its forms compared to the creation of religious cults that sought to take advantage of First Amendment protections while engaging in what many saw as outrageous behavior, often enriching individuals and endangering children (many of whom were unwitting victims at Jonestown) and susceptible young adults of all ages.

Following Jonestown, judges were called to rule on what was actually a new religion and what was actually a sham meant to benefit certain individuals or groups. It was often difficult to determine the difference between sincere religious creations and the cult of "anything goes" in the name of religious freedom.

Jim Jones decided to enter the ministry at the age of 21 in 1952, and started as a student pastor at an Indianapolis, Indiana, Methodist church. By 1956 he was running his own church called the People's Temple. In 1960 his church was accepted into the Disciples of Christ denomination and Jones was ordained as a minister. He was by then a graduate of Butler University.

In 1965 Jones relocated to northern California, establishing himself in the town of Ukiah. In October 1973 his rapidly growing People's Temple established a branch church and agricultural mission in Guyana, South America. Jones had previously visited Brazil in South America in 1962 as a recommended place to avoid the fallout from a nuclear war. The People's Temple built a settlement in Guyana called Jonestown. It would be the site of the mass suicide 15 years later.

In the meantime Jones became active in politics around San Francisco, helping liberal candidates to win office. He received a number of accolades for his humanitarian work, but trouble surfaced when a magazine report claimed that the People's Temple was actually an organization that was abusing people for the benefit of Jim Jones.

By September 1977 Jones and about 1,000 followers had relocated to Jonestown in Guyana. Stories began to circulate that Jones had become irrational and was practicing "White Night" suicide drills in response to perceived threats against his church. It was a series of investigations that culminated in Congressman Ryan's trip to Jonestown in November 1978. Ryan's death and the mass suicide in Jonestown followed.

June 1979— Evangelist Jerry Falwell (see listing for 1967) organized the Moral Majority. Several conservative activists had asked Falwell to undertake the task. They wanted to create a political lobbyist force consisting of fundamentalist Protestants to support the Republican Party and shape its party platform.

The immediate goal of the Moral Majority was to defeat President Jimmy Carter in the 1980 presidential elections. Its goal was realized when Ronald Reagan was elected president in 1980. Falwell's views that there should be no separation of church and state in terms of instilling Christian principles into the government made him an ideal leader for the Moral Majority.

Falwell would claim credit for helping to elect Republican presidents in 1980, 1984, and 1988. In 1989 he disbanded Moral Majority with the statement that "our mission is accomplished."

In 1987 Falwell was given control of Jim Bakker's *PTL Club* (see listing for January 13, 1974) after Bakker was embroiled in a series of financial and adultery scandals and was sentenced to what turned out to be five years in prison. Within just a few months after Falwell took over, the *PTL Club* filed for bankruptcy and Falwell and the board of directors resigned.

Falwell remained a contentious figure, but his most famous days ended with his disbanding of the Moral Majority in 1989. Falwell died at his home base in Lynchburg, Virginia, at the age of almost 74 in 2007.

1979

August 1, 1979—A Jewish woman named Linda Joy Holtzman was named the rabbi for the conservative Beth Israel congregation in Coatesville, Pennsylvania, a small town near Philadelphia. Holtzman thus became the first female rabbi to lead a Jewish congregation in the United States.

January 24, 1980—William Murray, son of famous atheist activist Madalyn Murray O'Hair (see listing for December 8, 1960), claimed to have had a dream this night that he believed was a religious vision from God.

Such dreams are a mainstay in the founding of many religious denominations, and Murray believed his dream was a directive from God to join a fundamentalist Christian church. Murray gave up drinking and smoking, and then worked to undo the effects of many of the court decisions regarding the separation of church and state his mother had struggled to obtain.

September 14, 1980—Dr. Robert H. Schuller, a pastor associated with the Reformed Church in America, dedicated the imposing Crystal Cathedral built in Garden Grove, California. The cathedral cost about $17 million to complete (about $55 million in 2007 dollars). The cathedral is the focal point of one of the most impressive megachurches in the United States.

The Garden Grove congregation numbers about 10,000 people, but the Crystal Cathedral Ministries reaches over 20 million people worldwide each week over its televised *Hour of Power* program. With operating offices literally around the world, it has been estimated that Reverend Robert H. Schuller, and now his son Reverend Robert A. Schuller, are the two most listened-to orators in the world.

Everything about the cathedral is best described in superlatives. It seats 2,890 persons, with room for over 1,000 singers and instrumentalists. Music is a big part of the services, and the pipe organ there is widely known for its size and quality, and is ranked among the five largest pipe organs in the world. The services can be viewed inside on a giant Jumbotron television screen, and outside on another giant screen for drive-in worshippers.

There is a professional audio studio and television production studio to support the televising of the *Hour of Power* program. These facili-

1982

ties include equipment to permit simultaneous translation of the services into five different languages. Dr. Schuller and his son are televangelists on a large and professional scale, but unlike many other televangelists there has never been a hint of scandal about their ministry.

Dr. Schuller came to Garden Grove in 1955, after five years of conducting services at a small church in Chicago that grew from a congregation of 38 to 500 during his tenure there. He started by renting the Orange Drive-In Theater and conducting Sunday services from the roof on the snack bar. Schuller's popularity was such that by 1961 his Garden Grove Community Church had moved to a new building, and by 1977 work on the Crystal Cathedral had begun.

Dr. Schuller retired on January 22, 2006, and turned his ministry to his only son, Robert A. Schuller, who was also an ordained minister and who had been involved in the activities of his father's church for most of his life.

June 25, 1982 — In a free-speech test, the United States Supreme Court ruled that the removal of certain books from the school libraries of the Island Tree Union Free School District was unconstitutional. The school district held that the books in question were "anti–American, anti–Christian, anti–Semitic, and just plain filthy."

The Court ruled, in a 5–4 decision, that although school boards have a vested interest in promoting respect for social, moral, and political community values, their discretionary power is secondary to the imperatives of the First Amendment.

School libraries are a center for the dissemination of information and ideas, and as such they have "a special affinity with the rights of free speech and press." Thus, the school board could not restrict the availability of books in their libraries simply because its members disagreed with their contents.

July 16, 1982 — The Reverend Sun Myung Moon, leader of the Unification Church, was sentenced in federal court to 18 months in prison for tax fraud and obstruction of justice. In spite of protests and appeals by his followers on freedom of religion and free speech issues, Moon went on to spend over a year in prison.

At the time, Moon had just finished conducting a mass marriage/

1983

blessing ceremony in June in Madison Square Garden in New York City for 2,075 couples. Many of the newlyweds were complete strangers to each other. Such mass marriages were, and continue to be, a staple of Moon's church.

Moon was born in Korea in 1920 and escaped what was essentially a death sentence to a labor camp in 1948 when forces of the United Nations freed him in 1950. He had had a religious revelation in 1935 in which he said he was asked by Jesus to complete the task of establishing God's kingdom on earth. Moon sees himself as the Second Coming of Christ and teaches that all people should strive to become perfect like himself and Jesus.

Moon founded what is now the worldwide Unification Church in Seoul, Korea, on May 1, 1954. He moved to the United States in 1971, and leads both his church and the larger Unification Movement. The movement owns, operates, or subsidizes many organizations involved in political, cultural, mass-media, and related activities. It has grown to be a multibillion dollar operation and includes the *Washington Times* newspaper and the Associated Press.

After his prison sentence, Moon continued to be very active in his mission "to unite Christianity and bring families back to God." In spite of many questions about the fund-raising activities of the Unification Movement, it continues to thrive. Analysts say Moon and his "moonies" could show a thing or two to the highly successful televangelists born and raised in the United States.

In April 2008, at the age of 88, Moon appointed his youngest son Hyung Jin Moon to be the leader of the Unification Church and the Unification Movement.

June 10, 1983—The Presbyterian Church (USA) was created in Atlanta, Georgia. The new church reunited the United Presbyterian Church (UPCUSA) and the Southern Presbyterian Church (PCUS). The branches had been divided since before the Civil War, a period of over 140 years.

June 4, 1984—The Southern Baptist Convention passed a resolution against ordaining women in the Baptist Church. The recent revolution in women's rights was not going to reach a number of church groups.

1985— Sex abuse of children by priests of the Catholic Church in the United States became a national issue for the first time when a Louisiana priest named Gilbert Gauthe pleaded guilty to 11 counts of molestation of boys.

Such sexual abuse cases would spiral into the thousands in the next two decades (see listing for February 17, 2004) and cause a huge black eye for the Catholic church. In many cases, a large amount of anger would be directed towards the church for not only the abuse by the priests, but also for the clumsy attempts by their superiors to cover up the crimes (see entry for 1992).

June 4, 1985— In another test of the First Amendment establishment clause forbidding the establishment of any religion by the government, the United States Supreme Court held that an Alabama law authorizing teachers to conduct regular religious prayer services and related activities in classrooms during the day was unconstitutional.

March 1986— Father Charles E. Curran, who held a position as a moral theologian at the Catholic University of America in Washington, D.C., revealed that the Vatican had given him an ultimatum. Curran was to retract his views on birth control, divorce, and other issues concerning sexuality, or he would lose his authority to teach Roman Catholic doctrine.

Thousands protested the issuance of the ultimatum, and Curran refused to retract his views. Curran said the church, in its effort to exercise its authoritarianism, was confusing what was essential to the faith and what was peripheral. Curran stated that the church was making a "belief in Jesus Christ of the same importance as 'no meat on Friday.'"

The Vatican, as usual, was in no mood to have its authority questioned or to consider issues of academic freedom or tenure. The Vatican ultimately revoked Curran's license to teach theology, and in 1987 suspended Curran from Catholic University completely.

January 1987— Television evangelist Oral Roberts (see listing for September 4, 1973), who had begun his ministry as a faith healer in a traveling tent show in the 1940s, claimed on his television show that he would be "called home" by God if he did not raise eight million dollars by March 31, 1987.

1987

The money was supposedly needed for medical missionary work in underdeveloped countries, although some suspected it would find its way to other uses in Oral Roberts University. Considerable ridicule was generated among commentators by the request, but Roberts' viewers had shown in the past their willingness to pour money into almost any request made by Roberts (and other televangelists for that matter).

This particular fund-raising drive proved to be successful when a Florida racetrack owner named Jerry Collins made up a shortfall of over one million dollars at the last moment.

Five months later, in June 1987, Roberts trained his credulity even further by claiming to have raised people from the dead. Roberts himself continued to benefit from his Oral Roberts Evangelistic Association formed four decades ago, but his favorite project, Oral Roberts University, started to fall on hard times.

In 1989, the City of Faith Medical and Research Center associated with the university was forced to close after being in operation only eight years. In 1993, Richard Roberts, Oral's son, was named president of the university. But the son was forced to resign in 2007 after a lawsuit claiming Richard Roberts had diverted money and resources from the university for the personal use of himself, his wife, and his children.

In early 2008 Oral Roberts, then age 90, was semiretired and living in the posh community of Newport Beach, California. Roberts reportedly continues to draw $83,505 a year from his Oral Roberts Evangelistic Association.

April 20, 1987—In Columbus, Ohio, three Lutheran groups merged to form the Evangelical Lutheran Church in America (ELCA). This merged group was the largest Lutheran denomination in the United States. However, the ELCA did not officially incorporate until the following year.

June 19, 1987—In yet another case dealing with the teaching of evolution, the United States Supreme Court found unconstitutional a Louisiana law entitled Balanced Treatment for Creation-Science and Evolution-Science in Public School Instruction Act. This act stated that evolution could not be taught in the schools unless accompanied by "creation science" based on biblical beliefs.

The Supreme Court held that the primary effect of the Louisiana law was to advance the viewpoint that a supernatural being created humankind, and the promotion of this viewpoint was clearly unconstitutional.

August 1987— In New Hampshire, a court of the United Methodist Church suspended lesbian minister Rose Mary Denman. The charge was that she had violated a rule prohibiting a practicing homosexual from being in the clergy.

October 1, 1987— Television evangelist Pat Robertson (see listing for October 1, 1961) announced that he was planning to seek the Republican nomination for president of the United States.

Most observers felt that Robertson was not a serious candidate for president, but was rather trying to be sure his views were reflected in the building of the Republican Party platform.

The majority of the television evangelists of the time reflected fundamentalist Protestant principles, and they felt the Republican Party was the place to stress their principles rather than the Democratic Party. The evangelists saw the Democrats as much too liberal and not sufficiently God fearing.

Robertson's quest for the Republican presidential nomination was not successful, and for the rest of the 1900s and into the 21st century, Robertson concentrated on his televised *700 Club* and the Christian Broadcasting Network (CBN) that carried the program.

The *700 Club*, starting essentially as a Christian variety program and moving towards a talk show format, became very successful. It has been broadcast in over 70 languages. CBN became a production company, producing the *700 Club* and other syndicated programs. Its full network operations were sold and appeared as the Family Channel in several versions on several other networks.

Pat Robertson became wealthy and influential, and is still recognized as an evangelistic spokesman for conservative religious causes. He still is controversial because of his firm fundamentalist views, but unlike so many other televangelists, Robertson has never been accused of using his work as a source of questionable funds to line his own pockets.

April 8, 1988— Televangelist Jimmy Swaggart was defrocked by his Assemblies of God denomination after he confessed on his February 21, 1988, television show that he had visited a prostitute. Swaggart said on

1988

that show that he would leave his ministry for an unspecified length of time. But Swaggart returned soon. Television evangelists had no desire to stay away from their revenue source for any length of time.

Swaggart's confession resulted from a clear case of "tit for tat." Swaggart had accused competing televangelist Martin Gorman in 1986 of an adulterous affair. This act eventually led to Gorman being defrocked by the Assemblies of God and losing a lucrative ministry.

Similarly, in 1987, Swaggart jumped on the bandwagon of accusations of adultery against televangelist Jim Bakker (see listing for January 13, 1974, et al.) that eventually led to Bakker's defrocking by the Assemblies of God and a prison term for fraud.

Gorman was anxious to repay Swaggart in kind and hired a detective who uncovered Swaggart's tryst with a prostitute. This led to Swaggart's confession on his television show and his defrocking by the Assemblies of God.

Up to the time of Swaggart's defrocking, his life could have served as the template for a whole family of televangelists of his type. Swaggart was born in 1935 in the South into a family of fundamentalist Baptists with musical ability. Swaggart began to preach on street corners and lead congregations in singing at the age of nine.

At the age of 23 Swaggart became a traveling preacher and led revivals as a licensed minister of the Pentecostal Assemblies of God. He expanded slowly in radio broadcasting and then television broadcasting. Ultimately he owned a number of radio and television stations and became one of the most popular televangelists in the United States with his combination of singing ability and dramatic preaching.

Eventually, almost inevitably, Swaggart was caught up in a scandal as described above that involved the sins he preached so firmly against. In the next few years Swaggart was caught again with prostitutes, but by now he had evolved into telling his television audience he had been told by the Lord to tell Swaggart's listeners it was "none of their business."

Swaggart's son Donnie (with the help of Swaggart's wife Frances), and even a grandson, tried to make a success of what remained of the once grandiose Jimmy Swaggart Ministries.

May 1988—The United Methodist Church made a statement against pluralism at its General Conference in St. Louis. Bishop Jack Tuell was quoted as saying, "The time has come to say the last rites over the notion that the defining characteristic of United Methodist theology is pluralism."

Analysts said this statement was another example of Protestant groups in America turning towards more conservative theological, social, and political positions.

January 9, 1989—A district court in Mississippi ruled in favor of a woman named Jamie Dodge who had been fired from her job at the Salvation Army in August 1987 because she was a pagan. Dodge subsequently filed suit for religious discrimination.

The judge ruled that because the Salvation Army receives federal, state, and local funding, it is subject to the First Amendment, and must conform with federal rules against religious discrimination. It cannot fire a person for practicing a specific form of religion, or no religion at all.

July 2, 1989—Reverend George A. Stallings, Jr., a black Roman Catholic priest, established an independent black Catholic congregation in Washington, D.C. Stallings made the move in defiance of the orders of his archbishop.

Stallings claimed he wasn't trying to create a schism in the church, but was rather trying to create a church that was more sensitive to black needs. But he later said that his Imani Temple was no longer under the control of Rome, and would allow such things as abortion and the ordination of women.

Such practices, according to the Vatican, automatically produced the excommunication of Stallings.

January 1990—Catholic Auxiliary Bishop Austin Vaughn stated that New York Governor Mario Cuomo, who was a Catholic, was in "serious risk of going to hell" because Cuomo believed abortion was a matter of an individual woman's conscience.

1992—Catholic Bishops from all over the United States, meeting in South Bend, Indiana, admitted that some of their members had attempted to hide cases of sexual abuse by priests within their purview.

April 9, 1992—Writing in the newspaper *Catholic New York*, Cardinal John O'Connor stated that if "the Church's teaching is rejected on such a

1992

crucial question as human life [in the debate over abortion], ... then questioning of the Trinity becomes child's play, as does the divinity of Christ or any other Church teaching."

June 24, 1992— The United States Supreme Court ruled in a 5–4 decision that prayers delivered at a graduation ceremony by a religious authority that were instructed by school authorities were unconstitutional (*Lee v. Weisman*).

The decision added that the fact that students could voluntarily opt out of the ceremonies was specious because cultural pressures on teenage students to conform make the word "voluntarily" meaningless.

The Court made it clear that any apparent involvement of the authority of the school system in any apparent religious exercise of any nature was unconstitutional.

November 4, 1992— The Church of the Lukumi Babalu in Florida went to court to contest ordinances in the city of Hialeah banning animal sacrifice. The church finally won its case on the basis of religious freedom.

March 10, 1993— An antiabortion activist named Michael Griffin shot and killed Dr. David Gunn, an abortion provider, in Pensacola, Florida. This was the first known case of the emotional battle over abortion leading to murder.

However, just four months later on July 29, 1993, the Reverend Paul Hill shot and killed Dr. John Britton in a similar crime. Such killings and even bombings of abortion clinics unfortunately would continue to mar the debate over abortion.

April 19, 1993— The Bureau of Alcohol, Tobacco, and Firearms (ATF), along with other government agencies such as the FBI, made an assault on the so-called Branch Davidian compound in Waco, Texas.

The Branch Davidians was a religious sect led by a dictator-like man named David Koresh, and there were reports about people being held against their will, instances of child abuse (girls as young as 12 years old were being taken as "wives"), and firearms being stockpiled to defend the compound against "outsiders."

1993

The AFT assault unfortunately led to a fire that caused the compound to burn to the ground. Between 72 and 86 people were killed, including about 25 children and the self-styled leader, David Koresh. Nine members of the cult survived.

An independent investigation was held six years later from August 1999 through July 2000 that exonerated the federal agencies involved in the attack from causing the fire that basically produced the many deaths. The Branch Davidian sect was found to be the main culprit in creating the gun battles resulting in the attack, and starting the essentially suicidal fire that destroyed the compound.

The Branch Davidians traced their roots back to the Great Disappointment of October 22, 1844 (see listing), and the failed prophecy of the Second Coming of Christ on that date. The Seventh-Day Adventists (see listing for May 23, 1863) grew out of this event, and the sect that became the Branch Davidians separated in about 1929 from the group that were the descendents of the original Seventh-Day Adventists.

David Koresh (who changed his name from Vernon Wayne Howell at the age of 31 in 1990) was the most recent of a series of leaders who broke off and reassembled over the years from the Davidians. Koresh started the practice of having multiple wives (including a 12-year-old girl), and claimed in 1989 that all the wives of all the members of his followers were also his wives.

Koresh became increasing irrational as he tightened his dictatorial hold on his followers, and reports from ex-members triggered a series of investigations that finally led to the assault on April 19, 1993.

June 1, 1993—The United States Supreme Court declined to review a lower court case challenging the language of the Pledge of Allegiance. The challenge was based on the claim that the words "under God" in the pledge violate the separation of church and state specified in the Constitution.

In refusing to hear the case, the Supreme Court let stand a lower court ruling permitting the language. The assumption was that the Supreme Court considered that the phrase "under God" had become secularized and thus was not a violation of the First Amendment.

But the lower court ruling applied only to the Fifth Circuit (Texas, Louisiana, and Mississippi) where the case had been brought. It was correctly anticipated that the case would arise elsewhere in the future.

1993

June 7, 1993, Prayer in Schools— The Supreme Court declined to hear a case in the almost endless list of cases concerning prayer in public schools. This time, a lower court had ruled in *Jones v. Clear Creek Independent School District* that students can vote for a graduation prayer as long as the prayer is approved by the school as nonsectarian and nonproselytizing.

The Supreme Court allowed the ruling to stand. This puzzled many analysts who felt this was in conflict with a prior ruling that even nonsectarian prayers in public schools violate the Constitution. But in this case the students essentially initiated and led the prayer, which was sufficiently neutral to pass court muster.

The Supreme Court action (or inaction) delighted the American Center for Law and Justice (ACLJ). The organization issued a special bulletin to every public school district in the United States advising them how to have prayer included in graduation ceremonies, valedictorian addresses, and baccalaureate services.

The American Civil Liberties Union (ACLU) immediately prepared a press release taking issue with the ACLJ bulletin and the refusal of the Supreme Court to hear the case. The refusal of the Supreme Court to hear the case meant that the lower court ruling was only effective in the Fifth Circuit (Texas, Louisiana, and Mississippi) where the case had been originally brought. Thus, similar cases would almost surely arise again in other areas.

June 7, 1993, Free Speech— The United States Supreme Court ruled in favor of a religious group wanting to use school facilities after hours to show films on religious and family-oriented topics. The case was brought as a free speech issue, but the Court decision turned out to be based on establishment clause elements.

The case was brought by a religious group named Lamb's Chapel that argued a New York state law forbidding the use of school facilities even after hours by a religious group was violating the free speech rights of Lamb's Chapel to show its films on religious and family issues.

The Court ruled that, first of all, the New York law, which applied only to religious groups, was a violation of the establishment clause that required that use of public facilities in such cases be "viewpoint neutral," i.e., not opposed only to religious views. Second, permission for a religious group to use the facilities would not violate establishment laws because the showings would be neither school sponsored or closed to the public.

This ruling emphasized again that the Constitution prohibits both the government-sponsored promotion of a religion as well as the demotion, so to speak, of a religion. Public schools must take both sides into account when dealing with religious issues.

June 18, 1993—In yet another decision this month dealing ultimately with the establishment clause (see above listings for June 7, 1993), the Supreme Court of the United States announced that it was constitutional for parents to request that an interpreter be supplied by a Catholic school for a child who had been deaf since birth.

The parents had asked for help under the provisions of the Individuals with Disabilities Education Act (IDEA). A lower court had ruled that public funds could not be used for an interpreter because the interpreter would be a conduit for the student's religious inculcation and this would be a violation of the First Amendment.

The Court ruled in a 5–4 decision that IDEA provides help to handicapped children and it is the private decision of the parents as to what school the aid should apply to. IDEA is neutral in this issue, and thus the state has nothing to do with the choice. Thus, the state is not promoting a specific religion when the aid is provided.

June 1994—The administrative body for Reform Judaism in America, the Union of American Hebrew Congregations, considered and overwhelmingly rejected the application for membership of the Congregation Beth Adam in Cincinnati.

The Congregation Beth Adam had removed all references to God in its services. The synagogue said its members preferred to study their Jewish heritage and identity without the requirement to follow old theistic assumptions.

July 1994—A prominent leader of the United Methodist Church, the Reverend Jeanne Audrey Powers, made the announcement that she was gay. Powers was the highest-ranking member of that denomination to do so.

Powers said she took the step "as an act of public resistance to false

1994

teachings that have contributed to heresy and homophobia within the church itself."

August 1994— Molly Marshall, a teacher at the Southern Baptist Theological Seminary in Louisville, Kentucky, and the first woman to achieve tenure at that school, was forced to resign after several accusations were made that she was promoting liberal doctrines.

March 26, 1995— Pope John Paul II, in the encyclical Evangelium Vitae, instructed all Catholic voters, judges, and legislators to obey Vatican teachings in their votes and decisions. Critics immediately said it was an example of the Vatican trying improperly to interfere with the government of the United States.

The pope wrote that "in the case of an intrinsically unjust law, such as a law permitting abortion or euthanasia, it is never licit to obey it, or take part in a propaganda campaign in favor of such a law, or to vote for it." The critics added that the pope was coming uncomfortably close to urging Catholic judges and legislators to violate the law separating church and state in the United States. Judges specifically take an oath to support the law whether or not they personally agree with it.

March 31, 1995— The American Civil Liberties Union (ACLU) filed a complaint against local Judge Roy Moore of Alabama. The ACLU claimed that Moore's display of the Ten Commandments in his courtroom, and his practices of initiating courtroom proceedings with a prayer violate the First Amendment.

The ACLU action set off a chain of events that continued for more than the next eight years. The events included the building of a 5,000-pound granite display of the Ten Commandments set in the rotunda of the Alabama Judicial Building, votes in Congress about the affair (see listing for March 5, 1997), and the eventual removal of Moore from his final position of chief justice of the Alabama Supreme Court for his refusal to remove the display.

Ultimately the ACLU case was dismissed on technical reasons by the Alabama Supreme Court in 1998 after some earlier rulings and appeals. In the meantime growing publicity about the case brought it to national attention, with all of the attention being focused on the issue of the posting of the Ten Commandments (as noted, see the listing for March 5, 1997).

Somewhat ironically the issue of the opening courtroom prayer got lost in the shuffle. The practice had been going on in Alabama for many years before the ACLU suit, and, in fact, the practice continues in many Alabama state courtrooms to this day.

The Moore affair was carried out in the following years against the background of both individuals and state legislatures still trying to overturn the First Amendment and its effects more than 200 years after the amendment was first added to the Constitution.

November 1995 — Congressman Ernest Istook, a Republican representative from Oklahoma, introduced a bill to amend the United States Constitution. Istook's bill was intended to modify the separation of church and state by permitting organized prayer in public schools.

Istook's bill was supported by the Christian Coalition and other fundamentalist groups, but it was also opposed by other religious groups who favored the continued separation of church and state. The question of whether or not to continue the separation of church and state always depended, as usual, on whose religion was the favored religion.

The Istook bill finally passed through the committee stage in the House of Representatives nearly three years later on June 4, 1998, but it did not receive the two-thirds majority needed to pass it on to the Senate.

In the meantime, as noted previously, other individuals and state legislatures would continue to try to modify the separation of church and state to permit prayer in public schools, but none would prove ultimately successful.

1996 — The convictions in the notorious Kern County, California, daycare sexual abuse case were overturned. This essentially ended a 15-year period of such cases (the Kern County case started in 1982) that spread at one time across the United States and even into Canada.

These were not religious cases per se, although they included some lurid testimonies about witchcraft, Satan worship, and strange occult ceremonies. Almost all cases started with testimony by some distraught mother claiming strange things were happening to her children in child-care facilities.

1996

In many cases supposed experts discovered more "happenings" that mostly rather young children were anxious to provide under proper coaching by the supposed experts. Nearly all of the exotic testimony was eventually found to be false or non-creditable. Many times the children later admitted their testimony was simply made to satisfy the demands of their parents or to please the adults coaching them.

In the meantime lives and careers were ruined, such as in the Kern County case where some convictions were initially obtained. In another notorious case in California, the McMartin preschool was closed with serious financial losses to the owners, and at least one defendant was held several years in jail with extremely high bail. The case went on from 1983 to 1990, when all charges were finally dropped. The dropping of charges of course could not restore the years spent in jail or the ruination of the careers, the business, and reputation of the owners of the business.

The Little Rascals case in North Carolina has a similar history. Lurid charges and trials and convictions starting in 1989, and the dropping of all charges in 1997. In the meantime several people spent several years in jail.

Even though the PBS Network ran a documentary program saying the charges were clearly false, and even though the testimony by the children included babies being ritualistically killed and victims being thrown overboard, the cases went to trial and lifetime convictions were obtained. Everyone involved on the prosecution and jury side of the case said the children were "very convincing." Fortunately, the appeals judges were not so easily convinced.

The connection between these cases and this book was the similarity between these modern events and the Salem witch trials that happened nearly two hundred years earlier (see listing for 1692). Both events took place in an atmosphere of hysteria, and both featured testimony from young children that was swallowed whole and even embellished by adults trying to "help." Both events made it clear that proper allowances must be made for the quality of the testimony presented by young children, and that the adults involved do not have personal agendas that color their "help."

January 1996— The American Baptist Church of the West expelled four congregations from the San Francisco Bay area for welcoming homosexuals and not teaching that homosexual activity is a sin.

April 1996— The delegates to the General Conference of the United Methodist Church voted not to support a proposal that would have eliminated portions of church law declaring homosexuality to be "incompatible with Christian teaching."

April 15, 1996— The Catholic bishop of Lincoln, Nebraska, Fabian W. Bruskewitz, declared all Catholics in his diocese to be excommunicated if they continued to be members of organizations he said were "perilous to the Catholic faith."

The organizations banned by Bishop Bruskewitz included Planned Parenthood and Call to Action.

June 1996— The Southern Baptist Convention announced it was planning a boycott of all parks and products of the Disney Company. The boycott was in response to the company's plan to give insurance benefits to the partners of gay employees, and the fact that theme parks owned by Disney were hosting "Gay Days."

March 5, 1997— The United States House of Representatives voted 295 to 125 in favor of supporting Alabama Judge Roy Moore in his battle to keep a plaque of the Ten Commandments in his courtroom (see listing for March 31, 1995).

In connection with the case, Alabama Governor Fob James had promised to deploy the National Guard and state troopers to prevent the removal of the plaque. Eventually the plaque became a 5,000-pound monument made of granite when Moore was elevated to the position of the chief justice of the Alabama Supreme Court in November 2000. Moore had his monument installed in the rotunda of the Alabama State Judicial Building on July 31, 2002.

Moore made a point of publicizing his actions and indicating his plans of defying any directions to remove his monument. The ACLU took the bait and immediately filed suit, the trial over which began the following year on October 15, 2002. A decision against Moore was made on November 18, 2002 (see listing).

The United States Supreme Court ultimately became involved before the display was finally removed in August 2003, and Moore was removed from his post shortly after. As often happens in cases of this type there

1997

was much arm waving and posturing, but the First Amendment was finally upheld.

March 23, 1997 — The members of a tiny religious cult named the Heaven's Gate sect began to commit suicide in anticipation of some type of transfer to another world when the comet Hale-Bopp appeared. Thirty-nine members committed suicide in three groups over three days.

June 23, 1997 — The United States Supreme Court, as part of its continuing dealings with establishment clause issues of the First Amendment, announced it was reversing a decision made in 1985 (*Aguilar v. Felton*) concerning the use of public funds from Title I of the Elementary and Secondary Education Act of 1965 to pay salaries of state employees who teach in parochial schools.

In 1985, the Court ruled that such payments were not allowed because it would lead to the intrusion of church and state into each other's respective domain and this would violate the intent of the establishment clause.

In 1997, the Court ruled that there was no evidence that the problems they anticipated had actually taken place, and the careful way in which the funds were applied did not violate the establishment clause. Further, from now on only those policies that generate an excessive conflict between church and state would be deemed to violate the First Amendment.

The reversal demonstrated how carefully the Court reviews First Amendment cases, but it also demonstrated why First Amendment cases continually appear before the Court. One never knows when a fresh look at the issue may produce a different result, especially when so many decisions on First Amendment issues are decided by a 5–4 vote.

July 13, 1998 — The Catholic diocese of Dallas was required to pay more than $31 million to the victims of priest Rudolph Kos. The first legal proceedings against the diocese for the crimes of Kos began in 1993.

February 7, 1999 — Bills were proposed in the state legislature of Georgia requiring public school districts to display the Ten Commandments and to permit "student-initiated spoken prayer." It was another example of states seeking a way to bypass the First Amendment.

In the next month, a bill was introduced in the New Hampshire legislature to permit students to recite the Lord's Prayer, and a year later Kentucky called for the posting of the Ten Commandments in schools.

All of these bills were carefully written to try to anticipate objections based on the First Amendment and to make it appear that the required actions were voluntary and/or part of a historical lesson regarding the development of a Christian United States. There appeared to be no end to the efforts states and individuals would take to install religion (of course only their religion) in public schools while passing muster with the First Amendment.

June 19, 2000 — The razor-thin distinctions the United States Supreme Court makes in determining whether or not school policies about prayer at school-related activities violate the First Amendment were demonstrated in a case named *Santa Fe Independent School District v. Jane Doe*.

This case concerned student-led student-initiated prayer at school football games. The parents of two unnamed students (supported by the ACLU) objected to the prayer activities, and this time the Court supported them in deeming the activities unconstitutional.

This decision seemed to conflict with the Court's action in permitting student-led student-initiated prayer in a similar June 7, 1993, case (see listing). The present case seemed to turn on the fact that the prayers were before a football game rather than as part of a graduation ceremony as had been the case in 1993.

Once again the basis of Court decisions regarding school prayer was left unclear. One point was clear, and this was the fact that new cases would continually turn up in this area as proponents of school prayer kept trying to find new circumstances in which to inject prayer into school activities in a way that would pass Court muster.

January 9, 2002 — Cardinal Bernard Law of the diocese of Boston apologized to victims of former priest John Geoghan (indicted on child rape charges in 1999). Law promised to take a "tougher line" on abusive priests in the future.

Cardinal Law's promise of a tougher line may have been influenced by the publication the day before by the Vatican that issued guidelines on how to deal with pedophile priests. The guidelines said all such cases should be reported to Rome.

2002

Cynical observers said they had little faith such reports would do much good because they believed the Vatican was trying as hard as the Catholic Church in the United States to cover up such crimes (three months later on April 4, 2002, two individuals began legal action against the Vatican for its alleged role in covering up sex abuse cases).

Nine days after Cardinal Law's apology, on January 18, 2002, former priest Geoghan was convicted of his crimes and ultimately sentenced to 10 years in prison (Geoghan was later killed in a Massachusetts prison on August 24, 2003).

September 19, 2002— The Boston Archdiocese reached a settlement of $10 million with the victims of the abuse by former priest John Geoghan (see listing for January 9, 2002). This settlement represented the retraction of a previous settlement of $30 million that the church claimed would have bankrupted the archdiocese.

However, seven months later continued claims of abuse would result in the archdiocese arranging to sell land and buildings to create a fund of $100 million to settle abuse claims (see listing for April 2003).

November 13, 2002, Bishops— Catholic bishops from the United States met in Washington, D.C., to revise a prior policy reached on abusive priests. The prior policy resulted from an emergency meeting in Rome called by Pope John Paul II seven months earlier on April 23, 2002. The meeting was called to discuss the mushrooming sexual abuse scandal in the United States.

The bishops responded on June 13, 2002, by adopting a zero tolerance national policy on such abuse, but then the Vatican demanded changes to protect the rights of priests. The November 13, 2002, meeting reflected those changes.

Critics complained that the Vatican was now copying typical criminal defense lawyer loud cries about the rights of criminal perpetrators, while the rights of criminal victims are mentioned in quiet mumbles, if at all.

November 13, 2002, Activists— On the same day Catholic bishops in the United States were bowing to Vatican pressure as noted above, Catholic activists from the Survivors First group launched an online database listing 573 priests in the United States who had been accused of involvement in pedophilia just since 1996.

Further investigation resulted in the dropping of 100 names, leaving an astounding 473 names on the list.

November 18, 2002— United States District Judge Myron Thompson of Montgomery, Alabama, ruled that the monument showing the Ten Commandments that had been installed in the rotunda of the Alabama Judicial Building was unconstitutional.

This ruling summarized the federal response to Judge Roy Moore's defiant public posting of the Ten Commandments (see listing for March 5, 1997) and, in essence, other state attempts to post the Ten Commandments on government-owned property including public schools.

Judge Thompson wrote in his decision that "the Ten Commandments monument, viewed alone or in the context of its history, placement, and location, has the primary effect of endorsing religion."

This decision was typical of the care the federal courts took in trying to determine if a specific action a government entity (including state or local governments) took was an endorsement of a specific religion in the way forbidden by the First Amendment.

The decision withstood appeals to the Supreme Court of the United States and the monument was ultimately removed by the end of 2003 (along with the removal of Judge Moore by the state of Alabama for his refusal to comply with court orders).

December 3, 2002— A new bombshell was dropped on Cardinal Bernard Law (see entry for January 9, 2002) and his archdiocese of Boston when new revelations were made about eight priests in the Archdiocese who were accused of abusing women and girls. The priests allegedly took drugs and also supplied drugs in return for sexual favors.

Only a month earlier on November 3, 2002, Cardinal Law had apologized for making "decisions which led to suffering" in the recent past. Three days later on December 6, 2002, Cardinal Law left on a trip to the Vatican. It was the same day he reportedly was ordered to appear before a grand jury investigating sex abuse allegations in his archdiocese. One week later on December 13, 2002, Cardinal Law resigned as archbishop of the diocese of Boston.

2003

March 16, 2003 — Catholic Archbishop Oscar Lipscomb of the Archdiocese of Mobile, Alabama, admitted that he had permitted Reverend J. Alexander Sherlock to remain in the pulpit of a church in Montgomery, Alabama, even though Sherlock had admitted in 1998 to sexual abuse of a teenage boy in the 1970s.

This incident was only one of thousands (see listing for February 17, 2004) in the United States that would create a crisis in the Catholic Church in the 21st century. But it was somewhat unique in that not only did a priest confess of being guilty of sexual abuse, his superior confessed to essentially covering it up. More typically, the leaders of the Catholic Church took great pains to avoid the disclosures of sexual abuse. Court damage awards would produce bankruptcies in Catholic dioceses and require apologies from the pope himself during his 2008 visit to the United States.

April 2003 — The Boston Archdiocese avoided bankruptcy by making an agreement to sell land and buildings it owned for more than $100 million to create a fund to make legal settlements to more than 500 victims abused by priests.

August 5, 2003 — During its meeting in Minneapolis, the Episcopal General Convention created outrage in Anglican churches worldwide by electing an openly gay man named Gene Robinson as bishop-designate of New Hampshire.

This election initiated the opening of a schism in the Episcopal Church, with conservatives beginning to move away from a leadership they felt was becoming heretical.

August 20, 2003 — Today was the specified deadline for Judge Roy Moore to move his monument of the Ten Commandments from the Alabama Judicial Building (see listing for November 18, 2002).

Moore continued to refuse, and the next day the eight associate justices ruled that the monument must be moved because "they are bound by solemn oath to follow the law, whether they agree with it or not." Some onlookers noted that this is a concept beyond the understanding of the Vatican (see listing for March 26, 1995).

Within a week the state Judicial Inquiry Commission suspended

Moore for refusing to obey a court order and the monument was moved. By November Moore was removed from his post of chief justice of the Alabama Supreme Court.

February 2004 — The United States Supreme Court drew another line in the sand in the education/religion debate when the Court ruled in favor of the state of Washington in a case where a college student claimed his right to the free exercise of religion was violated by the state's refusal to grant scholarships for the study of theology.

The Court ruled the state had the right to deny publicly funded scholarship money to the student.

February 17, 2004 — A survey conducted by Cable News Network (CNN) reported that during the last 52 years, more than 11,000 allegations of sexual abuse by Catholic priests were made. The 4,450 priests involved made up about 4 percent of the priests who served during that period.

This was convincing proof that the many incidents of sexual abuse by Catholic priests reported in this chronology were far from isolated incidents. The story of sexual abuse by Catholic priests would become one of the biggest of the first decade of the 21st century. There was no way to tell how far the repercussions would extend into the rest of the century.

July 7, 2004 — The Catholic Archdiocese of Portland, Oregon, took the unprecedented action of filing for bankruptcy when it determined it would be unable to cover the costs of lawsuits being brought against its priests for sexual abuse.

One immediate result of this strategy was the halting of a trial of a lawsuit seeking damages of $155 million against the late Reverend Maurice Grammond, who was accused of molesting more than 50 boys in the 1980s.

November 15, 2004 — Roman Catholic bishops in the United States elected Bishop William Skylstad of the Washington diocese as their new president. To show how persuasive the problem of priestly sexual abuse was in the United States, Skylstad's own diocese was facing bankruptcy because of the huge dollar amount of lawsuits brought in the diocese to settle claims of sexual abuse by priests.

2004

December 3, 2004— The diocese of Orange County, California, settled a sex abuse lawsuit against its priests brought on behalf of 87 plaintiffs for a sum later revealed to be $100 million. It took over two years of talks to reach a settlement, but the cases were finally settled without the diocese claiming bankruptcy.

This example spreads throughout the state, as settlements are reached in Sacramento in June 2005 for $35 million for 33 victims, and in Oakland in August 2005 for $56 million for 56 victims.

2005, Disciples of Christ— The General Assembly of the Christian Church (Disciples of Christ), the official name of the denomination since an organizational meeting in 1968, meeting in Portland, Oregon, voted almost unanimously for Sharon Watkins as the first woman to hold the position of general minister and president of the denomination.

2005, Southern Baptists— The Southern Baptist Convention (SBC), formed in 1845 because of tensions with northern Baptists due to the struggle over slavery (see listing for May 12, 1845), declined at its annual meeting to change its name to better indicate its now national scope.

Suggestions for a new name included the North American Baptist Convention and the Scriptural Baptist Convention. The latter name would keep the same initials SBC. But the proposals to adopt a new name were defeated. The existing SBC had been steadily growing since its founding 160 years ago, and it saw no need for a change.

The SBC claims to have 44,000 churches throughout the United States with a membership of over 16 million. As such the SBC has more congregations in the nation than any other denomination, including the Roman Catholic Church. The Catholic membership is three times as large as that of the SBC, although the SBC is the largest single Protestant denomination in terms of members.

The SBC has 1,200 local associations, 41 state conventions and fellowships among the 50 states, and over 10,000 missionaries in the United States and around the world. Thus, although it has its largest concentration in the southern United States where it started, it truly is a worldwide organization.

July 31, 2006— An article in the *San Diego Union Tribune* noted the failure of the latest attempt by the dioceses of Los Angeles and San Diego to further delay the cases of sex abuses charges filed against priests within the dioceses.

In the last four years, thousands of such lawsuits in locations across the nation have been settled for a total of about $1.5 billion. Closer to home, the diocese of neighboring Orange County, California, settled 87 lawsuits for $100 million in December 2005 (see listing).

But about 160 cases in the San Diego diocese and about 560 cases in the Los Angeles diocese, which have been combined into one action by the courts, have remained unsettled since 2003. This total of about 720 cases is the largest number of unsettled cases anywhere in the nation.

Cardinal Roger Mahoney of the Los Angeles Archdiocese has been severely criticized for his clumsy attempts to delay the trials and cover up the abuse. Mahoney has claimed that discussions between an abusive priest and his bishop is privileged information and must be kept confidential.

In April the United States Supreme Court denied Mahoney's claim, affirming a lower court ruling. An independent Catholic review board sharply criticized Mahoney's actions for harming the church's reputation.

December 2006—The Archdiocese of Los Angeles reached a partial settlement in the lawsuits filed against its priests for sexual abuse by agreeing to pay $60 million to 45 victims. This still left over 500 cases to be settled, but it was an important precedent.

Cardinal Mahoney of the Los Angeles Archdiocese had been stalling the settlements (see listing for July 31, 2006), and the diocese of San Diego, combined by the courts with the Los Angeles cases, had been making noises about threatening to file for bankruptcy, which would delay the cases further.

The partial Los Angeles settlement on this date led to final settlements of all cases in 2007 (see listing for July 2007).

July 2007—The Los Angeles Catholic Archdiocese settled its remaining 508 claims against its priests for a record-breaking $660 million. The archdiocese had already made a payment of $60 million dollars in December 2006 (see listing) to settle other cases.

The settlement was reached just before the scheduled beginning of a series of abuse trials dating as far back as the 1940s. This timing was typical of many such settlements because the church wanted to avoid at nearly

2007

all costs any trials in open court that would reveal not only the detailed abuses of the priests, but the efforts of their superiors to cover up the crimes.

Cardinal Roger Mahoney of the Los Angeles Archdiocese had been roundly criticized by judges, newspapers, the public, and the national Catholic Church itself for his truly clumsy attempts to cover up the crimes of his priests and to delay the settlement.

The event of the final settlement of the Los Angeles cases triggered the settlement of cases involving the diocese of San Diego, the processing of which had been combined by the courts with the Los Angeles cases. The San Diego diocese agreed in September 2007, to pay $198 million to settle 144 claims of sexual abuse by the clergy of its diocese.

July 2, 2007 — The *Michigan Daily*, the student newspaper at the University of Michigan, carried an article about the planned construction at its Dearborn, Michigan, campus of facilities that would provide foot baths.

There are a number of Muslim students at the Dearborn campus, and many use bathroom sinks to complete the washing rituals they must go through before daily prayers. This practice was raising concerns about safety and sanitation according to campus officials.

Objections were being raised about First Amendment violations involved with the school building facilities for a specific religious group, but the school claimed the facilities would be open to all students, not just Muslims, and thus no First Amendment requirements would be violated.

School officials said some student athletes had indicated they would use the foot baths, and officials noted that such facilities were already in use at other schools including Boston University, the University of Wisconsin at Madison, and Eastern Michigan University.

October 2007 — An analysis of the Seventh-Day Adventist Church that was founded about 144 years ago by a few people (see listing for May 23, 1863), showed that the denomination now included about 15.4 million people worldwide. An estimated 25 million people come weekly to worship in its churches.

However, only about 10 percent of its membership is located in the United States. The majority of its membership is located in Africa and Central and South America. The Adventists have a missionary presence in over 200 countries, and have a reputation for providing humanitarian aid in the form of hospitals and schools, especially in developing countries. The Adventist Development and Relief Agency (ADRA) is famous around the world.

The Adventists have become a truly worldwide church in spite of its relatively humble origins and low-profile presence in the United States.

December 7, 2007—Mitt Romney, a candidate for the Republican nomination for president of the United States in 2008, made a speech in Houston, Texas, designed to answer questions about his Mormon faith as it affected his suitability for the nomination.

The announcement of Romney's planned speech had evoked memories of a similar-themed speech made by John F. Kennedy in Houston in 1960 (see listing for September 12, 1960) to answer questions about his Catholic faith as it impacted his suitability to be president of the United States.

Considering the fact that Kennedy's speech was made over 47 years ago, Romney was bold enough to take issue in an intelligent, moderate way with some of Kennedy's points. But the fact was that Kennedy's speech is well remembered not so much for its theological insight, but because it was well delivered before a hostile audience and was considered an important factor in Kennedy's subsequent election victory.

Romney had no such hostile audience, and the real concern key Republican voters had was not so much the issue of Mormonism (which Romney handled satisfactorily), but the issue of Romney's shifting personal views on items such as abortion, gun rights, and immigration.

Romney had been the Republican governor of Massachusetts, probably the most liberal Democratic state in the country. His views on these issues as governor were quite different than those he espoused as a potential Republican nominee. Saying he had simply changed his mind was hard to swallow for many voters.

It would happen in 2008 that Romney would not win the nomination, so his religious speech, however well crafted, could never have the same historical glow as that of winner Kennedy.

January 27, 2008—Gordon B. Hinckley, the oldest man ever to serve as the president of the Mormon Church (officially The Church of Jesus

2008

Christ of Latter-day Saints or the LSD Church) died at the age of 97. Hinckley had been president for 13 years, starting on March 12, 1995, just three months short of his 85th birthday.

This chronology is filled with the travails of the Mormon Church, and the battles it had fought with various governments, including that of the United States, since it was born in 1830 (see listing). But the Mormons entered the mainstream when they gave up the practice of polygamy early in the 1900s.

Tiny splinter groups whose leaders cling to the practice have gathered lurid headlines even up to the present, but they represent less than 1 percent of Mormons around the world. The basic Mormon Church headquartered in Salt Lake City has been one of the fastest growing and most successful churches anywhere.

Gordon Hinckley increased the number of operating Mormon temples around the world from 47 when he became president in 1995 to 124 when he died in 2008. Another 14 had been announced or were under construction. Hinckley was a very successful president of a very successful church.

February 25, 2008—A report was released summarizing parts of a 2007 survey taken by the Pew Forum on Religion and Public Life in the United States. The Pew Forum called the 35,000-person poll the United States Religious Landscape Survey.

The survey was not meant to discover how many people were in a given religious denomination (for one thing only adults were surveyed and children were not included), but rather to indicate adult preferences with respect to religious affiliations and how those preferences were changing.

One major point of the survey was that Protestants of all types only accounted for 51.3 percent, barely keeping Protestants in the position of being the religious affiliation of the majority of the people in the United States. Catholics numbered 23.9 percent to bring the total number of Americans who are "Christian" to 75.2 percent.

The most notable point of the survey was the churning that was going on within the defined categories of religious affiliation. About 28 percent of American adults have left the church of their childhood, and if the people who have only moved from one Protestant denomination to another are included, the number switching affiliations grows to 44 percent. Thus, nearly half of all people in the United States have changed their religious childhood affiliation.

More detailed study shows larger changes than meet the eye. For example, a third of Catholics have left the church since 1972. But the total Catholic population has remained relatively constant because the growing number of Hispanic immigrants coming to the United States since that time is nearly all Catholic. As a result, nearly half of all Catholics under 30 years of age are Hispanic.

Determining winners and losers in terms of religious affiliation also requires a number of caveats. The "most stable" title goes to Hindus, 84 percent of whom retain their childhood religion. The "least stable" are the Jehovah's Witnesses, 63 percent of whom have changed their affiliation since childhood. But the Jehovah's Witnesses are such fervent converters that their door-to-door campaigns keep the tiny group at nearly a constant level of members.

The biggest winner in terms of change is the unaffiliated category. It stood at 16 percent whereas only 7 percent were brought up that way. However, even that category lost 50 percent of its original members to one church or another. The key lesson from the survey is one of dynamic change everywhere.

A final note of interest is that the categories most likely to marry within their affiliations are the Hindus at 90 percent and the Mormons at 83 percent.

March 3, 2008—The *Los Angeles Times* reported on a story about an Internet battle between supporters and detractors of Scientology. Since it was founded over 50 years ago in 1954 (see listing) by science fiction writer L. Ron Hubbard (who died in 1986), Scientology has been embroiled in a constant battle between detractors who see it as a money-making fraud and supporters (often highly visible figures such as famous actors and actresses) who see it as a modern kind of religion.

The latest battle was triggered by a video shown in January 2008 of a television appearance by actor Tom Cruise defending Scientology. Cruise, who recently had been appearing somewhat unstable, was subject to ridicule by anti–Scientologists.

Also, three young women who were raised as Scientologists started a Web site last week called ExScientologyKids.com describing how they

2008

escaped from the indoctrinations of the religion. Because two of the three were a daughter and a niece of high-ranking officials of Scientology, the Web site immediately attracted attention.

The events appeared to be yet another skirmish in the battle between those attacking Scientology and the officials of Scientology defending the organization (and its revenues).

March 4, 2008—The Associated Press announced that Harvard University has banned men from one of its gyms for a few hours each week to accommodate Muslim women who, for religious and cultural reasons, cannot exercise comfortably in the presence of men.

The policy, which went into effect on a trial basis a month ago on February 4, 2008, has evoked the usual debate in a pluralistic society. Some women, including Lucy Caldwell, a columnist on the campus newspaper the *Harvard Crimson* finds the policy sexist in that it discriminates against men.

Some Muslim women think it is a natural thing to offer such courtesy to a religious minority. Harvard spokesman Robert Mitchell agrees, saying "we get special requests from religious groups all the time, and we try to honor them whenever possible." He noted that the school has already designated spaces for Muslim and Hindu students to pray.

The general attitude on campus seemed to be that although strictly speaking the policy is sexist and discriminatory, it is on such a small scale considering the number of gyms available on campus and that the designated gym is only unavailable six out of the 70 hours a week it is open, it is reasonable to make the exception.

March 21, 2008—In an example of how deeply black churches get involved in every aspect of the lives of their members, it was announced that the FAME Assistance Corporation, the economic development branch of the First African Methodist Episcopal (FAME) Church in South Los Angeles is trying to raise $50 million to help families facing foreclosure of their homes.

FAME Corp. proposes to use the funds in their communities to buy repossessed properties and mortgages headed for or already in default. FAME then would offer more affordable mortgages to those who met its financial and other criteria.

The success of the plan would depend on present lenders essentially being willing to take a loss on the sale to FAME on the basis that loss, in the long run, would be no worse than foreclosing on the properties and being unable to sell them profitably in the present struggling real estate market.

No company has yet signed onto the FAME plan, and chances of success are at best marginal. But the example of the church trying to come to the aid of its members in every way is one reason black churches are supported so strongly by their members.

April 15, 2008— Pope Benedict XVI arrived in the United States for a visit that ended on April 20, 2008. He was the third pope to visit the United States. Pope Paul VI visited in 1965, and Pope John Paul II made seven visits to the United States during his tenure as pope.

This trip was unique because a number of pointed questions were directed at the pope about the story of longtime sexual abuse by Catholic priests that had occupied the news headlines in the United States for much of the beginning of the 21st century. There was a widespread feeling that the Vatican had not paid proper attention to the abuse, and that what attention it did pay was directed towards covering it up.

The questioning began even before the pope set foot in the United States. On the plane bringing him to the United States, the pope answered some questions previously submitted by reporters. The pope said he was "deeply ashamed" by the actions of pedophile priests. He added that "It's difficult for me to understand how it was possible that priests betrayed in this way their mission to give healing, to give the love of God to these children."

The pope said the church would work to exclude pedophiles from the priesthood, noting that "It is more important to have good priests than to have many priests." The pope's words were the strongest he had ever made on this issue, and although many persons wanted him to say more, the large majority were pleased that he was addressing the issue directly and not trying to deflect it or give it "spin."

Later, the pope met privately with some victims of sexual abuse by priests. This group was specifically from Boston because the pope was not able to include Boston in the itinerary for his trip. The pope also said of the scandal that "it was sometimes very badly handled." The pope visited

2008

Ground Zero, the site of the September 11, 2001, terrorist attacks, and also had a private meeting with some of the relatives of victims of the attacks, some survivors, and some rescue workers.

Observers said that the private meetings with sex abuse victims and the September 11 group did more than any of the more formal aspects of the visit to make the pope seem like a more human and respected figure to people in the United States. These observers noted that the Catholic Church had spent about two billion dollars to settle the sexual abuse claims in the United States, and as some of these claims went back to the 1940s, the church was essentially starting with a clean slate as of the pope's visit.

Thus, hopefully there would be far fewer sex abuse claims in the future as priests were more carefully screened, and, of equal importance, were more forcefully dealt with by the church when problems occurred. The pope's visit could be the symbol of a new day in this respect in the Catholic Church in the United States.

May 4, 2008—The Rockville Centre Catholic Diocese in Long Island, New York, announced it expects to ordain nine priests this June compared to a single priest just nine years ago. The number of seminarians at Rockville is up to 31 compared to single digits in recent years.

More than a third of those studying to be priests are older men, many in their 40s. The increased number of older men taking up the priesthood has been a boon to the Catholic Church, which now has only about 29,000 priests in the United States, 20 percent fewer than 40 years ago.

For the last decade, the median age for priests at ordination has averaged about 38. In the 1960s it was 26. Part of this increase is because more priests get a master of divinity degree rather than a bachelor of divinity degree, but a large part reflects the fact that potential priests are deciding later in life to seek fulfillment through the priesthood when events in their life turned out not to be as fulfilling as they had hoped.

June 9, 2008—The *Los Angeles Times* carried an advertisement (presented as if it were an article) for the Good News Mission Church. The article/ad was written by Pastor Ock So Park, a Korean-born minister.

According to a blog posted about the subject, "Ock So Park is one of the 'New Messiahs' that Korea seems to be producing at a prodigious rate." The blog stated that Park was perhaps less "malevolent" than Sun

2008

Myung Moon (see listing for July 16, 1982), but he was not totally benevolent either.

Park was born in Korea in 1944, educated at the Shield of Faith mission school run by missionaries Dick York and Marlin Baker from the United States, and ordained by York in 1971. Park founded the Good News Mission Church in the 1980s and took it around the world, including the United States.

June 23, 2008—More data were released from the survey on religion in the United States taken in 2007 by the Pew Forum on Religion and Public Life. It is the second release of data this year. The first release was on February 25, 2008 (see listing).

The data recently released focused more on individual attitudes towards religious feelings than on the overall changes in general religious affiliations that were at the core of the prior release on February 25, 2008.

The new data showed that 70 percent of Americans believed that "many religions can lead to eternal life," and over two-thirds say that there is more than one true way to interpret their religious teachings. Only 63 percent believe "holy scripture" is the word of God. But Mormons and Jehovah's Witnesses disagree significantly with the view of variable interpretations.

Although 92 percent say they believe in the existence of God or a universal spirit (even about 70 percent of those who say they are unaffiliated with any religious group believe so), the number of all Americans who believe in life after death was put at 74 percent.

Less than half (39 percent) of Americans attend religious services at least once a week, but 58 percent say they pray privately every day.

June 25, 2008—A television clip on CBS gave a report on the school district program in the town of Modesto, California, which requires students to take a course on world religions and religious liberty. The schools avoid First Amendment problems by scrupulously presenting the course as history. The course objectively describes religions rather than trying to evaluate their merits. As one teacher said, "we can't preach, but we can teach."

The course had its roots in 1997 when some Modesto religious groups were battling the school board over a policy of tolerance for homosexual

2008

students. Out of a series of discussions came an effort to create safe schools for all students and end bullying due to differences in sexual orientation, race, ethnicity, and religion. As part of this effort, the religion course was one of several proposed to end some practices of intolerance by educating all students about the differences demonstrated in these areas by some students.

Despite fears of lawsuits about First Amendment issues, which scare off almost all school districts from touching religion in any way, the Modesto schools started the new century in 2000 with its world religions education course.

Word got around about the unique course, and from October 2003 through January 2005, two college professors with an interest in social science who were studying religious freedom in the United States conducted a survey to determine if the program actually was making a difference in attitudes towards religion.

The professors, named Emile Lester and Patrick S. Roberts, surveyed more than 400 Modesto students, and interviewed students, teachers, administrators, and community leaders. The professors found a definite increase in the students' respect for religious rights and liberties. They also found a better respect for the same things among the community, which has representatives of Sikhs, Buddhists, Muslims, evangelistic megachurches, mainline Protestants, and Roman Catholics among its many churches as well as a flourishing Jewish community. The town of about 190,000 probably has what can be considered a normal mix of religions in a pluralist state such as California, but the high school religious history course appears to have a better understanding of the mix among its citizens.

The results appear to be universally positive, but so far as is known Modesto appears to be the only school district in the United States that requires students to make a study of all major religions to graduate.

June 27, 2008, Presbyterians— At a meeting in San Jose, California, the general assembly, the national governing body of the Presbyterian Church (USA) voted to ordain homosexuals, overturning a long-standing ban on the practice. However, a majority of the 173 regional presbyteries in the United States must also agree on the practice in the next year for it to become church law, and some observers predicted such a vote would fail (the general assembly only voted 56 percent to 44 percent in favor of the ruling).

The action of the general assembly was the latest attempt by mainstream Protestant churches to address the issue of homosexuality. Many churches are leaving their national groups because they still consider homosexuality to be a sin while the national leadership is trying to stay relevant in a world where homosexuality is becoming more generally accepted.

The Presbyterian General Assembly showed it was still split on the issue by refusing to sanction same sex marriage after agreeing to ordain homosexuals. The general assembly maintained its definition of marriage as a "covenant between a woman and a man."

Many denominations of Protestant churches are struggling with such issues. Only those churches that maintain a hard line against homosexuality feel no sense of a struggle. They refuse to seek any accommodation with homosexuals, no matter how many individual members may desire to make such a move. The result will probably be a continuation of the splintering of mainstream Protestant denominations that has been going on for one reason or another over the last half century.

June 27, 2008, Episcopal— Circuit Judge Randy I. Bellows of Fairfax, Virginia, issued a 49-page ruling upholding a state law permitting congregations to secede from their parent denominations. The judge found that the state law breaks no rules governing the separation of church and state.

The ruling was a victory for eleven conservative Episcopal churches who invoked the Virginia law to split from the Episcopal Diocese of Virginia over the issue of the role of homosexuals in the church. This is not just a philosophical issue as the churches deciding to split plan to take tens of millions of dollars of property with them.

The diocese claimed it was entitled to the properties and has a right to settle church disputes without state interference. The ruling today supported the dissenting churches. Observers say other such actions are sure to follow in other denominations because the issue of homosexuality has caused similar disputes between denominational ruling bodies and their individual churches.

July 19, 2008— Pope Benedict XVI wrapped up a nine-day trip to Australia by meeting privately with four sex-abuse victims of Catholic priests

2008

and apologizing for the actions of the priests. The meeting appeared to be an attempt to use the same technique he had used during his visit to the United States in April (see listing for April 15, 2008) to put a more humane face on the crimes and acknowledge errors made by the Vatican in the handling of the scandal.

It was not clear if the results of the pope's apologies would be as effective in Australia as they had been in the United States, but at least the pope was continuing to meet the crisis head-on rather than attempting to apply spin.

August 16, 2008— Rick Warren, pastor of Saddleback Church in Lake Forest, California, arranged a forum in which he separately question presidential contenders John McCain and Barack Obama, on issues relative to their religious beliefs. Saddleback Church is a 23,000-member megachurch that is typical of the direction the Protestant Church has been taking in the last several decades.

Warren is the author of the best-selling book *The Purpose Driven Life* which has sold upward of 30 million English-language copies and 40 million around the world. The book is essentially a "how to" guide about extending your Christian life beyond going to church. It is filled with exercises and homilies. But it has struck a chord worldwide and is still selling since its publication in 2002.

Warren, 54, is called by many the most influential churchman in the United States, and has been called the "next Billy Graham." Others see him as simply the next evangelistic superstar to arise out of the Southern Baptist Convention's long list of charismatic preachers. Warren's father was one of a chain of such pastors.

At any rate, Warren has ambitions to spread peace around the world by delivering humanitarian and developmental aid to poor countries. His present efforts are focused on Rwanda in Africa. The fact that he could attract both presidential contenders to an event organized by himself is an indication of his present influence in the United States and beyond.

September 5, 2008— Archbishop George Niederauer of San Francisco said that Nancy Pelosi, Speaker of the United States House of Representatives, was in error when she made recent comments about abortion and the position of the Catholic Church on the subject.

2008

Pelosi said last month, on *Meet the Press*, that "doctors of the church" disagreed on when life begins, and that abortion "continues to be an issue of controversy" in the Catholic Church. Niederauer said Pelosi's comments "are in serious conflict with the teachings of the Catholic Church."

At least 10 Catholic bishops have condemned Pelosi's remarks, pointing out that the Catholic Church has said consistently since the first century that abortion is wrong. Many other Catholics have written to Niederauer saying Pelosi should be denied communion because of her views. Neiderauer added that Catholics should not "pick and choose" which teachings of the church to follow, and that moral issues should not be dictated by opinion polls.

A letter from Pelosi was hand delivered to Niederauer today accepting an invitation to discuss her views further. The issue was another example of how politicians try to dance around controversial issues such as abortion, trying to mask their disagreement with their church and trying not to lose any votes on either side of the issue.

APPENDIX 1:
RELIGIOUS GROUPS IN THE UNITED STATES

Figure 1 shows the distribution of major religious groups in the United States. These data are based on surveys conducted by the Graduate School of the City of New York in 2001 that was called the American Religious Identity Survey (ARIS). This survey was not intended to be a total count of various religious groups. It involves only adults over the age of 18, and is intended only to show the distributions of religious groups in the sample interviewed.

Thus, the most useful data in the survey are the percentages shown for the various groups identified. In a sense this survey resembles the common political survey in which questions are posed to a sample group and the percentages of the responses are applied to the nation at large. The quality of the data accumulated depends on the skill of the interviewer, the relevance of the questions asked, and the honesty of the respondents.

Even with these caveats, the data provide a very good snapshot of religious preferences in the United States. The recent PEW study results described in the chronology during 2008 show that more recent studies indicate a great deal of switching among denominations in the United States, and less attention being paid to specific denominations. However, the data being presented in this appendix are greatly simplified. The appendix thus presents an excellent picture at a glance of religious preferences in the United States.

Figure 1 shows the major religious groups in the United States among about 208 million persons greater than the age of 18 as of 2001. By far the

Appendix 1. Religious Groups

largest group is the Christians (basically Catholics and Protestants) at 76.5 percent (greater detail among the Protestants is shown in Appendix 2).

The next largest group at 19.7 percent consists of those who profess to have no religious inclinations at all. Agnostics and atheists make up only a small portion of this group (less than 1 percent combined). This means that 96.2 percent of the people in the United States are either Christians or nonbelievers.

The remaining 3.8 percent are either Jewish (1.3 percent) or other religions of the world, none of which exceed 1 percent of the total. Muslims and Buddhists share second place behind the Jewish entry. The fact that there are over 20 named groups in this category shows that the United States is open to literally any religion in the world, even if the overwhelming predominant religion is the Christian religion.

Also, the fact that nearly 20 percent of the people in the nation profess to be nonreligious demonstrates the total freedom of religion in the United States, i.e., freedom from religion as well as freedom of religion.

Figure 1. Religious Groups in the United States in 2001 Among Adults Older Than 18

	Millions	*Percent*
Christian	159.0	76.5%
Catholic and Protestant		
Jewish	2.8	1.3%
Muslim	1.1	0.5%
Buddhist	1.1	0.5%
Hindu	0.8	0.4%
Unitarian/Universalist	0.6	0.3%
Other (15+ names)	1.6	0.8%
Subtotal	8.0	3.8%
None	39.1	18.8%
Agnostic	1.0	0.5%
Atheist	0.9	0.4%
Subtotal	41.0	19.7%
Total	**208.0**	**100.0%**

Appendix 2: Christian Religious Groups in the United States

Figure 1 shows the distribution of various religious denominations in the United States contained within the category of Christian. As shown in Appendix 1, the Christian category makes up 76.5 percent of all religious groups in the United States. These data are based on surveys conducted by the Graduate School of the City of New York in 2001 that was called the American Religious Identity Survey (ARIS). This survey was not intended to be a total count of various religious groups. It involves only adults over the age of 18, and is intended only to show the distributions of religious groups in the sample interviewed.

Thus, the most useful data in the survey are the percentages shown for the various groups identified. In a sense this survey resembles the common political survey in which questions are posed to a sample group and the percentages of the responses are applied to the nation at large. The quality of the data accumulated depends on the skill of the interviewer, the relevance of the questions asked, and the honesty of the respondents.

Even with these caveats, the data provide a very good snapshot of religious preferences in the United States. The recent PEW study results described in the chronology during 2008 show that more recent studies indicate a great deal of switching among denominations in the United States, and less attention being paid to specific denominations. However, the data being presented in this appendix are greatly simplified so that it presents an excellent picture at a glance of religious preferences in the United States.

Appendix 2

Figure 1 shows that about 159.0 million persons over age 18 identified themselves as Christians. This is 76.5 percent of the total of 208.0 million persons in the United States who were above the age of 18 in 2001 at the time of the survey.

Catholics were projected to be 53.6 million or 33.7 percent of those 159.0 million identifying themselves as Christians. The remaining 105.4 million or 66.3 percent were identified as Protestants. However, the word Protestant in this data needs to be thought of in the broadest possible way. In addition to the traditional denominations that are thought of when one thinks of the word Protestant, there are groups included in Figure 1 that are perhaps best thought of as Christians who are not Catholic.

Figure 1 shows the top six Protestant groups that have easily recognized names, and these denominations represent over 70 percent of the groups listed as Protestant. However, there are over 30 other names listed in the Protestant group that would not be as familiar to most people.

Even in the denomination listed as Pentecostal in Figure 1, four subgroups including Charismatic, Assemblies of God, Holiness, and Foursquare Gospel are part of the total. Some people might not recognize these names, but they are clearly Christian denominations with a strong belief in God and Jesus. They have unique methods of worship, and make up one of the largest Christian denominations around the world (with numbers perhaps ten times larger than in the United States). But the word Protestant is used to include them, even if they did not originate per se in the time of the Reformation in Europe and England. The same thing is true of many other denominations shown for convenience in the Protestant category.

With this caveat, the largest Protestant denomination by far is the Baptist denomination at 22.5 percent of the Christian category, and 33.9 percent of the Protestant category. It was pointed out in the chronology that even though the Baptists trail the Catholics in the Christian category by 33.6 percent for the Catholics to 22.5 percent for the Baptists as shown in Figure 1 here, the Baptists had more total churches in the United States.

It must be noted again that all the totals shown here do not include children under the age of 18. Thus, membership totals for the various denominations will not agree with other sources. As emphasized before, the percentages shown are key to any analysis.

The more familiar Protestant denominations of Methodists, Luther-

Christian Religious Groups

ans, Presbyterians, and Episcopals trail the Baptists in that order, with the Pentecostals being inserted in fifth place as discussed above.

Figure 1. Christian Religious Groups in the United States in 2001 Among Adults Older Than 18

	Millions	*Percent of Christians*
Catholic	53.6	33.7%
Protestants	105.4	66.3%
Total Christian	**159.0**	**100.0%**

Protestant Categorization			*Percent of Protestants*
Baptist	35.7	22.5%	33.9%
Methodist	15.6	9.8%	14.8%
Lutheran	10.3	6.5%	9.8%
Presbyterian	6.4	4.0%	6.1%
Pentecostal	6.4	4.0%	6.1%
Episcopal	3.7	2.3%	3.5%
Other (30+ names)	27.3	17.2%	25.9%
Total Protestant	**105.4**	**66.3%**	**100.0%**

Bibliography

This bibliography lists the key references consulted in putting together this chronology. There are several excellent histories of religion and the role it has played in both shaping and reflecting United States history and cultural life. By far the most useful book was *A Religious History of America*, by Edwin Scott Gaustad. As Gaustad notes in his preface to the revised edition, his goal is to "portray the role of religion in all stages of this country's development" since for all intents and purposes the history of religion in the United States is "a veritable whirlwind of energies and contrary forces in the latter half of the twentieth century," and certainly continues to be so. Gaustad's book is a very detailed analysis and contains much useful information.

In addition to the books listed in this bibliography, the Internet has been a useful research source. No attempt has been made to compile a list of specific Internet sources for this book because most Internet-based material in the book is a combination of facts drawn from several different Internet sources. Also, Internet information constantly changes as it is updated. In the world of today, the Internet has to be used as a major source in any research activity, and much use was made of it in writing this book.

Selected Bibliography

Ahlstrom, Sydney E. *A Religious History of the American People*. New Haven: Yale University Press, 1972.

Crews, Clyde F. *American and Catholic: A Popular History of Catholicism in the United State*s. Cincinnati, OH: St. Anthony Messenger Press, 1994.

Gaustad, Edwin Scott. *A Religious History of America*, new rev. ed. New York: Harper & Row, 1990.

Bibliography

Hill, Frances. *A Delusion of Satan: The Full Story of the Salem Witch Trials*. Cambridge, MA: Da Capo Press/Perseus Books Group, 2002.

Jones, C. Alan, ed. *The World Almanac and Book of Facts, 2008*. New York: World Almanac Books/A Reader's Digest Company, 2008.

Krakauer, Jon. *Under the Banner of Heaven: A Story of Violent Faith*. New York: Doubleday, 2003.

Neuser, Jacob, ed. *World Religions in America: An Introduction*, rev. and exp. Louisville, KY: Westminster John Knox Press, 2000.

Porterfield, Amanda. *The Transformation of American Religion: The Story of a Late Twentieth-Century Awakening*. New York: Oxford University Press, 2001.

Roach, Marilynne K. *The Salem Witch Trials: A Day-by-Day Chronicle of a Community Under Siege*. Lanham, MD: Taylor Trade Publishing, 2004.

Sachar, Howard M. *A History of the Jews in America*. New York: Alfred A. Knopf, 1992.

Wright, Russell O. *Chronology of Education in the United States*. Jefferson, NC: McFarland, 2006.

Index

Abbelen, P.M. 1886 Abbelen
ABC 9/30/1951
Abstinence Society 2/13/1826
Act of Tolerance 1649
Adams, President John 1816 John Adams, 1818 Connecticut
Addams, Jane 1889
Adventalism 5/10/1939
Adventist Churches 10/22/1844
Adventist Development and Relief Agency (ADRA) October 2007
Adventist Movement 5/23/1863
Africa October 2007
African Americans August 1619
African Methodist Episcopal (AME) Church July 1794, 2/16/1801, 1821, 1852, 4/14/1906
Aguilar v. Felton 6/23/1997
Akron, Ohio 6/10/1935
Alabama 1764 St. Louis, 6/4/1985, 3/1/1995, 3/5/1997, 11/18/2002
Alabama Judicial Building 3/31/1995, 3/5/1997, 11/18/2002, 8/20/2003
Albany, New York 1629
Alcoholics Anonymous (AA) 6/10/1935
Allen, John 1772
Allen, Richard April 1787, July 1794, 2/6/1801
Alton, Illinois 11/7/1837
American Baptist Church of the West January 1996
American Bible Society 1816 Bible Society
American Center for Law and Justice (ACLJ) 6/7/1993 Prayer in Schools
American Christian Temperance movement 12/27/1899
American Civil Liberties Union (ACLU) 7/10/1925, 11/26/1956, 6/7/1993 Prayer in Schools, 3/31/995, 3/5/1997, 6/19/2000
American Temperance Society 2/13/1826
American Temperance Union 2/13/1826
American Tract Society 1825 Tract Society
American Unitarian Association (AUA) 1961
Amherst College 1847 Theological Society
Amish June 1683, 1709, 5/15/1972
Angelus Temple 1/1/1923, 1927
Anglican May 1607, 12/16/1653, 2/13/1689, 1704, 1707 New York, December 1712, 1740 George Whitfield, 1744, 1754 King's College, 1759 Anglicans, 1768, 1776, 1784 Catholics, 1785 Madison, 7/17/1836, 1840 Shakers, 8/5/2003
Anti-Defamation League 1913
Anti-Saloon League 2/13/1826, August 1874, 1895, 1895 Russell, 12/18/1917
Appalachian Mountains 1811
Applied Christianity: Moral Aspects of Social Questions 1886 Gladden
Arabella 1630
Archdiocese, Boston 9/19/2002, 12/3/2002, April 2003
Archdiocese, Los Angeles 7/31/2006, December 2006, July 2007
Archdiocese, Orange County, California 12/3/2004
Archdiocese, Portland, Oregon 7/7/2004
Archdiocese, San Diego 7/31/2006, December 2006, July 2007
Ark 3/25/1634
Art of Living 1952

Index

Asbury, Francis 1784 Methodists, April 1787, July 1794
Asbury, John 1773
Assembly of God 4/14/1906, April 1914, 9/4/1973, 4/8/1988
Associated Press 7/16/1982, 3/4/2008
Atlanta, Georgia 6/10/1983
Augsburg 1643
Augusta, Georgia 5/12/1845
Austin, Ann July 1656
Australia 1886 Abbelen, 7/9/2008
Azusa Street 1/1/1901, 4/14/1906, April 1914
Azusa Street Revival 4/14/1906

Badin, Stephen 1793
Baker, Marlin 6/9/2008
Bakker, Jim 1/13/1974, June 1979, 4/8/1988
Bakker, Tammy Faye 1/13/1974
Balanced Treatment for Creation-Science and Evolution-Science in Public School Instruction Act 6/19/1987
Baltimore, Maryland 1784 Methodists, 1805, 1811, 1815, 1829, 1854, 1887, 12/8/1960
Baptist 1609, August 1619, 1639, 12/16/1653, 1707 Philadelphia Baptists, 1740 George Whitfield, 1754 Baptists, 1759 Anglicans, 1763 Brown University, 1772, 1776, 1790 George Washington, 1790 Leland, 12/15/1791, May 1800, 8/6/1801, 1817, 5/1/1845, 1857, 12/31/1894, 1907, 5/10/1939, 9/30/1951, 4/23/1968, 6/4/1984, 4/8/1988, January 1996
Baptist Bible College 6/19/1956
Barbados April 1670, 1692 Salem
Barbour, N.H. 1872
Bardstown, Kentucky 1793, May 1800, 1811, April 1812
Barrows, John Henry 1893 World Parliament
Battle Creek, Michigan 5/23/1863
Baughn, Bishop Austin January 1990
Beecher, Lyman 1832
Belgium 1815, 1840 Pierre DeSmet
Bellows, Judge Randy I. 6/27/2008 Episcopal
Benedict XVI, Pope 4/15/2008, 7/9/2008
Benezet, Anthony 1772
Berle, Milton 1951

Bethel Bible College 1/1/1901
Bible Institute for Home and Foreign Missions 1875 Moody, 3/21/1900
Bill for Establishing Religious Freedom 1777
Bill of Rights (United States) 1619, 1662, 2/13/1689, December 1712, 1774, 1785 Madison, 1/1/1786, September 1787, March 1789, 1790 George Washington, 12/15/1791, 7/19/1825, 1/18/1844
Birmingham, Alabama 3/9/1965
Blackwell, Antoinette Brown 1853
Blair, James 1693
Blanton, Smiley 1952
Blavatsky, Madame H.P. 1875 Blavatsky
Book of Mormon Spring 1820, 9/2/1823, 3/26/1830, 9/9/1850, 1876
Booth, Ballington 1/19/1889
Booth, Bramwell 1/19/1889
Booth, Catherine 1/19/1889
Booth, Evangeline 1904
Booth, Maud 1/19/1889
Booth, William 1/19/1889
Boston, Massachusetts 1609, December 1620, 1630, October 1635, July 1656, 6/1/1660, May 1664, May 1682, 1685, 1753, 1772, 1785 King's Chapel, 12/25/1789, 1793, May 1800, 7/19/1825, 2/13/1826, 1834, 1835 Channing, 12/29/1851, 1875 Moody, 1879, 1/9/2002, 12/3/2002, April 2003, 4/15/2008
Boston University 7/2/2007
Branch Davidian 4/19/1993
Bray, Thomas 1699, 1707 New York
Brazil 1654
Bresee, Phineas F. 1895 Nazarene
British Parliament 1718 Scotch-Irish
Britton, Dr. John 3/10/1993
Brown University 1764 Brown University
Bruskewitz, Fabian W. 4/15/1996
Bryant, William Jennings 7/9/1896, 7/10/1925
Buchanan, James 1/18/1844, 7/13/1857
Buddhism 1893 World Parliament, 4/24/1898, 1954, 6/25/2008
Bunyan, John September 1675
Bureau of Alcohol, Tobacco, and Firearms (ATF) 4/19/1993
Burger, Chief Justice Warren 6/28/1971
Burnt-over District 3/31/1848, 1876

210

Index

Bushnell, Howard 7/19/1825, 1865
Butler University 11/18/1978

Cable News Network (CNN) 2/17/2004
Caldwell, Lucy 3/4/2008
California 8/29/1852
Calvary Church, New York City 6/10/1935
Calvert, Cecil (Lord Baltimore) 3/25/1634
Calvert, Sir George (Lord Baltimore) 3/25/1634
Calvert, Leonard 3/25/1634
Calvin, John December 1620, 1706
Cambridge Synod September 1646
camp meeting May 1800
Campbell 1/1/1832
Canada 1764 St. Louis
Cane Ridge, Kentucky 8/6/1801, 1/1/1832, May 1880
Carolina Territory April 1670
Carroll, Charles 3/25/1634, 1784 Catholics, November 1789
Carroll, John 1784 Catholics, November 1789, 11/10/1791, 1793, 1811, 1815
Carter, President James June 1979
Carthage, Illinois 6/27/1844
Catholic 1610, 1629, 3/25/1634, 12/16/1653, 1654, April 1670, 1674, 1685, 2/13/1689, 1718 Scotch-Irish, August 1727, February 1732, 1740 The Garden of the Soul, 1750, 1764 St. Louis, 7/16/1769, 1772, 1784 Catholics, November 1789, 1790 George Washington, 11/10/1791, 12/15/1791, 1793, May 1800, 1805, 1815, 1822, 1829, 1834, 1836, 10/22/1844, 5/1/1845, 1846, 1850, 10/2/1881, 1885 Strong, 1887, 1893 Toomy, 1893 World Parliament, 12/31/1894, 1897 Church of God, 4/24/1898, January 1899, 6/29/1908, 6/4/1919, 9/15/1923, 1926 Klan, 1928, November 1936, 1951, 9/30/1951, 5/17/1954, 9/12/1960, November 1960, 3/27/1962, 11/18/1966, 2/13/1973, 1985, 7/2/1989, January 1990, 1992, 6/18/1993, 3/26/1995, 4/15/1996, 7/13/1998, 1/9/2002, 11/13/2002 Bishops, 11/13/2002 Activists, 11/13/2002 Bishops, 11/15/2004, 2005 Southern Baptists, 12/7/2007, 2/25/2008, 4/15/2008, 5/4/2008, 6/25/2008, 9/5/2008
Catholic Benevolent League 10/2/1881
The Catholic Hour 1951
Catholic New York newspaper 4/9/1992
Catholic Order of Foresters 10/2/1881
Catholic Review Board 7/31/2006
Catholic University of America March 1986
The Catholic Worker 1933
Catholic World 1893 Toomy
Catholic Young Men's National Union 1910
CBS November 1936, 6/25/2008
Central America October 2007
Central Conference of American Rabbis 1918, 1931 Federal Council of Churches
Challoner, Richard 1740 The Garden of the Soul
Champain, Illinois 3/8/1948
Channing, William Ellery 1819 Channing, 7/19/1825, 1835 Channing
chaplain July 1775
Chapman, John 3/29/1772
Charles I, King 3/25/1634
Charles II, King October 1635, May 1681
Charleston, South Carolina 1685, April 1670, 1740 George Whitfield, 1822, 1829
Chase, Samuel November 1789
Chauncy, Charles 1742 Chauncy, 1784 Chauncy, 7/19/1825
Chautauqua, New York August 1874
Cherry Street Synagogue 1782
Chicago, Illinois 1857 Moody, 1889, 1893 Toomy, 1893 World Parliament, 3/21/1900, 9/14/1980
Chief Justice, Alabama Supreme Court 3/5/1997
China 4/24/1898
Christian August 1619
Christian Broadcasting Network (CBN) 10/1/1961, 10/1/1987
Christian Church (Disciples of Christ) 1/1/1832
Christian Coalition November 1995
Christian Endeavour Society of Missouri 7/20/1910
Christian Science Monitor 1879
Christmas May 1682, 12/25/1789, 6/26/1870

211

Index

Church of Christ, Scientist 1879
Church of England 1619, December 1620, 3/25/1634, 1649, 1662, April 1670, September 1675, 1740 George Whitfield, 1784 Methodists
Church of God in Christ 1897 Church of God, 1/1/1901, 4/14/1906, 1927
Church of Jesus Christ of Latter-Day Saints (LDS) 3/26/1830, 1/27/2008
Church of the Lukumi Babalu 11/4/1992
Church of the Nazarene 1895 Nazarene
Cincinnati, Ohio 1832, 10/3/1875, June 1994
City of Faith Medical and Research Center January 1987
Civil War (United States) 1772, July 1794, 1818 Presbyterians, 1840 Shakers, 5/1/1845, 3/31/1848, 1858 Revivalism, 1862, 4/22/1864, 7/28/1868, 1875 Blavatsky, 1875 Moody, 1/1/1901, 1902, 7/10/1925, 1926 Klan, 3/9/1965, 6/10/1983
Clarke, John 1639
Cleveland, President Grover 1/19/1889
Cleveland, Ohio August 1874
Coatesville, Pennsylvania 8/1/1979
Coke, Thomas 1784 Methodists
College of William and Mary 1693
Collins, Jerry January 1987
Columbia 1754 King's College
Columbus, Ohio 1886 Gladden, 1900, 4/20/1987
Columbus Day 10/2/1881
Complex Marriage 1847 Oneida
Confucianism 4/24/1898
Congregation Beth Adam June 1994
Congregation of Jeshuat Israel 1763
Congregation Shearith Israel 1654
Congregational Christian Church 6/25/1957
Congregational Church September 1646
Congregationalist 6/1/1660, May 1664, May 1675, 1701, 1740 George Whitfield, July 1741, 1748, June 1750, 1770, 12/15/1791, 1818 Connecticut, 7/19/1824, 1832, 1833, 1853, 1875 Moody, 1885 Strong, 1886 Gladden, 1893 World Parliament, 12/31/1894, 1897 Sheldon, 4/24/1898, 1900
Connecticut 1701, 1818 Connecticut
conscientious objectors 1840 Shakers

Constitution (United States) 2/13/1689, 1785 Madison, 1/1/1786, September 1787, March 1789, 12/25/1789, 1790 Leland, 1818 Connecticut, 2/13/1826, 1/18/1844, 7/28/1868, 4/24/1898, 5/13/1925, 1940, 2/13/1973, 6/1/1993, 6/7/1993 Free Speech, 3/31/1995, November 1995
Cornbury, Lord 1707 New York
Coughlin, Father Charles E. November 1936
Cox, Harvey 1965
Cromwell, Oliver 12/16/1653
"Cross of Gold" speech 7/9/1896
Cruise, Tom 3/3/2008
crusades 2/17/1889
Crystal Cathedral Ministries 9/14/1980
Cuba 4/24/1898
Cumming, Alfred 7/13/1857, 6/26/1858
Cumorah 9/21/1823, 3/26/1830
Cuomo, Governor Mario January 1990
Curran, Father Charles E. March 1986
Czechoslovakia 1886 Abbelen

Dallas, Texas 4/23/1968, 7/13/1998
Darrow, Clarence 7/10/1925
Dartmouth 1770, 1819 Dartmouth, 1847 Theological Society
Darwin, Charles 11/24/1858
Daughters of Isabella 10/2/1881
David, John Baptist April 1812
Davies, Samuel 1744
Day, Dorothy 1933
day-care sexual abuse 1996
Dayton, Tennessee 7/10/1925
Dearborn, Michigan 7/2/2007
Declaration of Independence (United States) 2/13/1689, 1746, July 1775, 1776, 1777, 1784 Catholics, November 1789, 4/24/1898
Declaration of Religious Tolerance 1707 New York, 1744
Delaware May 1681, 1707 New York, April 1787
Denman, Rose Mary August 1987
Denmark 1890
Deseret 9/9/1850
The Deseret News 9/9/1850, October 1910
DeSmet, Pierre Jean 1815, 1840 Pierre DeSmet
Detroit, Michigan November 1936

Index

Dewey, John 1929
Dianetic Research Foundation 1954
Dianetics: The Modern Science of Mental Health 1954
Disciples of Christ 12/31/1894, 11/18/1978
Disney Company June 1996
Doctrines and Covenants 3/27/1836
Dodge, Jamie 1/9/1989
Douglass, Frederick 1846, 1852
Dove 3/25/1634
DuBourg, Bishop William 1815, 1840 Pierre DeSmet
DuMont (network) 1951
Dutch Reformed Church 1629, 1647, 1707 New York, 1765
Dyer, Mary 6/1/1660, May 1682

Earl of Dartmouth 1770
East London Christian Mission 1/19/1889
Eastern Anglican Church 1784 Methodists
Eastern Michigan University 7/2/2007
Echo Park (Los Angeles) 1/1/1923
Eddy, Mary Baker 1879
Edict of Nantes 1685
Edmunds Act 3/22/1882
Edmunds-Tucker Act 1887, March 1887, 10/6/1890
Edwards, Jonathan July 1741, June 1750
Egypt 1885 Strong
Eighteenth Amendment to the Constitution 2/13/1826, August 1874, 1895 Russell, 12/18/1917
El Camino Real 7/16/1769
Elizabeth I, Queen May 1607
Emancipation Act 1/1/1863
Emerson, Ralph Waldo 3/29/1772, 7/19/1825, 1838
Emery, Philip 1773
Emmetsburg, Maryland 1805
Emmy Award 1951
Endicott, Governor 1639
England May 1607, 1609, December 1620, 1629, 1630, 3/25/1634, 1639, 1643, 1647, 1649, 12/16/1653, September 1675, May 1681, June 1683, 2/13/1689, 1692 Maryland, 1693, 1699, 1704, 1706, 1730, 1740 The Garden of the Soul, July 1741, 1742 Muhlenberg, 1744, 1746, 1750, 1759 Anglicans, 1768, 1773, August 1774, 1784 Catholics, 1785 Madison, 7/17/1836, 1840 Shakers, 12/29/1851, 11/24/1859, 1875 Moody, 1/19/1889, 1/1/1901, 1915
England, John 1822, 1829
English Bill of Rights 2/13/1689
English Civil Wars 12/16/1653
"Enthusiasm Described and Cautioned Against" 1742 Chauncy
Episcopal May 1607, 1785 King's Chapel, July 1794, 1886 Huntington, 12/31/1894, 9/6/1976, 6/27/2008
Episcopal General Convention 8/5/2003
Erie Canal 1876
establishment clause 6/7/1993 Free Speech
Evangelical and Reformed Church 6/25/1957
Evangelical Lutheran Church in America (ELCA) 4/20/1987
Evangelical Society 1857 Moody
Evangelical United Brethren 4/23/1968
Evangelium Vitae 3/26/1995
evolution 11/24/1858, 7/9/1896, 7/10/1925, 6/9/1987
ExScientologyKids.com 3/3/2008

Fairfax, Virginia 6/27/2008 Episcopal
Faith Is the Answer: A Psychiatrist and a Pastor Discuss Your Problems 1952
Falwell, Jerry 6/19/1956, 1967, 1/13/1974, June 1979
Family Channel 10/1/1987
FBI 4/19/1993
Federal Council of Churches 1908, 1931 Federal Council of Churches
Fifth Circuit 6/1/1993, 6/7/1993 Prayer in Schools
Finney, Charles G. 1835 Finney, 1876
First African Methodist Episcopal (FAME) 1821, 3/21/2008
First Amendment to the Constitution 1692 Salem, 1790 George Washington, 12/15/1791, 1818 Connecticut, 1834, 1836, 4/22/1864, 7/28/1868, 6/26/1870, 1885 Strong, 4/24/1898, 5/13/1925, November 1936, 1940, 3/8/1948, 6/19/1956, 1962, 6/28/1971, 11/18/1978, 6/25/1982, 6/4/1985, 1/9/1989, 6/1/1993, 6/18/1993, 3/31/1995, 3/5/1997, 6/23/1997, 2/7/1999, 11/18/2002, 7/2/2007, 6/25/2008

Index

Fisher, Mary July 1656
Flaget, Bendick Joseph 1811
Florida 1815, 5/13/1925, January 1987 11/4/1992
Ford, Henry 1913
Fort Orange 1629
40Plus 1952
Fosdick, Harry Emerson 5/21/1922
Fourteenth Amendment to the Constitution 7/28/1868, 6/4/1923
Fox, George 1651
Fox, Kate 3/31/1848
Fox, Margaret 3/31/1848
Fox sisters 1876
France 1685, 1718 Scotch-Irish, August 1727, 1764 St. Louis, 1790 George Washington, 1815, 1845
Franciscan Friars 1610
Frankel, Rabbi Jacob 9/10/1862
Franklin, Benjamin November 1789
Free African Society April 1787, July 1794
Freeman, James 1785 King's Chapel
Freeman, Joseph, Jr. 6/8/1978
Freemasons 10/2/1881
French-Indian War 1742 Muhlenberg, 1750
Fulton Sheen Program 1951

Gallagher, Michael November 1936
Garden, Alexander 1740 George Whitfield
Garden Grove, California 9/14/1980
Garden Grove Community Church 9/14/1980
The Garden of the Soul 1740 The Garden of the Soul
Gaustad, Edwin 12/31/1894
Gauthe, Gilbert 1985
Gay, Ebenezer 1759 Ebenezer Gay
"Gay Days" June 1996
General Assembly 6/27/2008 Presbyterians
General Assembly of the Christian Church (Disciples of Christ) 2005 Disciples of Christ
General Conference (United Methodist Church) May 1988
General Conference of the United Methodist Church April 1996
Geneva, Switzerland 1706
Geoghan, John 1/9/2002, 9/19/2002

Georgetown November 1789
Georgia 1740 George Whitfield, 2/7/1999
German Palatine 1709
Germantown June 1683
Germany 1643, June 1683, 1709, 1742 Muhlenberg, 1829, 1834, 1850, 1886 Abbelen 1902, 6/4/1923, November 1936
Gibbons, James Cardinal 1887
Gladden, Washington 1886 Gladden, 1900
Glorious Revolution of 1688 12/16/1653, 2/13/1689
Goebbels, Joseph November 1936
Good News Mission Church 6/9/2008
Gorman, Martin 4/8/1988
Graham, Reverend Billy 9/30/1951, 8/16/2008
Grammond, Reverend Maurice 7/7/2004
Grant, Ulysses S. 6/26/1870
Great Awakening July 1741, 1835 Finney, 1858 Revivalism, May 1880
Great Basin, Utah 2/4/1846
Great Disappointment 3/21/1843, 10/22/1844, 5/23/1863, 1876, 4/19/1993
Great Lakes 1811
Great March West 2/4/1846
Great Salt Lake 2/4/1846
Greater Houston Ministerial Association 9/12/1960
Greece 1885 Strong
Greenwich, Connecticut 12/29/1851
Griffin, Michael 3/10/1993
Ground Zero 4/15/2008
Guam 4/24/1898
Guideposts 1952
Gulf of Mexico 1764 St. Louis
Gunn, Dr. David 3/10/1993
Guyana, South America 11/18/1978

Hale-Bopp 3/23/1997
Hallelujah Army 1/19/1889
Harvard October 1635, May 1664, 1693, 1759 Ebenezer Gay, 1813, 3/4/2008
Harvard Crimson newspaper 3/4/2008
Harvard Divinity School 1838
Haun's Mill December 1840
Hawaii 4/24/1898
Hayes, President Rutherford B. 3/22/1882
Haymarket Riots 1886 Huntington

214

Index

Heaven's Gate 3/23/1997
Hebrew 1885 Strong
Hebrew Union College 10/3/1875
Henrietta Marie, Queen 3/25/1634
Henry, Patrick 1785 Madison
The Herald of the Morning 1872
Herrick, Governor Myron T. 1895 Russell
Herzl, Theodor 1896 Herzl, 5/14/1948
Hialeah, Florida 11/4/1992
Hill, Reverend Paul 3/10/1993
Hinckley, Gordon B. 1/27/2008
Hindu 1893 World Parliament, 2/25/2008, 3/4/2008
Hingham Association 1759 Ebenezer Gay
Hispanic immigrants 2/25/2008
Hitler, Adolf 1875 Blavatsky, November 1936
Holiness movement 1/1/1901
Holland August 1619, 1620, 1629, 1643, 1647, 1742 Muhlenberg
Holmes, John Hayes 1915
Holtzman, Linda Joy 8/1/1979
Holy Spirit 1/1/1901, April 1914
Hoover, President Herbert 1928
Hospitality Houses 1933
Hot Springs, Arkansas April 1914
Houdini, Harry 3/31/1848
Hour of Decision 9/30/1951
Hour of Power 9/14/1980
House of Representatives, United States 3/5/1997, 9/5/2008
House Un-American Activities Committee (HUAC) 7/21/1953
Houston, Texas 4/14/1906, 12/7/2007
How the Other Half Lives 1890
Howell, Vernon Wayne 4/19/1993
Hubbard, L. Ron 1954, 3/3/2008
Huguenots April 1670, 1685
Hull House 1889
Hungary 1896 Herzl
Huntington, Bishop Frederick D. 1886 Huntington
Hutchins, Julia 4/14/1906
Hutchinson, Anne March 1638
Hydesville, New York 3/3/1848, 1876

Illinois 2/4/1846, November 1960
Imani Temple 7/2/1989
"In God We Trust" 4/22/1864

In His Steps 1897 Sheldon
Independence, Missouri 3/26/1830
Independent Order of Good Templars 2/13/1826
India 1875 Blavatsky
Indianapolis, Indiana 11/18/1978
Individuals with Disabilities Education Act (IDEA) 6/18/993
International Bankers November 1936
International Church of the Foursquare Gospel 1/1/1923, 1927
Ireland 12/16/1653, 2/13/1689, 1706, 1718 Scotch-Irish, 1773, 1834, 1850, 10/2/1881, 1886 Abbelen
Ireland, Archbishop John 4/24/1898
Irish-American 10/2/1881
Islam 1893 World Parliament
Island Tree Union Free School District 6/25/1982
Israel 1896 Herzl, 5/14/1948
Istook, Ernest November 1995
Italy 1885 Strong, 1886 Abbelen

James, Governor Fob 3/5/1997
James, Henry, Sr. 3/29/1772
James, William 1893 World Parliament
James I, King May 1607, December 1620
James II, King 2/13/1689
Jamestown May 1607, August 1619, 1622
Japan 4/24/1898
Jefferson, Thomas August 1727, 1776, 1777, 1/1/1786, March 1789, 1815, 1818 Connecticut
Jefferson Park Presbyterian Church 2/17/1889
Jehovah's Witness 1872, 1931 Witnesses, 2/25/2008, 6/9/2008
Jesuit 1815
Jewish 1647, 1654, 1763, 1782, 1790 George Washington, 9/10/1862, 10/3/1875, 1893 World Parliament, 12/31/1894, 1896 Herzl, 1897 Solomon, 1902, 1910, 1912, 1913, November 1936, 9/30/1951, 8/1/1979, 6/25/2008
Jewish Community Centers (JCC) 1854
The Jewish State 1896 Herzl
Jewish Theological Seminary 1902, 1912
Jewish Welfare Board 1854
John Paul II, Pope 1951, 10/16/1978, 3/26/1995, 11/13/2002 Bishops, 4/15/2008

215

Index

John Street Methodist Church 1821
Johnny Appleseed 3/29/1772
Jones, Absalom April 1787, July 1794
Jones, Jim 11/18/1978
Jones v. Clear Creek Independent School District 6/7/1993 Prayer in Schools
Jonestown 11/18/1978

Kansas 7/13/1857
katydid 6/9/1848
Keller, Helen 3/29/1772
Kellogg, W.K. 5/23/1863
Kennedy, President John F. 1834, 1928, 9/12/1960, November 1960, 12/7/2007
Kentucky 1793, 1811, 2/7/1999
Kern County, California 1996
Key to the Scriptures 1879
King, J.H. 1/1/1901
Kingdom of God 3/21/1843
King's Chapel 1785 King's Chapel
King's College 1754 King's College
Kirkland, Ohio 3/27/1836
Knights of Columbus 10/2/1881
Knights of Labor 1887
Knox, John 1706
Koran 11/26/1956
Koresh, David 4/19/1993
Kos, Rudolph 7/13/1998
KSFG (radio station) 1/1/1923
Ku Klux Klan 9/15/1923, 7/21/1953

Lake Erie 1876
Lake Forest, California 8/6/2008
Lamb's Chapel 6/7/1993 Free Speech
Las Vegas, Nevada 8/29/1852
Lathrobe, Benjamin 1784 Catholics
Latter-Day Saints 10/6/1890
Law, Cardinal Bernard 1/9/2002, 12/3/2002
Lee, Ann August 1774
Lee, John Doyle 7/13/1857, 3/23/1877
Leland, John 1776, 1790 Leland
Lemke, William November 1936
Lemon v. Kuraman 6/28/1971
Leo XIII, Pope 9/4/1893, January 1899, 1931 Federal Council of Churches
Lester, Emile 6/25/2008
Lexington, Kentucky 8/6/1801
Lexington, Mississippi 1897 Church of God

Liberty Baptist University 1967
licensed exhorter April 1787
Life Is Worth Living 1951
Lincoln, President Abraham 3/31/1848, 1862, 1/1/1863, 1865
Lincoln, Mary Todd 3/31/1848
Lincoln, Nebraska 4/15/1996
Lippman, Walter 1929
Lipscomb, Archbishop Oscar 3/16/2003
Little Rascals 1996
Livingston, William 1754 King's College, 1768
Logan County, Kentucky May 1800
London, England 1846, 1/19/1889
Long Island, New York 5/4/2008
Lord's Prayer 2/7/1999
Los Angeles, California 4/14/1906, April 1914, 1/1/1923, 1927, 9/30/1951, 7/31/2006, 3/21/2008
Los Angeles Times newspaper 3/3/2008, 6/9/2008
Louisiana 1815, 4/28/1930, 3/27/1962, 1985, 6/1/1993, 6/7/1993 Prayer in Schools
Louisiana Purchase 1815, August 1727
Louisville, Kentucky 5/1/1845, August 1994
Love, E.K. 1896 Love
Lovejoy, Elijah P. 11/7/1837
Low Hampton, New York 1876
Luther, Martin 1643
Lutheran 1629, 1643, 1709, 1742 Muhlenberg, 1852, 12/31/1894, 6/4/1923, 4/20/1987
Lutheran Church-Missouri Synod 4/26/1847
Lynchberg Christian Academy 1967
Lynchburg, Virginia 6/19/1956
Lynn, Massachusetts 1879

Madison, President James 1774, 1776, 1777, 1785 Madison, 1/1/1786, March 1789
Madison Avenue Hall 1875 Moody
Madison Square Garden 7/16/1982
Mahoney, Cardinal Roger 7/31/2006, December 2006, July 2007
Maine October 1649
Makemie, Reverend Francis 1706, 1707 New York
Manhattan 1629

Index

Marble Collegiate Church, Manhattan 1952
Marechal, Ambrose 829
Marshall, Molly August 1994
Mary II, Queen 2/13/1689
Maryland April 1649, 1692 Maryland, February 1732, 1750, 1773, 1784 Catholics, November 1789, 5/27/1924, 11/26/1956, 6/17/1963
Massachusetts 1619, December 1620, May 1631, October 1635, 1639, September 1646, May 1675, May 1682, 1754 Baptists, 1759 Ebenezer Gay, July 1775, 1776, 12/15/1791, 1818 Connecticut, 1833, 10/2/1881, 1961, January 1697, 12/7/2007
Massachusetts Bay 1609, December 1620, 1630
Massachusetts Bay Colony October 1635, March 1638
Mather, Cotton May 1664, 1692 Salem, April 1693
Mather, Increase May 1664, 1692 Salem, April 1693
Maurin, Peter 1933
Mayflower December 1620
Mayhew, John 1748, 1753
McCain, John 8/16/2008
McCarthy, Senator Joseph 7/21/1953
McGivney, Father Michael J. 10/2/1881
McGuffey Readers 12/15/1791, 1836
McKinley, President William 7/9/1896, 4/24/1898
McMartin Preschool 1996
McPherson, Aimee Semple 1/1/1923, 1927
Mecham, Joseph August 1774
Medicine Lodge, Kansas 12/27/1899
Meet the Press 9/5/2008
"Memorial and Remonstrance" 1785 Madison, 1/1/1786
Mennonites June 1683, 5/15/1972
metaphysical 1875 Blavatsky
Methodist August 1619, May 1623, 12/16/1653, 1772, 1773, April 1787, 1784 Methodists, 12/15/1791, July 1794, May 1800, 8/6/1801, 5/1/1845, 1857, 1/19/1889, 12/31/1894, 1895 Nazarene, 1/1/1901, 5/10/1939, 1952, 7/21/1953, 4/23/1968, 11/18/1978, July 1994
Methodist Episcopal Church 1773, 1784

Methodists, 5/1/1845, 1895 Nazarene, 1/1/1901, 5/27/1924, 5/10/1939
Methodist Episcopal Church, South 5/1/1845, 1870, 5/10/1939
Meurin, Sebastian 1764 St. Louis
Mexico 7/16/1769
Michigan Daily newspaper 7/2/2007
Millennialism 3/21/1843
Miller, William 3/21/1843, 10/22/1844, 5/23/1863, 1876
Millerism 1876
Millerites 1876
mind-cure institute 1875 Blavatsky
Minneapolis, Minnesota 8/5/2003
Mississippi 1764 St. Louis, 1817, 1847 Theological Society, 1/9/1989, 6/1/1993, 6/7/1993 Prayer in Schools
Mississippi River 1764 St. Louis, 1811, 11/7/1837
Missouri December 1840
Mitchell, Robert 3/4/2008
Mobile, Alabama 3/16/2003
Modesto, California 6/25/2008
Monk, Maria 1834
Montgomery, Alabama 11/18/2002, 3/16/2003
Moody, Dwight L. 1875 Moody, 3/21/1900
Moody and Sankey Hymnbook 1875 Moody
Moody Bible Institute 3/21/1900
Moon, Hyung Jin 7/6/1982
Moon, Reverend Sun Myung 7/16/1982, 6/9/2008
Moore, Judge Roy 3/31/1995, 3/5/1997, 11/18/2002, 8/20/2003
Moral Majority 1967, June 1979
Mormon Spring 1820, 3/26/1830, 3/27/1836, December 1840, 7/12/1843, 6/27/1844, 2/4/1846, 6/9/1848, 8/29/1852, 7/13/1857, 1862, 10/2/1871, 1876, 1885 Strong, 1885 Taylor, March 1887, 10/6/1890, 12/31/1894, October 1910, 6/8/1978, 12/7/2007, 1/27/2008, 2/25/2008, 6/23/2008
Mormon War 6/26/1858, 1862
Mormonism Unveiled 3/23/1877
Moroni 1876
Morrill Anti-Bigamy Act 1862, 3/22/1882
Morse, F.B. 1834
Mother Ann 1840 Shakers

217

Index

Mott, Lucretia 1853
Mount Hermon (school for boys) 1857 Moody
Mountain Meadows Massacre 7/13/1857, 3/23/1877
Muhlenberg, Henry 1742 Muhlenberg
Murray, William 1/24/1980
Muslim 7/2/2007, 3/4/2008, 6/25/2008
Mussolini, Benito November 1936
"The Mystery Hid from Ages and Generations" 1784 Chauncy

Nation, Carrie 12/27/1899
National Association of Broadcasters (NAB) November 1936
National Baptist Convention 1896 Love
National Catholic Church July 2007
National Catholic War Council 1917
National Catholic Welfare Conference 1917, 1931 Federal Council of Churches
National Conference of Catholic Charities 1910
National Council of Catholic Bishops 2/13/1973
National Council of Churches 1952, 7/21/1953
National Council of Jewish Women 1897 Solomon
National Lutheran Conference 10/8/1924
National Prohibition Party 2/13/1826
National Shrine of the Little Flower Church November 1936
Native American (Indian) May 1607, 1610, 1614, 1622, 1629, October 1635, June 1683, 1693, 1718 William Penn, 1718 Scotch-Irish, 1764 St. Louis, 7/16/1769, 1815, 1840 Pierre DeSmet,
Nauvoo, Illinois December 1840, 2/4/1846, 9/9/1850
Nazi November 1936
Nebraska 6/4/1923
Nerinckx, Charles April 1812
New Amsterdam 1629, 1647, 1654
New England 1630, October 1635, September 1646, 6/1/1660, May 1675, 1692 Salem, 1740 George Whitfield, 1763 Brown University, 1784 Chauncy, 1832, 1847 Theological Society, 4/24/1898, 7/19/1825
New Hampshire 1840 Shakers, August 1987, 2/7/1999, 8/5/2003

New Jersey 1707 New York, 1726
New Lights July 1741
New Netherlands 1629
New Orleans, Louisiana August 1727, 1764 St. Louis, 3/27/1962
New Sweden 1643
New Thought 1875 Blavatsky
New York 1629, 1654, 1685, 1707 New York, 1773, 1793, May 1800, 3/27/1836, 1876, 10/2/1881, 1915, 10/8/1924, January 1990, 6/7/1993 Free Speech
New York City 1629, 1654, April 1730, 1754 King's College, 1821, 1854, 1875 Moody, 1876, 1890, 1902, 1912, 5/21/1922, 1926 Klan, 6/10/1935, 1952, 7/16/1982
Newport, Captain Christopher May 1607
Newport, Rhode Island 1639, 1790 George Washington
Newport Beach, California January 1987
Newport News, Virginia May 1607
Niederauer, Archbishop George 9/5/2008
NINA (No Irish Need Apply) 1834
Nineteenth Amendment to the Constitution 6/4/1/1919
Nixon, President Richard M. November 1960
North American Baptist Convention 2005 Southern Baptists
North Carolina 1740 George Whitfield, 1754 Baptists
Northampton, Massachusetts June 1750
Northfield, Massachusetts 1875 Moody
Norton, Andrews 1813, 1833
Noyes, John 1847 Oneida

Oakland, California 12/3/2004
Obama, Barack 8/16/2008
Oberlin College 1835 Finney, 1853
O'Connor, Cardinal John 4/9/1992
O'Hair, Madalyn Murray 12/8/1960, 1/24/1980
Ohio 1709, 1895 Russell
Oklahoma November 1995
Old Lights July 1741
Omaha, Nebraska 2/4/1846
Oneida, New York 1847 Oneida
Oneida Community 1847 Oneida, 1876
Oral Roberts Evangelistic Association January 1987

218

Index

Oral Roberts University 9/4/1973, January 1987
Orange (Holland) 2/13/1689
Orange, California 9/14/1980
Orange County, California 12/3/2004, 7/31/2006
Oregon 6/1/1925
The Origin of Species by Means of Natural Selection 11/24/1858
Our Country: Its Possible Future and Its Present Crisis 1885 Strong
Oxford Group 6/10/1935
Oxnam, Bishop G. Bromley 7/21/1953

Palmyra, New York Spring 1820, 1876
Parham, Charles F. 1/1/1901, 4/14/1906
Park, Pastor Ock So 6/9/2008
Parris, Abigail 1692 Salem
Parris, Betty 1692 Salem
Parris, Samuel 1692 Salem
Parthenon (Rome) 1784 Catholics
Paul VI, Pope 11/18/1966, 11/10/1977, 4/15/2008
Payne, Daniel 1852
PBS (Public Broadcasting Service) Network 1996
Peale, Dr. Norman Vincent 1952
Peck, John Mason 1817
Pelosi, Nancy 9/5/2008
Penn, William 1622, October 1635, May 1681, June 1683, May 1700, 1718 William Penn
Pennsylvania 1643, 1651, June 1683, 1685, May 1700, 1707 Philadelphia Baptists, 1709, 1718 William Penn, 1718 Scotch-Irish, 1726, February 1732, 1744, 1750, 1763 Brown University, 1782, 1784 Catholics, 4/26/1847, 11/26/1956, 12/8/1960, 6/17/1963, 6/28/1971
Pensacola, Florida 3/10/1993
Pentecostal 12/31/1894, 1895 Nazarene, 1897 Church of God, 1/1/1901, 4/14/1906, April 1914, 1/1/1923, 1927, 5/10/1939, 9/4/1973, 9/6/1976, 4/8/1988
Pentecostal/Charismatic Churches of North America 1927
Pentecostal Fellowship of North America 1927
People's Temple 11/18/1978
Pew Forum on Religion and Public Life in the United States 2/25/2008, 6/23/2008
Philadelphia, Pennsylvania May 1681, 1706, 1707 Philadelphia Baptists, February 1732, 1742 Muhlenberg, 1750, 1772, 1782, 1793, 1794, April 1787, May 1800
Philadelphia Association 1707 Philadelphia Baptist
Philippines 4/24/1898
Phipps, Sir William 1692 Salem
Pilgrim December 1620, 1630
Pilgrim's Progress September 1675
Pius X, Pope 6/29/1908
Pius XI, Pope 1931 Federal Council of Churches
Pledge of Allegiance 10/2/1881, 6/1/1993
Plenary Council of American Bishops 11/10/1977
Plymouth, England December 1620
Plymouth, Massachusetts 1629, 1639
Plymouth Rock December 1620
Pocahontas 1614, 1622
Poland 1829, 1886 Abbelen, November 1936, 5/17/1954, 10/16/1978
polygamy 8/29/1852, 1862, 10/2/1871, 3/23/1877, 3/22/1882, 1885 Strong, 10/6/1890, October 1910, 1/27/2008
Pope 1836, 1885 Strong
Porters 1692 Salem
Portland, Oregon 7/7/2004, 2005 Disciples of Christ
Portugal 1886 Abbelen
Post Office, United States November 1936
The Power of Positive Thinking 1952
Powers, Reverend Jeanne Audrey July 1994
Praise the Lord (PTL) Club 1/13/1974
A Preface to Morals 1929
Presbyterian 1629, 12/16/1653, 1706, 1718 Scotch-Irish, 1726, 1740 George Whitfield, 1744, 1746, 1754 King's College, 1768, 1772, 1776, 12/15/1791, May 1800, 8/6/1801, 1818 Presbyterians, 1/1/1832, 15/1/1845, 1/7/1837, 1852, 12/31/1894, 1915, 5/21/1922, 5/10/1939
Presbyterian Church (USA) 6/10/1983, 6/27/2008 Presbyterian
Presbyterian Church, Southern (PCUS) 6/10/1983

219

Index

Priestly, Joseph 1794
Princeton University 1726, 1746
Prohibition May 1623, 2/13/1826, August 1874, 2/17/1889, 12/27/1899, 12/18/1917
Protestant April 1670, 1685, 2/13/1826, 1836, 5/12/1845, 1857, August 1874, 1885 Strong, 1887, 12/31/1894, 1896 Love, 7/9/1896, 4/24/1898, 4/14/1906, 1908, 1910, 5/21/1922, 1926 Klan, 5/10/1939, 6/3/1959, 9/12/1960, 12/8/1960, 3/9/1965, 4/23/1968, June 1979, 10/1/1987, May 1988, 2005 Southern Baptists, 2/25/2008, 6/25/2008, 6/27/2008
Protestant Episcopal 7/17/1836
Protestant Episcopal Church 1785 Madison
Providence, Rhode Island October 1635, 1639, 1763 Brown University
PTL (Praise the Lord) Club June 1979
Puerto Rico 4/24/1898
Puritan 1609, December 1620, 1630, May 1631, October 1635, 1639, 12/16/1653, July 1656, May 1675, September 1675, 1692 Salem, 1701, 1748, 1 June 1750, 1770
The Purpose Driven Life 8/16/2008
Putnam 1692 Salem
Putney, Vermont 1847 Oneida

"Quadragesimo Anno" 1931 Federal Council of Churches
Quaker 1629, 1647, 165112/16/1653, July 1656, 6/1/1660, May 1681, May 1682, May 1700, 1718 William Penn, 1742 Muhlenberg, 1772, August 1774, April 1787, September 1787, 1790 George Washington, July 1794, 1853, 1889,
Queen's College 1765
Quimby, Phineas P. 1879
Quincy, Illinois December 1840

Randolph, Ann Page 1825 Ann Randolph
Rauschenbusch, Walter 1907
Reader's Digest 1954
Reagan, President Ronald June 1979
Reed, Reverend James J. 3/9/1965
Reform Judaism June 1994
Reformed Church 1952, 9/14/1980
Regents of New York State 1962, 6/17/1963

Restoration Movement 1/1/1832
Revolutionary War 3/25/1634, 1685, 1730, 1742 Muhlenberg, 1754 King's College, 1774, 1776, 1784 Catholics, 1784 Methodists, April 1787, 1790 Leland, 1822, 1833, 1834, 7/17/1836, 1840 Shakers, 4/26/1847
Rhineland 1709
Rhode Island 1609, October 1635, 1643, 1651, 1704, 1763, 6/28/1971
Riis, Jacob 1890
Riverside Church 5/21/1922
Roberts, Oral 9/4/1973, January 1987
Roberts, Patrick S. 6/25/2008
Roberts, Richard January 1987
Robertson, Pat 10/1/1961, 10/1/1987
Robinson, Gene 8/5/2003
Rochester, New York 1907
Rockefeller, John D. 5/21/1922
Rockville Centre Catholic Diocese 5/4/2008
Rolfe, John 1614, 1622
Rome, Italy 1772, 1784 Catholics, November 1789, 1885 Strong, 1887, January 1899, November 1936, 9/12/1960, 7/2/1989, 1/9/2002, 11/13/2002 Bishops
Romney, Mitt 12/7/2007
Roosevelt, President Franklin 1931 Federal Council of Churches, November 1936
"Root Races" 1875 Blavatsky
Royal Oak, Michigan November 1936
Rummel, Archbishop Joseph F. 3/27/1962
Russell, Charles Taze 1872, 1931 Witnesses
Russell, Howard H. 1895 Russell
Russia 1875 Blavatsky, 1902, 1951
Rutgers 1765
Rutherford, Joseph F. 1931 Witnesses
Rwanda 8/16/2008
Ryan, Monsignor John A. 1917
Ryan, Congressman Leo 11/18/1978

Sacramento, California 12/3/2004
Saddleback Church 8/16/2008
St. Augustine, Florida 1674
St. Clements Island, Maryland 3/25/1634
St. George's Methodist Church April 1787, July 1794
St. Joseph's (Philadelphia) February 1732

Index

St. Joseph's Academy 1805
St. Louis, Missouri 1764 St. Louis, 1815, 1817, 1840 Pierre DeSmet, May 1988
St. Thomas Seminary April 1812
St. Thomas's African Episcopal Church July 1794
Salem, Massachusetts 1630, 6/1/1660, May 1664, 1692 Salem, 1996
Salem Witch Trials 1692 Salem, April 1693, January 1697
Salt Lake City, Utah 6/9/1848, 8/29/1852, 6/26/1858, 10/2/1871, October 1910, 1/27/2008
Salt Lake Tribune 10/6/1890, October 1910
Salvation Army 1/19/1889, 1904, 1/9/1989
San Carlos Mission 7/16/1769
San Diego, California 7/16/1769, 7/31/2006, December 2006, July 2007
San Diego Union Tribune newspaper 7/31/2006
San Francisco, California 11/18/1978, 9/5/2008
San Francisco Bay Area January 1996
San Jose, California 6/27/2008 Presbyterians
San Miguel Chapel 1610
Sankey, Ira D. 1875 Moody
Santa Fe, New Mexico 1610
Santa Fe Independent School District v. Jane Doe 6/19/2000
Satolli, Archbishop Francesco 9/4/1893
Savannah, Georgia 1740 George Whitfield
Scandinavia 1643
Schaff, Philip 1893 World Parliament
Schechter, Rabbi Solomon 1902
Schempp, Ellery 11/26/1956
Scherlock, Reverend J. Alexander 3/16/2003
Schuller, Robert A. 9/14/1980
Schuller, Dr. Robert H. 9/14/1980
Science and Health 1879
Scientific American magazine 3/31/1848
Scientology 1954, 3/3/2008
Scientology: A History of Man 1954
Scopes, John 7/10/1925
"Scopes Monkey Trial" 7/9/1896, 7/10/1925
Scotch-Irish 1706, 1718 Scotch-Irish, 1746

Scotland 12/16/1653, 2/13/1689, 1706, 1746
Scriptural Baptist Convention 2005 Southern Baptists
seagulls 6/9/1848
Sebert Commission 3/31/1848
Second Great Awakening May 1880
The Secular City 1965
Security and Exchange Commission (SEC) 1967
Selma, Alabama 3/9/1965
Seneca Falls, New York 1876
Seneca Falls Convention 1876
Seoul, Korea 7/16/1982
separate but equal 5/17/1954
September 11, 2001 terrorist attack 4/15/2008
Serra, Junipero 7/16/1769
Seton, Elizabeth Baley 1805
Seton, William 1805
Settlement House 1889
700 Club 10/1/1987
"Seven Sermons" 1748
Seventh-Day Adventist 3/21/1843, 5/23/1863, 1876, 4/19/1993, October 2007
Seventh-Day Adventist Church 5/23/1863
Seymour, William J. 4/14/1906
Shakers August 1774, 1840 Shakers, 3/21/1843, 1876
"Shall the Fundamentalists Win?" 5/21/1922
Shearith Israel April 1730
Sheen, Bishop Fulton J. 1951
Sheldon, Charles M. 1897 Sheldon
Shield of Faith 6/9/2008
Shinto 4/24/1898
Shirley, Lieutenant Eliza 1/19/1889
Shoemaker, Reverend Dr. Sam 6/10/1935
Sikh 6/25/2008
Simpson, A.B. 1/1/1901
Sinatra, Frank 1951
"Sinners in the Hands of an Angry God" July 1741
Sioux 1840 Pierre DeSmet
Sisters of Charity 1805, 1910
Sisters of Charity of Nazareth April 1812
Sisters of Loretto April 1812
Sisters of Mercy 1910

Index

Sisters of St. Joseph 1910
Sisters of the Holy Names of Jesus and Mary 6/1/1925
Skelton, Samuel 1630
Skylstad, Bishop William 11/15/2004
slave trade 1772
slavery August 1619, April 1670, May 1700, 1730, 1744, April 1787, 1790 Leland, July 1794, 1818 Presbyterians, 1825 Ann Randolph, 1835 Channing, 11/7/1837, 1840 Shakers, 5/1/1845, 5/12/1845, 1846, 1852, 1857, 1858 Revivalism, 1/1/1863, 7/28/1868, 2005 Southern Baptists
Smith, Alfred E. 1928
Smith, Dr. Bob 6/1/10/1935
Smith, Emma 6/27/1844
Smith, Hyrum 6/27/1844
Smith, John "Raccoon" 1/1/1832
Smith, Joseph 9/21/1823, 3/26/1830, December 1840, 7/12/1843, 6/27/1844, 2/4/1846, 1876, 3/23/1877
Smith, Joseph, Jr. Spring 1820
Smyth, John 1609
Social Justice November 1936
"Society for Promoting Christian Knowledge" 1699
Society for the Promotion of Collegiate and Theological Education 1847 Theological Society
Society for the Propagation of the Gospel 1699, 1707 New York
Society of Friends 1651, May 1681
Society of St. Vincent de Paul 1845
Solomon, Hannah 1897 Solomon
Sons of Temperance 2/13/1826
South America October 2007
South Bend, Indiana 1992
South Carolina December 1712, 1740 George Whitfield
Southern Baptist Convention (SBC) 5/12/1845, 6/4/1984, June 1996, 2005 Southern Baptists
Southern Baptist Theological Seminary August 1994
Southern Presbyterian Church (PCUS) 4/28/1960
Soviet Union 3/9/1965
Spain May 1607, 1610, 1674, 7/16/1769, November 1789, 1815, 1885 Strong, 4/24/1898

Spaulding, Bishop John Lancaster 4/24/1898
Special Olympics 10/2/1881
spiritualism 3/31/1848, 1875 Blavatsky, 1876
Springfield, Massachusetts 12/29/1851
Springfield, Missouri 6/19/1956, 9/4/1973
Stalin, Joseph 1951
Stallings, Reverend George A. 7/2/1989
Stamp Act 1768
Stanton, Elizabeth Cady 1876, 1895 Stanton
Statuary Hall August 1874
Statute for Religious Freedom 1/1/1786
Sterns, Shubal 1754 Baptists
Stone, Barton 8/6/1801, 1/1/1832
Stoughton, William 1692 Salem
Stowe, Harriet Beecher 1858 Revivalism
Strawbridge, Robert 1773
Strong, Josiah 1885 Strong
Stuyvesant, Peter 1629, 1643, 1647,
Sunday, Billy 2/17/1889, 9/30/1951
Sunday Law December 1712
Superior of Missions 1784 Catholics
Supreme Court, Alabama 3/31/1995, 3/5/1997, 8/20/2003
Supreme Court, Arkansas 11/12/1968
Supreme Court, Tennessee 7/10/1925
Supreme Court, United States 1770, 12/15/1791, 1819 Channing, 1/18/1844, 3/22/1882, March 1887, 10/6/1890, 6/4/1923, 5/13/1925, 6/1/1925, 7/10/1925, 4/28/1930, 1940, 3/8/1948, 5/17/1954, 12/8/1960, 1962, 3/27/1962, 5/21/1963, 6/17/1963, 11/12/1968, 5/15/1972, 6/25/1982, 6/4/1985, 6/9/1987, 6/24/1992, 6/1/1993, 6/7/1993 Prayer in Schools, 6/7/1993 Free Speech, 6/18/1993, 3/5/1997, 6/23/1997, 6/19/2000, 11/18/2002, 7/31/2006, February 2004
"Survivors First" 11/13/2002 Activists
Swaggart, Donnie 4/8/1988
Swaggart, Frances 4/8/1988
Swaggart, Jimmy 4/8/1988
Sweden 3/29/1772
Swedenborg, Emmanuel 3/29/1772
synagogue 1654, April 1730, 1763, 6/4/1919, June 1994
Szold, Henrietta 1912

Index

Taylor, John 3/23/1877, 1885 Taylor, March 1887
telegraph 1834
Templars of Honor and Temperance 2/13/1826
Temple Emmanu-El 1926 Klan
Ten Commandments 3/31/1995, 3/5/1997, 2/7/1999, 11/18/2002, 8/20/2003
tenements 1890
Tennant, William 1726
Tennessee 7/10/1925
testem benevolentiae January 1899
Texas November 1960, 6/1/1993, 6/7/1993 Prayer in Schools
Theosophical Society 1875 Blavatsky
third "Great Awakening" 1858 Revivalism
Thomas Road Baptist Church 6/19/1956
Thompson, Judge Myron 11/18/2002
Time magazine 1951, 7/21/1953
Toomy, Alice T. 1893 Toomy
Topeka, Kansas 1897 Sheldon, 1/1/1901, 4/14/1906
Touro Synagogue 1763
Transcendentalism 7/19/1825, 1838
Truman, President Harry S 5/14/1948, 9/30/1951
Tuel, Bishop Jack May 1988
Tulsa, Oklahoma 9/4/1973
"Twelve Steps" 6/10/1935
typhoid fever 3/31/1848

Ukiah, California 11/18/1978
Uncle Tom's Cabin 1858 Revivalism
Unification Church 7/16/1982
Union of American Hebrew Congregations 10/3/1875, June 1944
Union of Soviet Socialist Republics (USSR) 5/14/1948
Union Party November 1936
Unitarian 1742 Chauncy, 1748, 1753, 1759 Ebenezer Gay, 1785 King's Chapel, 1794, 1813, 1833, 1835 Channing, 1838, 1915, 3/9/1965
Unitarian Christian Fellowship (UCF) 1961
Unitarian Christianity 1819 Channing
Unitarian Church 6/3/1959
Unitarian-Universalist Association 1961
Unitarian-Universalist Christian Fellowship 1961

United Church of Christ 6/25/1957
United Methodist Church August 1987, May 1988
United Nations 7/16/1982
United Presbyterian Church (UPCUSA) 5/21/1963, 6/10/1983
United Society of Believers in Christ's Second Appearing August 1774
United Society of Believers in Christ's Second Coming 3/21/1843
United States Army 6/26/1858, 9/10/1862
United States Catholic Miscellany 1822
United States Religious Landscape Survey 2/25/2008
Universalist Church 6/3/1959
Universalist Church of America (UCA) 1961
University of Michigan 7/2/2007
University of Pennsylvania 3/31/1848
University of Southern California 1895 Nazarene
University of Wisconsin, Madison 7/2/2007
Ursaline August 1727
USO 1/19/1889
Utah 2/4/1846, 6/9/1848, 9/9/1850, 7/13/1857, 6/26/1858, 1862, 10/6/1890

Van Buren, Martin 6/27/1844
Vatican 1886 Abbelen, 1887, November 1936, March 1986, 7/2/1989, 3/26/1995, 1/9/2002, 11/13/2002 Activists, 8/20/2003, 4/15/2008
Vicar Apostolic of London 1784 Catholics
Vietnam 3/9/1965
Virgin Queen May 1607
Virginia May 1607, 1619, August 1619, 1622, May 1623, 1629, 1649, 1662, 1692 Maryland, 1693, 1744, 1754 Baptists, 1759 Anglicans, 1774, July 1775, 1776, 1777, 1785 Madison, 1790 Leland, 1825 Ann Randolph, 1/1/1786

Waco, Texas 4/19/1993
Wales 1/1/1901
Walton, John 9/15/1923
War of 1898 4/24/1898
Ware, Henry 1813
Warner, D.S. 1/1/1901
Warren, Rick 8/6/2008

Index

Washington February 2004
Washington, D.C. August 1874, March 1986, 7/2/1989, 11/13/2002 Bishops
Washington, George July 1775, 1790 George Washington, 11/10/1791
Washington Times newspaper 7/6/1982
The Watchtower Announcing Jehovah's Kingdom 1931 Witnesses, 1872
"Water Wagon" 2/17/1889
Watkins, Sharon 2005 Disciples of Christ
Wesley, John 1773, 1784 Methodists, 1895 Nazarene, 1/1/1901
West India Company 1629
West Indies April 1670
West Indies Company 1647
"What Would Jesus Do?" 1897 Sheldon
Wheeler, Wayne B. 1895 Russell
Wheelock, Eleazer 1770
White, Ellen Harmon 5/23/1863
White, James 5/23/1863
White, William 7/17/1836
Whitfield, George 1740 George Whitfield, July 1741
Whitfield, James 1829
Widney, Dr. Joseph Pomeroy 1895 Nazarene
Willard, Frances E. August 1874
William and Mary 12/16/1653
William III, King 2/13/1689
Williams (College) 1847 Theological Society
Williams, Roger 1609, October 1635, March 1638, 1639, 1651
Wilmington, Delaware 1643
Wilson, Bill 6/10/1935
Wilson, President Woodrow 1915
Winthrop, John 1630
Wisconsin 5/15/1972
Wise, Rabbi Isaac Meyer 10/3/1875
Wise, Rabbi Stephen 1915
wise men 5/14/1948
Witherspoon, John 1746
Wittenmeyer, Annie August 1874

WJR (radio station) November 1936
Women's Bible 1876, 1895 Stanton
Women's Christian Temperance Union (WCTU) 2/13/1826, August 1874, 1893 Toomy, 1895 Russell, 12/18/1917, 6/4/1919
women's suffrage 6/4/1919
Women's Zionist Organization of America 1912
Woodruff, Wilford March 1887, 10/6/1890, October 1910
World Assemblies of God Fellowship April 1914
World War I 1915, 3/31/1848, 2/17/1889, 6/4/1923
World War II 1931 Federal Council of Churches, 1933, 1952, 10/1/1961
World's Parliament of Religions 1893 World Parliament
Wright, Lucy August 1774
Wyoming 8/29/1852

Yale University 1701, 1754 King's College, 1770, 1847 Theological Society, 1865
York, Dick 6/9/2008
Young, Brigham December 1840, 6/27/1844, 2/4/1846, 9/9/1850, 8/29/1852, 7/13/1857, 6/26/1858, 1862, 10/2/1871, 3/23/1877
Young Men's Christian Association (YMCA) 12/29/1851, 1854, 1858 YWCA
Young Men's Hebrew Association (YMHA) 12/29/1851, 1854
Young Women's Christian Association (YWCA) 12/29/1851, 1858 YWCA
Young Women's Hebrew Association (YWHA) 1854

Zionism 1896 Herzl
Zionist 5/14/194
Zion's Watch Tower Tract Society 1872